AF839545

UNIVERSITY OF EXETER

THE LIBRARY

This Item must be returned on or before the date marked below. A fine on each volume will be incurred if this rul is not observed.

N 2004

WITHDRAWN

30 0159208 9

TELEPEN

EUROPEAN TRANSNATIONAL CONCENTRATIONS

Top Management's Perspective on the Obstacles to Corporate Unions in the EEC

European Transnational Concentrations

Top Management's Perspective on the Obstacles to Corporate Unions in the EEC

RENATO MAZZOLINI

Assistant Professor of Business Policy and International Business
Graduate School of Business
Columbia University, New York

London · New York · St Louis · San Francisco · Düsseldorf
Johannesburg · Kuala Lumpur · Mexico · Montreal · New Delhi
Panama · Paris · São Paulo · Singapore · Sydney · Toronto

Published by McGRAW-HILL Book Company (UK) Limited
MAIDENHEAD · BERKSHIRE · ENGLAND

Library of Congress Cataloging in Publication Data

Mazzolini, Renato, (Date).
European transnational concentrations.

Bibliography: p.
1. Consolidation and merger of corporation—European Economic Community countries. 2. International business enterprises. I. Title.
HD2741.M35 658.1'6'094 74-5457
ISBN 0-07-084444-5

Copyright © 1974 McGraw-Hill Book Company (UK) Limited.

All rights reserved. No part of this publication may be reproduced, stored in a retrieval system, or transmitted, in any form or by any means, electronic, mechanical, photocopying, recording, or otherwise, without the prior permission of McGraw-Hill Book Company (UK) Limited.

PRINTED AND BOUND IN GREAT BRITAIN

To the memory of my brother Massimo

CONTENTS

PREFACE

The EEC Commission and the academic community have devoted considerable effort to the problem of eliminating the many barriers to international concentration (or merger, to use a more readily recognized term). An analysis of their work led the author to doubt the effectiveness of this effort. Specifically, the *description of the problem* appears inadequate. While their aim has been to make the task of concentration easier for the firms involved, no one has ascertained what obstacles corporate strategists actually encounter and what recommendations they might make.

Using over one hundred and fifty interviews with top executives in the original six EEC countries plus Great Britain, this study attempts to supply the missing knowledge. Two obstacles were found to be of prime importance. The first is strategic inertia: concentration does not receive adequate analysis by corporate strategists, hence its desirability is not recognized. The second is management's resistance to merger. Four principal causes for this were found: resistance to change *per se*; perceived threat to personal position in a concentration; nationalism; and misconceptions about foreigners. Moreover, a major constraint is the opposition of governments: public authorities tend to resist transnational concentration. In some instances, serious difficulties arise because of state ownership of industry. National differences may also present problems: labour codetermination becomes an issue when a German and a non-German company concentrate; macroeconomic uncertainty may hamper concentration with an Italian firm. These combined with many other obstacles make the implementation of a concentration quite complex.

While the literature stresses legal and fiscal barriers, it has been found that the juridical impossibility of merging is not fundamental. Other legal structures are available, which (from the managerial point of view) give results similar to the *de jure* merger. Fiscally, the most important stumbling block is operating taxes, i.e., taxes which concern the operations of the concentrated group (as opposed to taxes concerning the set-up of the concentration). Moreover, serious problems are created by top management's exaggerated perception of the juridical difficulties encountered by a concentration.

The principal recommendations fall into three groups. First, individual top managements can improve corporate strategic planning in the total European environment, with particular emphasis on evaluating the potential benefits of concentration. Top management should also recognize that resistance to concentration can be reduced if the concentration is implemented in a gradual fashion. (A model for a gradual integration process is presented in this study.) Furthermore, the business community as a whole needs to make a concerted effort to remedy the inadequacy of business education—the source of many obstacles to international business collaboration (as well as a problem for European business in general). Finally, information and consulting expertise should be made available to assist companies which pursue concentration. The second set of recommendations is directed to governmental agencies, whose opposition to concentration is criticized as hindering European integration. The EEC Commission is advised that the statute for a European company which it advocates will not make a substantial contribution. Possible tax reforms and other measures are suggested. The third set of recommendations is addressed to prospective researchers. Highlighted here are the behavioural issues, where new knowledge would result in more effective corporate consolidation policies.

ACKNOWLEDGEMENTS

I would like to thank the members of the Stanford Business School faculty who assisted me in writing the Ph.D. dissertation on which this book has been based. Special appreciation is extended to Professor Gail Oxley, who provided guidance vital for the development of this study, and to Professor Henry Eyring, who has been an unfailing source of motivation. I would also like to acknowledge my indebtedness to my colleagues at the Columbia Business School who, in many ways, have contributed to this book; in particular, to Professor William Newman.

I would like to express my gratitude to the Institut Massimo Mazzolini, which generously sponsored my research.

The success of this study has been dependent upon the help and co-operation of scores of leading businessmen. Their co-operation has been invaluable and to them I offer my warmest thanks. The 155 companies and organizations that contributed to this study are listed in the following pages, but I would like to pay particular tribute to: Mr Eric Faulkner, Chairman of Lloyds Bank; Mr H. Stout, Chairman of Internatio-Müller; Mr Richard Herlin, Director-General of Minière et Métallurgique de Rodange; Mr Roberto Olivetti, Managing Director of Olivetti; Mr Arnaud de Vogué, President of Saint-Gobain–Pont-à-Mousson; Mr Herman Abs, Chairman of the Deutsche Bank; Mr D. J. Ezra, Chairman of the National Coal Board; Mr Furio Cicogna, President of Châtillon; Mr L. Wauters, Chairman of Kredietbank; Mr Walter Kolvenbach, Vice-Chairman of Henkel GmbH; Mr Pierre Champin, Chairman of Vallourec; Mr John Read, Chief Executive of EMI; Mr Ermanno Guani, Chairman of Fincantieri; Mr Allen Greenwood, Managing Director of the British Aircraft Corporation;

and Mr André Bénard, Managing Director of Royal-Dutch/Shell.
My greatest debt is to my family. Without the inspiration of my parents Ulisse and Luciana Mazzolini none of this would have been possible. My late brother Massimo has had a considerable influence over my work. It is to his memory that I dedicate this book.

LIST OF THE 155 COMPANIES AND ORGANIZATIONS INTERVIEWED

BELGIUM: total of 15 interviews

ACEC = Ateliers Constructions Electriques	Charleroi
Agfa–Gevaert	Mortsel
Banque Lambert	Bruxelles
Bekaert NV	Bruxelles
Cockerill–Ougrée	Seraing
Communauté Economique Européenne	Bruxelles
Europemballage (Continental Can)	Bruxelles
Fabrique Nationale d'Armes de Guerre	Herstal-les-Liège
FIV = Fédération Industrie du Verre	Bruxelles
Kredietbank	Bruxelles
Métallurgie Hoboken–Overpelt	Hoboken
Petrofina	Bruxelles
S. té Métallurgique Hainaut–Sambre	Couillet
Société Générale de Banque	Bruxelles
Solvay & Cie	Bruxelles

FRANCE: total of 34 interviews

Aérospatiale = SNIAS	Paris
Air France	Paris
Banque Nationale de Paris	Paris
Banque de Paris et des Pays Bas	Paris
CGE = Compagnie Générale d'Electricité	Paris
Compagnie du Nord = Banque Rothschild	Paris
Conseil National du Patronat Français	Paris
Crédit Industriel et Commercial	Paris

Crédit Lyonnais	Paris
Avions Marcel Dassault	Vaucresson
Esso Standard	Courbevoie
Eurofinance	Paris
Galeries Lafayette	Paris
Gervais–Danone	Courbevoie
IBM France	Paris
ITA = Institut Transport Aérien	Paris
Kodak–Pathé SA	Paris
Librairie Hachette	Paris
McKinsey & Company	Paris
Mobil Oil Française	Paris
Opera Mundi Europe	Paris
L'Oréal	Paris
Pechiney	Paris
Pechiney–Saint-Gobain	Neuilly-sur-Seine
Pétroles d'Aquitaine = SNPA	Paris
Rhône–Poulenc SA	Paris
Saviem	Suresnes
Saint-Gobain–Pont-à-Mousson	Neuilly-sur-Seine
Thomson CSF & Thomson–Houston–Hotchkiss–Brandt	Paris
Cie Française des Pétroles–Total	Paris
Cie Générale Transatlantique	Puteaux
Ugine Kuhlmann	Paris
UTA = Union Transports Aériens	Puteaux
Vallourec	Paris

GERMANY: total of 37 interviews

Bank für Gemeinwirtschaft	Frankfurt/M
Bayer Farbenfabriken AG	Leverkusen
BASF = Badische Anilin & Soda-Fabrik AG	Ludwigshafen
Bayerische Gemeindebank Girozentrale	München
BDI = Bundesverband der Deutschen Industrie	Köln
BMW = Bayerische Motoren Werke	München
Commerzbank	Frankfurt/M
Daimler Benz = Mercedes	Stuttgart
Degussa	Frankfurt/M
Demag AG	Duisburg
Deutsche Bank	Frankfurt/M
Deutsche Genossenschaftskasse	Frankfurt/M
Dresdner Bank	Frankfurt/M
Esso AG	Hamburg
VFW–Fokker	Düsseldorf

Ford–Werke AG	Köln
Gelsenberg AG	Essen
Glanzstoff AG	Wuppertal
Grundig Werke GmbH	Fürth/Bayern
GHH = Gutehoffnungshütte	Oberhausen
Henkel GmbH	Düsseldorf
Hoechst Farbwerke AG	Frankfurt/M
Hoesch*	Dortmund
Fried. Krupp GmbH	Essen
Klockner–Werke AG	Duisburg
Mannesmann AG	Düsseldorf
Mobil Oil AG	Hamburg
Metallgesellschaft AG	Frankfurt/M
Opel AG	Rüsselsheim
Röchling–Burbach Stahlwerke	Völklingen-Saar
Ruhrkohle AG	Essen
Salzgitter AG	Salzgitter
Schering AG	Berlin
Verband der Chemischen Industrie	Frankfurt/M
Volkswagenwerk	Wolfsburg
Westdeutsche Landesbank Girozentrale	Düsseldorf
Wirtschaftsvereinigung Eisen- und Stahlindustrie	Düsseldorf

GREAT BRITAIN: total of 23 interviews

BAC = British Aircraft Corporation	Weybridge
Barclays Bank	London
BEA = British European Airways	London
British American Tobacco	London
British Leyland	London
Burmah Oil Company Ltd	London
Chartered Bank	London
Confederation of British Industry	London
Dunlop	London
EMI = Electric & Musical Industries	London
GKN = Guest Keen & Nettlefolds	London
ICI = Imperial Chemical Industries	London
ICL = International Computers Ltd	London
Lloyds Bank	London
Midland Bank	London
National Coal Board	London
RHM = Ranks Hovis McDougall Ltd	London
RTZ = Rio Tinto Zinc	London
Society of Motor Manufacturers and Traders	London

* This company gave a written interview.

Spillers	London
TI = Tube Investments	Birmingham
Vickers	London
National Westminster Bank	London

ITALY: total of 33 interviews

Alfa Romeo	Milano
Alitalia	Roma
Arthur Andersen & Company	Roma
Associazione Industriali Lombarda	Milano
Banca Commerciale Italiana	Milano
Banca d'Italia	Roma
Banco di Roma	Roma
Buitoni–Perugina	Perugia
Credito Italiano	Milano
Châtillon SpA	Milano
Confindustria	Roma
CNEN = Comitato Nazionale Energia Nucleare	Roma
Costa–Navigazione	Genova
EFIM = Ente Finanziamento Industria Manifatturiera	Roma
ENI = Ente Nazionale Idrocarburi	Roma
Esso Standard Italiana	Roma
Falk Acciaierie Ferriere Lombarde	Milano
FIAT	Torino
Fincantieri	Roma
Finmare	Roma
Finmeccanica	Roma
Finsider	Roma
Flotta Lauro	Napoli
IMI = Istituto Mobiliare Italiano	Roma
IRI = Istituto Ricostruzione Industriale	Roma
Istituto Bancario San Paolo	Torino
Montecatini–Edison	Milano
Arnoldo Mondadori Editore	Milano
Olivetti	Milano
Pirelli SpA	Milano
La Rinascente	Milano
Snia Viscosa	Milano
Voxon–EMI	Roma

LUXEMBOURG: total of 3 interviews

ARBED	Luxembourg
Banque Générale du Luxembourg	Luxembourg
Minière et Métallurgique de Rodange	Rodange

THE NETHERLANDS: total of 10 interviews

Algemene Bank Nederland NV	Amsterdam
AMRO = Amsterdam-Rotterdam Bank	Amsterdam
DAF = Van Doorne's Automobielfabrieken	Eindhoven
Internatio Müller NV	Rotterdam
Hoogovens NV	Ijmuiden
KLM*–Royal Dutch Airlines	Amsterdam
Nederlandsche Middenstandsbank	Amsterdam
Philips Gloeilampenfabriken	Eindhoven
Royal-Dutch/Shell	Den Haag
Unilever NV	Rotterdam

* This company gave a written interview.

1.

INTRODUCTION

This introductory chapter is divided into three sections. The first presents the case for international consolidations and emphasizes the importance of knowing top management's point of view on the problems involved in these consolidations. The second section deals with the level of discourse and the third section briefly discusses methodology.

The problem

In the last decade there has been an increasing awareness in the European Economic Community (EEC) of the desirability of international consolidations. Although the economic necessity for them is not new, it has become dramatically apparent since 1967. Jean-Jacques Servan-Schreiber has argued convincingly in favour of these operations, and his writings have drawn wide attention to the issue.[1]

A study by Opera Mundi,[2] first quoted in the *Memorandum on Industrial Policy* of the EEC Commission,[3] has also increased public awareness of the necessity for such concentrations. This study makes a significant observation. Between 1961 and 1969, there were 820 international 'fusions' or 'majority control participations' involving a company of an EEC member state and a company of a non-member country (mainly the US). During the same period there were only 257 'fusions' or 'majority control participations' involving two EEC countries. Although Opera Mundi itself places limited confidence in the absolute figures, their ratio tells an interesting story. The number of international amalgamations between an EEC company and a non-EEC company is more than triple the international amalgamations within the

EEC. As the amalgamations involving a foreign partner are principally take-overs of European firms by US companies, one must conclude that European industry is being rationalized under the auspices of American industry. The fact that the real value of US investment in the EEC is close to $40 billion (including 80 per cent control of the total production of electronic calculators and 95 per cent of integrated circuits) 'poses an unprecedented threat to Europe's continued independence'.[4] The need for a European solution to Europe's industrial inefficiencies is urgent not only because Europe is losing ground on a world basis, but also because it is becoming a vassal of foreign economic powers. Increasingly, the answer appears to lie in international concentration among EEC corporations.

International concentration in the EEC should be put in historical perspective. Compared with US industry, European industry has always been fragmented and dispersed. As US firms increased their commitment in Europe and industry became dominated by rapidly changing technology requiring ever larger R & D investments, isolated small European firms were unable to sustain effective performance. They were at a disadvantage both in economies of scale and in ability to attract managerial talent.

The response to these pressures has been a proliferation of domestic mergers. Opera Mundi estimates that between 1961 and 1969, 1861 national amalgamations took place in the six EEC countries.[5] As Robert Mattson commented: 'The entrance of large efficient global firms into Europe has prompted concern that European industries are fragmented and overpopulated by small family-owned companies with limited managerial and financial resources. The response has been a wave of European [national] mergers . . .'[6] Antitrust in Europe traditionally has been far less restrictive than in the US, and national mergers have encountered little opposition from public agents charged with the preservation of economic competition. On the contrary, domestic concentration has been encouraged by European governments for the protection of their industrial independence. To them, the solution to their relative weakness appeared to be the creation of large industrial units through a pooling of resources of the many small national firms and for the firms themselves domestic concentration has seemed the most obvious route if growth is to be pursued through link-ups with external partners. Examples can be found in every EEC country. In Italy, Montecatini, the country's largest chemical corporation, joined forces with Edison, the largest electric company. In France, the electronic and appliance giant, Thomson–Houston–Hotchkiss–Brandt, was created by a succession of mergers. British Leyland resulted from a series of mergers of virtually all national automobile manufacturers. An illustration of governmental approval of such concentration was embodied in the creation in 1965 of the Industrial Reorganization Corporation (IRC) to promote domestic pooling of resources in the United Kingdom.[7] In France, a main aim of Le Plan, the centralized economic programme of the nation, is the encouragement of national consolidations.[8] In Italy, the state itself often brings industrial units together: through its wholly owned holding company, IRI, it acquires companies and incorporates them in a single structure.

These concentrations, however, have not reached the size necessary to meet US competition and the opportunities offered by the developing Common Market. When domestic mergers produce one or a few giants in each country for sectors which are still not internationally competitive, the alternative of transnational consolidation is attractive. This situation exists in many fields: in the high-technology sectors such as electronic computers, aircraft industry, and chemicals, and in the more mature sectors such as automobiles and mining.

At this point, let us consider some of the advantages of international concentration.

As already pointed out, the first reason for consolidation is the increased R & D requirements in many industries. Particularly in the advanced sectors where Europe suffers the greatest gap in relation to the US, American companies have a considerable competitive edge in technical know-how. For example, ICL, Europe's largest computer manufacturer, has a sales revenue smaller than IBM's R & D budget.[9] There is much to be gained from the creation of a large European company that would avoid wasteful duplication of R & D among various national firms.

A second advantage is marketing. In many sectors an international marketing organization is needed to distribute a product throughout Europe. For example, the chairman of a large EEC automobile company stated that to support an adequate marketing organization a company must produce 1·6 million vehicles a year.[10] Virtually no European car manufacturer has reached such a figure.

A third advantage is the increased financial leverage. Two merging companies of different nationalities gain the flexibility of a multinational firm. They are then able to raise funds in capital markets where money is cheapest, and invest where opportunities are most attractive. They are also able to hedge against international monetary fluctuations. In general, the new transnational group will have greater opportunities to raise funds on the basis of sheer size. Smaller companies obviously encounter more difficulties in raising money than do larger industrial units.[11]

A fourth advantage to international consolidation lies in reaping the benefits of internal complementarity. Frequently, European firms of different nationalities have dissimilar strengths which fit together well. An example of this is German technical know-how in synergistic combination with an abundant Italian labour supply.

A fifth advantage is the possibility for European firms to pool resources to penetrate a third market. Particularly in the US, it is difficult, because of the high start-up costs involved, for a European organization to penetrate a third market alone.

A sixth advantage has to do with the learning process. The growing opportunities offered by international business require that European firms broaden their scope to multinational dimensions. Traditionally, however, European companies have had a national orientation. Geographical mobility is limited and there is not enough internal flexibility to meet the challenge of going abroad. The international concentration route offers an attractive opportunity for an organization to learn to operate at an international level. (Naturally, this feature will come up again when dealing with the obstacles to international concentration.)

A seventh advantage is that of balancing out political risk. In some cases, as in Italy today, there is great incentive for management (which is also often ownership) to export capital through a concentration with a foreign partner. Exchange of shares between two firms of different nationalities provides an easy way to bypass exchange controls and to diversify stockholders' risk as a function of political uncertainty.

It should be noted that the traditional argument of production economies of scale is not included among the above advantages. Economic studies have shown that the optimal size of plant can normally be reached within national boundaries.[12] For example, the automobile company chairman cited previously stated that in his industry the optimal size of plant corresponds to a minimum production of 300,000 vehicles per year, a figure sustainable by any of the big national companies of the major EEC countries.

The above motives relate to the managerial point of view. There are also attractive features to international concentration from the macro point of view.

The first advantage is the avoidance of national monopolies. If the present trend of domestic mergers continues, a situation may well develop in which there will be but one giant company in a given sector and in each country operating as a complete monopoly, undisturbed by its foreign counterparts. An understanding may be reached that each national giant will refrain from expanding outside its own market. Indeed, this is quite plausible in Europe where cartel agreements are not uncommon. Such restraint of competition along geographical lines can be avoided by European mergers that create multinational groups competing across national boundaries.[13] Moreover, it has often been argued that, far from reducing competition, large European companies would increase it on a global basis. This is true for high-technology industries like computers or aeronautics. The only hope for any competition with IBM, for example, is the creation of its European counterpart through a pooling of resources of ICL, Siemens, CII,

Philips, and others. If these companies continue to operate alone, they have no chance in the computer market, except for some small specialized niche which the US giant neglects.

The second advantage is less economic than sociopolitical. European industrial collaboration will be a force for European integration. European societies have little feeling of cohesiveness; they are used to autonomy and rivalry. National identity is strong, and European community spirit virtually non-existent. The behavioural sciences have amply demonstrated that in this type of situation a common purpose can best foster group cohesiveness.[14] Because it can benefit in the most immediate and tangible fashion from transnational collaboration, industry can be the catalyst in making the European concept operative. Co-operation for common objectives will eventually weaken nationalism and strengthen European solidarity. As Professor Reuter has stated: 'It is the industrialists who will create Europe.'[15] Without arguing the desirability of European integration, it is clear that industry's contribution to such integration cannot be overemphasized. The United States of Europe is first of all an economic need, and it is the integration of economic factors which will lead to social and political integration. Consequently, industry's attempts to co-operate should be welcomed, and governmental agencies should be committed to policies facilitating such concentrations.

These arguments for international concentration are by no means exhaustive. Nor are we implying in this study that international mergers are always desirable. Rather, the assumption is that international consolidations should be a strategic choice available to European companies. This is in fact akin to the official position of the EEC as specified in Article 220 of the Rome Treaty: 'Member States shall engage in negotiations with each other with a view of ensuring . . . the possibility for companies subject to the municipal law of different Member States to form mergers.'[16]

The objective, then, should be to eliminate the barriers which prevent an international consolidation from taking place. This is the position of the EEC Commission, as expressed in its *EEC Memorandum*, and of academic circles as well.[17] That it is also the desire of the firms themselves was quite clear from the field work of this study.[18] Indeed, this study unconditionally endorses the goal of eliminating the barriers to international concentration in the EEC.

There have been many efforts in this direction: first, within the EEC Commission itself (e.g., the work on a statute for a European company or on the directives for tax harmonization[19]); second, in academic research (e.g., Sanders,[20] Brosio,[21] Goldman[22]); third, within the framework of professional associations such as UNICE or CNPF.[23]

It would be inappropriate here to engage in a detailed survey of this work, particularly because the juridical issues involved will be taken up later on in this study. For the present, it is enough to indicate the main emphasis of this literature. It deals essentially with technical problems of international concentration, company and fiscal laws receiving most of the attention. First, it is recognized that a merger in the legal sense of the word is impossible. There is no juridical instrument specifically dealing with international mergers. A great deal of thought has been devoted to the development of such an instrument. Second, the literature focuses on the tax problems of an international merger both at the moment the merger takes place and at the operating level. Considerable effort has been devoted to finding ways to eliminate these fiscal barriers.

All this work, however, has a common feature which casts some doubt upon its usefulness. There has been no real effort to define the problem as seen by the interested parties themselves, namely, the companies which are potential merger candidates. Virtually no mention is made of non-technical problems (such as managerial or psychological issues), and one suspects that the problem is superficially defined; this, in turn, may lead to a misallocation of the resources devoted to the elimination of the barriers to international concentration. The aim is to make the task of concentration easier for the firms, but no one has ascertained what difficulties the firms actually encounter, let alone suggestions regarding the elimination of these difficulties. As still happens too often in Europe, the literature has become normative too soon. For example, a number of interviews with EEC officials showed that the massive work that went into the proposed statute for a European company had never really been preceded by any formal field research with management, aimed at defining what legal problems actually arise in an international merger.

There has been little effort to investigate 'in the field' the practical difficulties faced by the companies themselves, the few exceptions being the work by Christopher Layton,[24] Werner Feld[25] and the CEPES,[26] as well as two doctoral dissertations by Paul Goldberg[27] and Milton Hochmut.[28] Studies such as these, however, touch upon the obstacles to international concentration only as a by-product of other interests. Their focus is different; hence their treatment of the barriers to international concentration cannot be considered as definitive.

The result of such inadequate efforts to define the obstacles is that work to date may be emphasizing only part of the problem—and probably only the less important part. In other words, there has been an effort to treat symptoms before performing a thorough diagnosis of the disease. This study is designed to supply the missing information. Specifically, it turns to the top management of European firms to determine the obstacles encountered in concentrations. The principal objective is to define the problem from the point of view of 'corporate strategists'. An effort is made to appraise the relative importance of each problem and to indicate which obstacles are more acute in particular types of businesses. Where appropriate, an attempt is also made to discuss likely reasons for the existence of particular obstacles. Finally, recommendations for overcoming these obstacles are developed.

The relevance of this study can be seen in three ways. First, for European companies it should help develop more effective transnational concentration policies by indicating what problems should be anticipated. As will be shown later, there are many misconceptions about the barriers that exist; if they are pointed out, strategic planning should become more realistic. Further, it should specify solutions to the various obstacles. By drawing on the experiences of companies that have made international consolidations, policies for best implementing these operations can be developed.

Second, recommendations are made to governmental or public agencies regarding the facilitation of international concentration. Defining the problem of concentration will help to identify new issues which should receive the attention of public agents. Also, suggestions for resolving these issues are offered. A further contribution should be that of setting more realistic priorities. As will be seen later, governmental agencies are currently working on problems which are relevant only after other problems are solved. This study should help redirect official attention to the latter.

Third, this study should make future research more meaningful. The technical literature (e.g., fiscal or legal) should benefit from awareness of the problems companies face and the opinions of experienced professionals about the most rewarding directions in which to look for solutions. Finally, the potential contribution of specialized researchers such as behavioural scientists should be enhanced, their attention being directed to those issues of greatest concern to practitioners.

The level of discourse

Until now, the terms *concentration*, *consolidation*, and *merger* have been used loosely. It is important, at this point, to provide formal definitions. A *concentration* refers to an essentially permanent[29] collaborative endeavour by two or more economic entities adopting an integrated strategy in which the parties are vitally interdependent.[30] *Concentration* then refers to mergers or to *de facto* mergers. The term *merger* is not used in this study because it has legal connotations. The term *merger* refers to a legal operation in which two or more corporate bodies become a single one either by the incorporation of one into the other (i.e., the remaining body is one of the original ones) or by the creation of a new corporate body in which the two or more original bodies are absorbed. As defined by Cheris and Fischer: 'A merger, for our purposes, will be any transaction which produces a single legal entity to replace the two or more independent businesses in existence before the concentration.'[31] The *EEC Memorandum* has adopted a similar definition: 'A merger is the ultimate form of concentration in which the two partners lose their juridical identity and either are dissolved into a new juridical person or one of them is integrated into the other.'[32]

In contrast to the *de jure* merger is the *de facto* or economic merger, synonymous with *concentration.* This is the blending of the operational side of the enterprise and refers to a managerial or economic (as opposed to legal) process in which two companies unite their resources and adopt a common strategic posture. Two or more companies which form a concentration are what Friedrich Silcher calls 'a single economic entity'.[33] A concentration may, of course, be accompanied by a merger as defined above. The true test of a concentration is whether there is finally one decision-making unit.[34]

The above definition of a concentration refers to companies joining their forces on a long-term basis, indeed permanently, for the purpose of becoming a single unit. Such 'marriages' will be referred to by the synonyms *concentration*, *union*, *amalgamation*, *link-up*, and *consolidation.* The definition does not include 'one shot' joint ventures or limited partnerships for a particular line or function of business (e.g., R & D or marketing of one product). This type of operation will be referred to as *co-operative agreement*, whereby the parties involved retain their individual identities and do not adopt a single integrated strategy.

The question arises of whether or not the term concentration should include acquisitions (or take-overs). The notion of 'interdependence' embodied in the above definition suggests a mutual flow of influence and exchange of resources, a common strategy reflecting the inputs of all partners involved. Typically, this kind of situation does not occur in an acquisition. Here, one company is absorbed by another strong enough to unconditionally impose its structure and decision-making power. This distinction has been made by Krekel, Van der Woerd, and Wouterse:

> As soon as a firm decides, as part of a definite development plan, on full co-operation with another firm which must adapt itself completely to this plan, we speak of a take-over (acquisition). This, therefore, implies that the company being taken over unilaterally relinquishes its independence. If all those in the amalgamation relinquish independence (absolute independence may be replaced by some measure of independence), and the purpose of the co-operation and the way in which the co-operation will be realized are a matter of common consultation, we speak of a merger. Usually this situation arises where the partners are of approximately the same size, both in the number of employees and in turnover.[35]

However, the term concentration is applicable not only where the parties involved are of exactly equal size; it encompasses all operations in which parties are similar enough in size to make the concept of a pooling of interests meaningful, each party being able to retain an active role and to participate directly in policy decisions. The single decision-making unit should not be one of the original units; it should be an entirely new one, composed of the amalgamation of the two originals or, at least, a strongly modified version of one of the originals. All the contracting parties should share responsibility for the entire group's strategic commitment. The parties involved should be of sufficiently similar weight that a new organizational structure will emerge, instead of one party 'swallowing' the other. A few examples should help to clarify what this concept of concentration means in practice.

The VFW–Fokker link-up, clearly, is just such a concentration. The two companies are very similar in size and the consolidation is 'a marriage of equals'.[36] At the time the union took place the two companies had identical sales volume ($88 million).[37]

At the other extreme is the purchase by Ford Motor Company of the shares of De Tomaso, the small Italian sports car manufacturer. De Tomaso cannot be expected to have any influence on Ford's strategic decision-making process; at best it may be granted a certain autonomy which would fall under the label of decentralization. This clearly is not a concentration but an acquisition.

A less clear-cut case is the Fiat–Citroën operation. Fiat is much larger than Citroën (Fiat's sales were $2·7 billion as opposed to $1·4 billion for Citroën[38]), but certainly the original objective was to create a mutual flow of resources which would have had an impact on both. Had this reciprocal influence led to an integrated strategic posture, Fiat–Citroën could then have been considered a concentration.[39]

In sum, while it may be useful theoretically to regard the concept of concentration as a process in which the partners are of equal size, in practice it should be understood as including all those amalgamation processes in which the parties involved are able to exert an active influence on the strategic posture and organizational structure of the amalgamated group. Furthermore, it should be pointed out that the discussion of concentrations as defined in this dissertation, has relevance to outright acquisitions (and, for that matter, to other forms of joint operations). The acquisition poses problems similar to those of the concentration, although usually less complex. As Krekel, Van der Woerd, and Wouterse have stated: 'As a process it [the takeover] is comparatively uncomplicated, in sharp contrast to a merger. Nevertheless, much of what is said on mergers can be of a great value to those contemplating take-overs.'[40]

How many transnational concentrations have actually occurred? In his thesis, Paul Goldberg identified seven companies as transnational.[41] Among these he included Scandinavian Airlines Systems, which is neither in the EEC nor in Great Britain. The six others are:

- Royal-Dutch/Shell, an Anglo-Dutch concentration in the oil industry.
- Unilever, an Anglo-Dutch concentration in the food and chemical industry.
- Agfa–Gevaert, a concentration in the photographic industry, between a German and a Belgian firm.
- VFW–Fokker, a concentration between a German and a Dutch firm in the aircraft industry.
- Dunlop–Pirelli, an Anglo-Italian concentration in the rubber industry.
- Crédit Lyonnais–Commerzbank–Banco di Roma, an agreement between a French, a German, and an Italian bank.

Except for the last one, the above operations indeed appear to be transnational concentrations.[42] A few other examples are Akzo–Glanzstoff (a concentration between a Dutch and a German chemical firm) and, particularly, Hoesch–Hoogovens (a concentration between a German and a Dutch steel and mining firm). Several other cases are dubious (e.g., Arbed–Roechling–Burbach involving two steel companies of Luxembourg and Germany, or the already mentioned Fiat–Citroën case in the automobile industry). In any event there are at present only a limited number of transnational consolidations. Presumably, the reasons are precisely those obstacles to be analysed in this study. As Michael Stewart observes: 'Why has this fast short-cut been so slowly exploited? The answer lies in the immense obstacles in the path of the aspiring transnational.'[43]

Methodology

This section describes the essentials of the methodology of research in this study. (Appendix I presents further details on how the study was developed.) The frame of reference is the six original EEC countries and Great Britain. In accord with the belief that Europe should develop as a cohesive bloc around a well-defined community in which all members are formally committed to a common goal, the EEC provides an ideal framework. At the time the research was actually being done (1971–72) Great Britain, Denmark, and Ireland were not part of the Common Market. Great Britain was nevertheless included because the author believed that it should and would become part of the EEC in the near future. Other countries were also candidates to join the Community, but neither the probability of their entrance nor their economic importance was as great. Moreover, it was of interest to have a control group to ascertain whether or not the Common Market had changed the nature of the problem of international concentration in Europe. In other words, was the problem different if the partner was in another EEC country or in Britain?

The main source of data was the top management of Europe's largest companies because these companies are the prime candidates for transnational consolidations. Specifically, 155 companies were interviewed.[44] They included industrial and transportation companies as well as utilities and banks. The largest organizations in each country and sector were selected. It seemed of interest to include in the companies under investigation the largest US firms in the EEC in order to find out whether their perception of the problem is any different from that of their European counterparts. In addition, a deliberate effort was made to contact those who have effected an international concentration so as to establish the variance in views between managers who have had a direct experience and those who have not. Finally, the opinions of practitioners were corroborated by others who participated in a concentration in a staff or advisory position. These included consulting firms as well as professional and trade associations. The objective here was to supplement management's views in particular areas with the more detailed perception of specialists.

Although it was intended to restrict this study as much as possible to data from top management, there were two areas in which it had to be supplemented. First, in the legal and fiscal area top management was asked for an evaluation of the importance of obstacles, but an appropriate description of the technicalities involved was made from the literature. Second, as part of the problem resided in top management itself, namely 'barriers' within the decision-makers, self-evaluation alone would have been risky. A number of stratagems therefore had to be used to secure better information in this area. An effort was made to interview staff members in constant contact with the chief executive and therefore in an ideal position as observers. For example, heads of planning departments or economic advisers were contacted. Where possible, a foreign national within a company was asked to present his own views. Also, external observers with insight into the dynamics of top management's behaviour were approached; for example, consultants or academics with a seat on the boards of companies.

Moreover, top managers were encouraged to describe the problems encountered with foreign top managers—to judge not themselves but their potential foreign partners. Also, top managers were asked to judge other top managers of their own country who differed in their education, their career pattern, or the industry in which they worked. Finally, top managers were asked to judge top managers of other generations. The older honorary chairman was asked to describe his successor, and the younger executive vice president to talk about the present generation of chief executives.

Despite these techniques, it is recognized that conclusions presented here are somewhat tentative. However, it is hoped that useful areas for further behavioural research have been opened up.

Turning now to the research design, it was recognized at the outset that the processing of the data would probably reveal issues which needed further attention. Their importance might not have been immediately obvious, and respondents might have merely alluded to them during the interview. It seemed desirable to direct management's attention more closely to these problems. Hence, interviews were divided into two sets. The first was aimed at gathering the basic data, the question being 'What are the obstacles you see . . . ?' With the second set of managers, emphasis was on the problems requiring further analysis. These were more structured interviews.

The first set of interviews included 115 firms. As far as possible the researcher tried to be non-directive in order to avoid introducing bias in the discussion of obstacles. A few days prior to the interview, respondents were sent a brief statement informing them that they would be asked to identify the obstacles they perceived and emphasizing that the potential relevance and validity of the study would be enhanced by their detailed and specific description of the problem. The idea was to stimulate respondents to think through the obstacles they saw, in order to avoid eliciting responses on specific issues, a procedure which would have distorted the neutrality of the responses.

In the second set of 43 interviews,[45] the emphasis was on issues proposed by the researcher himself. These included obstacles needing further elaboration, those which the first set of respondents had inadequately described. Also, some issues might only have been mentioned by a limited number of respondents, and the question arose as to whether the issue was minor or obscure. This could be answered by the second set of interviews asking for comments. Further, an idea for solving a given problem might have been proposed by an individual respondent; it then became desirable to submit it to the reactions of others. Finally, the second set of interviews was designed to establish the soundness of the researcher's personal conclusions. It was possible to get managers' feedback on the analysis of the data of the first interviews. In other words, the second set was designed to corroborate the first set of interviews.

The data are presented and analysed in the following chapters. For convenience and cohesiveness the analysis accompanies the presentation of each obstacle. This approach seemed further justified by the research design, which permitted the analysis to be developed, to a certain extent, with the interviewees themselves. Conclusions were reached principally after the first set of interviews, but were then verified and completed during the second set. Consequently, data, analysis, and conclusions are interrelated.[46]

NOTES

1. Jean-Jacques Servan-Schreiber, *The American Challenge*, Atheneum, New York, 1968.

2. 'L'interpénétration dans le Marché Commun', Opera Mundi Europe (unpublished study), Paris, 1970.

3. *La politique industrielle de la Communauté: Memorandum de la Commission au Conseil*, Commission des Communautés Européennes, Brussels, 1970, pp. 89–95 (hereinafter cited as *EEC Memorandum*).

4. Robert N. Mattson, 'Mergers: European Style', *Mergers and Acquisitions*, Spring 1971, p. 27.

5. 'L'interpénétration dans le Marché Commun'.

6. Robert Mattson, 'Mergers: European Style', p. 27.

7. William Davis, *Merger Mania*, Constable, London, 1970, p. 50.

8. Robert N. Mattson, 'Mergers: European Style', p. 28.

9. Robert N. Mattson, 'Mergers: European Style', p. 29.

10. This information was collected in a field interview, and the author has expressed the wish to remain unidentified.

11. *EEC Memorandum*, pp. 185–220.

12. See: Jacques Houssiaux, 'Limites économiques des concentrations et fusions', *Revue du Marché Commun*, No. 109, January–February 1968, pp. 51–80; and H. W. De Jong, 'Economic Concentration', Judiciary Committee, US Congress, Part 7, p. 3617, April 1968.

13. Christopher Layton, 'European Advanced Technology: A Programme for Integration', *European Business*, July 1969, p. 33.

14. See: Muzafer Sherif, 'Experiments in Group Conflict', *Scientific American*, CXCV, 1956, pp. 54–58; and Thomas C. Schelling, 'Bargaining, Communication and Limited War', *Readings in Managerial Psychology* by Harold J. Leavitt and Louis R. Pondy, The University of Chicago Press, 1964, pp. 422–41.

15. Quoted in André Marchal, 'Nécessité économique des fusions et concentrations intracommunautaires', *Revue du Marché Commun*, No. 109, January–February 1968, p. 44.

16. *Treaty Establishing the European Economic Community* (referred to as Rome Treaty), Secretariat of the Interim Committee for the Common Market and Euratom, Brussels, 1958, p. 169.

17. See: Pierre-Henri Teitgen, 'Rapport de synthèse', *Revue du Marché Commun*, No. 109, January–February 1968, pp. 539–52.

André Marchal, 'Nécessité économique des concentrations et fusions intracommunautaires'.

Christopher Layton, 'Europe: It's Industry that Counts', *Vision*, May 1971.

18. Virtually every company interviewed expressed concern about the necessity for making international concentration easier to put into practice.

19. See: *Proposed Statute for the European Company*, Commission of the European Communities, Supplement to Bulletin 8, 1970, of the European Communities.

'Proposition de directive concernant le régime fiscal commun applicable aux fusions, scissions et apports d'actifs intervenant entre sociétés d'Etats Membres différents', COM (69) 5 final, Brussels, January 15, 1969 (hereinafter cited as 'EEC Draft Directive on Merger Taxation').

'Proposition de directive concernant le régime fiscal commun applicable aux sociétés mères et filiales d'Etats Membres différents', COM (69) 6 final, Brussels, January 15, 1969 (hereinafter cited as 'EEC Draft Directive on Parent-Subsidiary Taxation').

20. Peter Sanders, *The European Stock Corporation, Draft Statute with Commentary*, Commerce Clearing House, Chicago, 1969.

21. Guido Brosio, 'National Tax Hindrances to Cross-border Concentration in the European Economic Community', *Harvard International Law Journal*, II, 1970, pp. 311–57.

22. Berthold Goldman, 'Obstacles tenant au droit interne des sociétés', *Revue du Marché Commun*, No. 109, January–February 1968, pp. 297–316.

23. See: 'Les fusions internationales de sociétés dans la Communauté Economique Européenne', Union des Industries de la Communauté Européenne (UNICE), Brussels, 1967; and 'La politique industrielle européenne', Conseil National du Patronat Français (CNPF), Document de travail préparatoire, January 1971, Paris.

24. Christopher Layton, *European Advanced Technology—A Programme for Integration*, George Allen and Unwin Ltd., 1969; and *idem*, *Cross-Frontier Mergers in Europe*, Bath University Press, Bath, 1971.

25. Werner J. Feld, *Transnational Business Collaboration among Common Market Countries*, New York, Praeger, 1970.

26. *Grenzueberschreitende Unternehmenskooperation in der EWG*, Comité Européen pour le Progrès Economique et Social (CEPES), Stuttgart, Forkel Verlag, 1968.

27. Paul Morton Goldberg, 'The Evolution of Transnational Companies in Europe', Ph.D. Dissertation, Massachusetts Institute of Technology, Sloan School of Management, 1971.

28. Milton S. Hochmut, 'The Effect of Structure on Strategy: The Government sponsored Multinational Joint Ventures', DBA Dissertation, Graduate School of Business Administration, Harvard University, 1972.

29. The notion of a *permanent* collaborative endeavour refers to the *objective* of the concentration, i.e., two companies do a concentration with the aim of staying together. Indeed, in a successful concentration the companies are united forever.

30. This is a modified version of Werner Feld's definition in *Transnational Business Collaboration among Common Market Countries*, p. 4.

31. S. D. Cheris and E. R. Fischer, 'The European Company: Its Promise and Problems', *Stanford Journal of International Studies*, Vol. 6, Spring 1971, p. 115.

32. *EEC Memorandum*, p. 153, translated from the French text.

33. Friedrich Silcher, 'Coopérations, concentrations, fusions d'entreprises dans la CEE', *Revue du Marché Commun*, No. 109, January–February 1968, p. 178.

34. This is a modified version of Kindleberger's definition in 'European Integration and the International Corporation', *Columbia Journal of World Business*, Winter 1966, p. 68.

35. N. R. A. Krekel, T. G. Van der Woerd, and J. J. Wouterse, *Mergers—A European Approach to Technique*, Business Books, London, 1969, p. 6.

36. This expression was used by a Dunlop official to describe the Dunlop–Pirelli union. See: R. Marsh, 'The Dunlop–Pirelli Union', Speech given at the Institute of Chartered Accountants—Summer Conference, Oxford, July 1971.

37. P. M. Goldberg, 'The Evolution of Transnational Companies in Europe', p. 165.

38. 'The Fortune Directory of the 200 Largest Industrials outside the U.S.', *Fortune*, August 1971, p. 151.

39. The companies never reached a point where they were interdependent enough to be considered a consolidation. Moreover, they soon faced fundamental disagreements which hampered further integration. Indeed, these disagreements led, in June 1973, to a 'corporate divorce'. See: Giorgio Sansa, 'La Fiat e la Citroën rompono il "matrimonio"', *Corriere della Sera*, June 24, 1973.

40. N. R. A. Krekel, T. G. Van der Woerd, and J. J. Wouterse, *Mergers—A European Approach to Technique*, p. 7. For further discussion of the differences between a concentration and an acquisition, the reader is referred to chapter 1 of this book.

41. P. M. Goldberg, 'The Evolution of Transnational Companies in Europe', p. 13.

42. As will be seen in the next chapter, a concentration, typically, goes along with financial ties among the partners. The agreement among the three banks does not have such ties. Further, it is not clear to what extent the parties intend to adopt an integrated strategy.

Strictly speaking, there may be some doubts as to whether Dunlop–Pirelli really qualify as a concentration. As will be seen in chapter 2, unity of command is required in a concentration. Dunlop–Pirelli do not as yet have such unity (see note 38, chapter 2).

43. Michael B. Stewart, 'Transnational Enterprise: The European Challenge', *Columbia Journal of World Business*, July–August 1972, pp. 5–13, at p. 8.

44. The list of companies is given on pp. xiii–xvii.

45. This included three companies which had already been visited during the first set of interviews.

46. In addition to the data presented in the body of the book, the reader is referred to Appendix 2 in which quantitative data are given about the relative importance of the various obstacles to transnational concentration.

2.

LEGAL AND FISCAL ISSUES: DETERMINING THE JURIDICAL STRUCTURE

This chapter is devoted to the legal structure of an international concentration. The two main divisions of this problem are: company law and fiscal law. Although often dealt with separately in the literature, they interdependently determine the legal format of a concentration and businessmen tend to think of them simultaneously. It therefore seems more realistic to treat company and fiscal law together here.

As was pointed out in chapter 1, a great deal has been written on these problems, but there are some legitimate doubts about the appropriateness of the focus of this literature.[1] In fact, these doubts have been generally confirmed by the field research of this study, which has found substantial differences between the approach to these problems in the literature or by the EEC Commission, on the one hand, and by practitioners on the other.

While this chapter discusses the problem from the firms' point of view, attention is also given to existing work in the area. Specifically, the legislation has been analysed to establish juridical facts; and in view of legal and fiscal problems, the international merger in the legal sense has been deemed impossible in practice. Discussion follows of alternatives to the merger available to companies if transnational concentration is to be pursued. An evaluation is made of what governmental agencies are doing to facilitate international link-ups, and recommendations are formulated as to what they should do from management's point of view. Finally, the by-products of the legal format are analysed.

Legal and fiscal facts

The legal institution for domestic mergers is provided for by every EEC member state except the Netherlands.[2] French, Italian, and German legislation formally defines the notion of a merger between two or more companies, delineating the forms it may take (absorption of one company by another or the creation of a new corporate body which absorbs the participating companies) and regulating the implementation thereof. In these countries a merger takes place in direct compliance with national codes that make express provision for it. The same is true for Belgium and Luxembourg, though the term *merger* is not explicitly mentioned in their national codes. Dutch legislation, on the other hand, makes no provision for mergers, either explicitly or implicitly. Instead, fusions are accomplished by financial cross-holdings through either unilateral stock acquisitions or exchanges of shares. In all these countries, with the exception of the Netherlands, tax exemptions have been instituted to render mergers acceptable from the fiscal point of view. The most liberal of these are the French Law 65566 of 12 July 1965 and the Italian Law 170 of 18 March 1965 and its subsequent provisions.[3] In Great Britain the situation is similar to that in most of the EEC countries; domestic mergers are legally provided for and are quite feasible in practice.

While domestic mergers receive appropriate legal treatment, no comparable legal provision has been made for international ones.[4] Apart from the absence of legal provisions, there are other obstacles to international mergers. As noted in the *EEC Memorandum*, German law requires mergers to be judicially supervised.[5] Because the German court does not have jurisdiction over a foreign subject, a merger between a German and a foreign company is not possible. As the Netherlands do not provide for domestic mergers, they do not regulate international mergers either. In Belgium, France, Italy, and Luxembourg international mergers are possible when a foreign company is absorbed by a domestic one. When a domestic company is absorbed by a foreign one, Belgium, France, and Luxembourg require the unanimous consent of the stockholders. This is an insurmountable barrier in practice if the stock is widely owned by the public. However, the absorption could conceivably be carried out if the stock of the company in question is held by a closed group of owners, as in family-owned enterprises. 'In the United Kingdom, company law does not impose such restrictions and is closer to the U.S. model.'[6] In Italy, if a domestic company is to be absorbed by a foreign one, this unanimity is not required, but dissenting shareholders must be paid the market value of their stock or, if the stock is not listed, a value determined by a committee of the stock exchange.[7] Thus, from a strictly legal point of view, international mergers are in some instances theoretically feasible. However, fiscal barriers render these possibilities unacceptable.

The fiscal obstacles present entirely insurmountable barriers for both the merger and the contribution of assets.[8] These fiscal obstacles are of a double nature: those which concern the set-up of the merger itself and those which concern the subsequent operations of the merged company. Here, the discussion will deal only with those concerning the set-up because, as they virtually preclude the possibility of a merger, the problem of the operating fiscal burdens does not arise.[9]

Enterprises entering into a merger are immediately faced with a plethora of tax liabilities which hamper the transfer of assets. The taxation on capital gains is a tax on the difference between the real value of the contributed assets and their book value. This taxation thus affects the hidden reserves of the securities in the company's portfolio, as well as that portion of the true value of all assets which has hitherto remained undeclared. All declared reserve funds which are contributed are subject to taxation if no taxes have previously been paid on them, as is usually the case. From the merger itself, the internal revenue derives the right to tax the contribution of assets. It also imposes a tax on the delivery of shares from the absorbing company to the stockholders of the absorbed and dissolved company; the justification, according to the internal revenue, is that such an exchange creates a capital gain by enriching the stockholders of the absorbed company.[10] However, this is often untrue or only potentially true.

A tax on the exchange or voidance of stocks arises when one of the two corporations is a stockholder of the other one. That is, if the absorbing company holds shares of the absorbed company, it exchanges its shares of the absorbed company for those of the absorbing company (like other stockholders), thus receiving its own shares. If the company is not permitted to hold its own shares, then it must void the shares it receives from the exchange. On the other hand, if the absorbed company holds shares of the absorbing company, then, when the absorbing company receives the assets of the absorbed company, it will also receive a block of its own shares.[11] Again, if the company is not permitted to hold its own shares, then it must void them. The internal revenue claims that all these transactions create a profit: in some cases this may be true, but more often than not, any claimed added value is only an optimistic expectation. In any case, it is very difficult to evaluate precisely any eventual added value, whereas there is a great risk of double taxation:[12] first, on the potential added value at the moment of exchange or voidance; and, second, on the added value when actually realized. On the contrary, it is very possible that these transactions may result in a minus value, as when the absorbing company is a shareholder of the absorbed company. It is difficult to convince the internal revenue of the reality of a minus value. So, if it is not possible to deduct the minus value from the taxable profit, then the tax, which is in itself heavy, becomes unbearable.[13]

It is easy to see that if one adds to the juridical obstacles the burden of taxation, the international merger cannot be realized in practice.[14] This conclusion has also been reached by the fiscal Commission of UNICE[15] and by the EEC Commission:

> . . . operations of mergers and absorptions are virtually impossible between corporations of different nationalities, as the corporate laws of Member States pose obstacles which are difficult to surmount.[16]
>
> Apart from the legal impossibility . . . the fiscal cost of the operation constitutes in general a prohibitive obstacle.[17]

The above discussion refers to the international merger in its direct form, i.e., an operation leading to a merger by reference to a special legal institution purposely designed for this objective. This might correspond, on the international scale, to the US statutory merger. In addition to the direct merger, it is theoretically possible to achieve a merger across national boundaries by two indirect methods. The first is to liquidate one of the companies and transfer its assets to the other. The second is to transfer the registered office of one company to the country of another and then undergo a domestic merger. While these alternatives are sometimes legally possible, in practice they are not.

The liquidation of a company and the transfer of its assets to another implies that one corporation loses its juridical personality, by extinction thereof. This amounts to a winding off of its corporate body. Its assets are then transferred to the partner that takes on the activities of the liquidated company. Juridically, this is a feasible operation. Fiscally, however, it is unacceptable. It encounters the same obstacles as the direct merger discussed above.

The transfer of the registered office of one company to the country of another in order to perform a national merger is an alternative which requires more detailed attention.

The juridical concern of the different member states focuses on the problem of whether a company's relinquishing its original nationality and acquiring a new nationality automatically causes dissolution and reincorporation in the new country. In Italy and France a transfer to another country is permitted and does not represent, in principle, a cause for dissolution. A foreign company which transfers its registered office to Italy or France does not have to be reincorporated *in toto*, though it must adjust its by-laws to conform to local legislation. In Italy the transfer of a domestic company to a foreign country is decided by the majority of a general meeting of stockholders; the dissenting stockholders have the right to be reimbursed for their shares at their market value (Articles 2369 and 2437 Italian Civil Code).[18] In France the unanimity of the stockholders is required unless the domestic company intends to transfer to a country which has signed a protocol with France providing uninterrupted legal status, in which case a quorum (as determined in the company's by-laws) suffices. In Germany, Belgium, the Netherlands, and Luxembourg the transfer of a domestic company to a foreign country causes dissolution; the foreign company which intends to transfer its registered office to one of these countries must reincorporate *in toto* according to the local law. In Great Britain the transfer of the company's registration from one location (office) to another is not permitted.

The position of the internal revenue on transfers generally corresponds to its position on mergers or other concentrations between companies of different nationalities: it considers a transfer from the native country as a form of dissolution even if the dissolution is not juridically compulsory, and thus taxes the profits of liquidation and contribution of assets. Italy (the most liberal state in this situation) makes an exception: transfers to foreign countries do not necessarily imply juridical dissolution, and as a coherent consequence no dissolution taxes are imposed. With the exception of Italy then, the transfer of a company abroad runs into the same set-up fiscal problems as the direct merger. In Italy, in addition to a host of practical difficulties (e.g., exchange controls),[19] such a transfer is *de facto* unrealizable because of the fiscal cost of the transfer of assets, both at the Italian level and at the level of the recipient company's country.[20]

At present the mutual recognition of companies and the transfer of their registered office between member states are regulated by a system of bilateral agreements. This system, however, is incomplete and precarious.[21] These agreements are of short duration and run into a number of limitations which render their applicability quite uncertain. Further, they do not include the legal persons of public law, which is not congruent with Article 58 of the Rome Treaty providing for them. While Article 220 of the Rome Treaty contains a commitment by member states to provide for the mutual recognition of companies and the transfer of their registered office, the problem remains unsolved. This is true despite the fact that member states have signed an agreement designed to meet this commitment.[22] The agreement has not yet come into force,[23] and it is not possible to predict when it will.[24] Furthermore, it contains a major limitation which renders its applicability uncertain. This arises from the possible abuses of the clause of 'public order' as a unilateral source of refusal or revocation of a transferred company's legal recognition. This clause gives each country the right to evaluate the appropriateness of recognition of a company according to unilateral and unquestionable criteria of public order (e.g., public health, public safety, morality, etc).[25] Thus, in the present situation, transfers of companies have no practical potential.

It can thus be concluded that for all practical purposes the international merger in the juridical sense is impossible because there is no appropriate tool. European national legislation renders it infeasible, while tax hindrances create further insurmountable obstacles.[26]

Practitioners' solutions

In view of this *de facto* impossibility of merging, what legal format should a concentration take? This section answers the question from the companies' point of view. Although there are many variations, seven basic models of the legal structure of international consolidations can be identified. Because they fall short of a true legal merger, they are referred to as hybrid solutions, or what the Germans call *Ersatzloesungen* (substitute solutions). They are legal structures which, from the managerial point of view, give virtually the same results as the merger, i.e., they permit full integration of the operational side of the enterprise. All seven hybrid models have three main characteristics in common.

First, they preserve the juridical persons of the companies involved; there is no extinction of any of the participating corporate bodies. The concentration is formalized through other mechanisms than the legal institution of the merger. Second, they provide that the companies participating in the concentration have a common top management—that there is a single group of strategists for all the parties involved in the amalgamation. Indeed, unity of command is an essential ingredient for a successful concentration to occur, precisely because it is the precondition for implementing an integrated strategy. Third, they call for financial ties between the companies taking part in the concentration. Such ties are designed to formalize the amalgamation; they serve as a contract welding the parties together. They unite their financial fates, thus providing a permanent link. Indeed, these financial ties reinforce the notion of vital interdependence. In more prosaic terms, the two latter elements ensure that the companies are 'in the same boat'.

Hybrid solution I can be referred to as the Unilever model, because it is this organization which first used it. Two or more companies formalize their consolidation by some special arrangements designed to link the parties together, while leaving the juridical structure basically unaltered. In the case of Unilever there are two of these special arrangements.[27] The first ensures that the boards of the two companies are of identical composition, that is, that the top management of the concentration is one group of people. 'This is accomplished by a series of deferred shares, so-called because they rank after the ordinary shares in the annual profit appropriation. These shares are held 50 per cent each by two companies, N. V. Elma, a subsidiary of N. V. [the Dutch partner] and United Holdings, Ltd., a subsidiary of Limited [the British partner]. The articles of the two parent companies provide that the holders of these shares alone shall be entitled to nominate persons for appointment as directors. These two companies together, therefore,

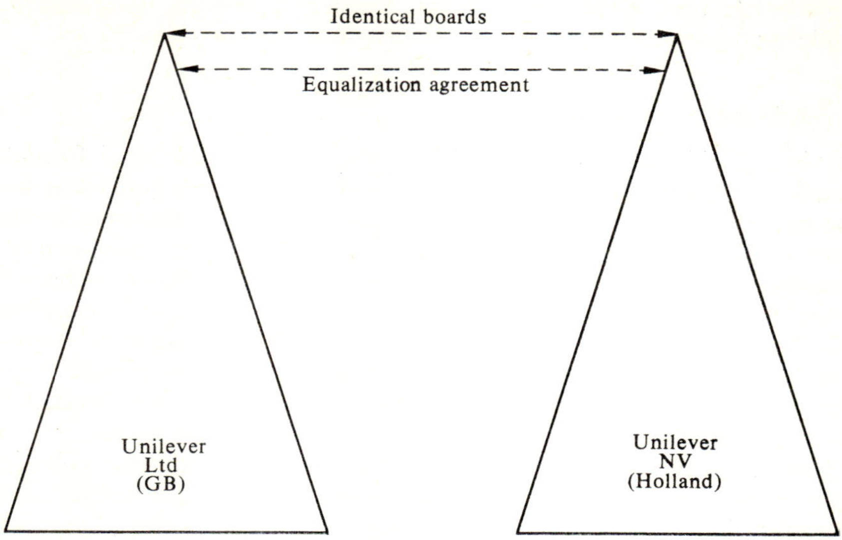

Fig. 2.1

draw up binding nomination agreements with identical parties on both lists.'[28]

The second of these special arrangements is the so-called Equalization Agreement. This is a financial arrangement which regulates the rights of the shareholders of the two companies. 'The principal object of the Equalization Agreement is to secure that the rights attaching and the benefits accruing to each unit of ownership [of the two companies] . . . shall as nearly as possible be the same as if each such unit formed part of the ordinary capital of one and the same company.'[29] In other words, it is basically an arrangement by which the stockholders of both corporations receive the same benefits, although the individual performance of each corporation may differ.

Beyond these two arrangements, the two corporations are legally independent. As one company official put it: 'There are two legally autonomous pyramids. The two special arrangements suffice to bring about total integration from the internal point of view.'

The legal structure of this type of concentration can be viewed in Fig. 2.1.

Hybrid solution II consists of the creation of a common joint subsidiary. Two or more companies get together and found a subsidiary owned and led by the group of companies involved. This solution was adopted, for example, by BAC (British Aircraft Corporation), MBB (Messerschmitt–Boelkow–Blohm of Germany), and Aeritalia (of Italy) when they joined forces to form a joint subsidiary—Panavia—to build military airplanes. This solution can be pictured in Fig. 2.2.

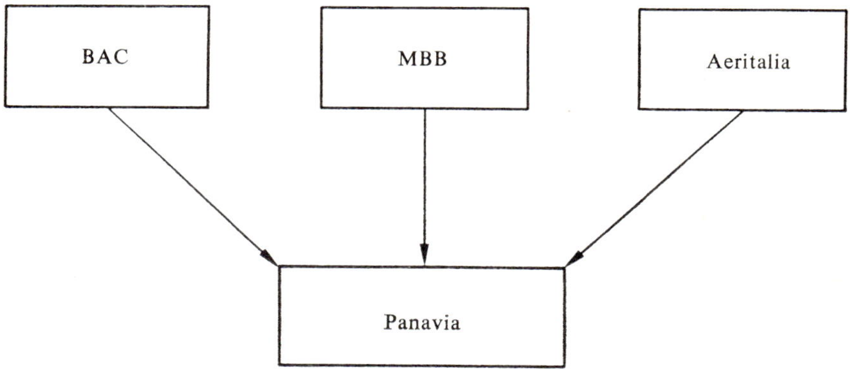

Fig. 2.2

The joint subsidiary is the operating company, and the founding corporations become its holding companies. This set-up cannot really fall under the heading of concentration unless it is understood that the subsidiary will gradually take over all the activities of the companies involved; in other words, that the founding companies will eventually be merely holding companies leaving the subsidiary as the only operating unit of the group.[30] There can be a number of variations to this model. For example, the joint subsidiary can take the form of an entity without autonomous legal personality (e.g., permanent establishment) as in the case of international consortia.[31]

Hybrid solution III is a unilateral stock purchase. This solution was adopted by Fiat–Citroën.[32] It consists of one company buying up the stock of the other. Clearly, this solution is most useful where there is a substantial imbalance in the size of the firms involved. Unity of command is brought about by the fact that the board of the acquiring company assumes leadership for the whole group, although it is more than likely that in a true concentration the influence of the acquired company will make itself felt in the other's board.[33]

There can be some refinements of the simple stock purchase. In the case of Fiat–Citroën, the Italian company agreed to put its shares of Citroën in a newly formed holding company (Participation et Développement Industriels) together with another major stockholder of Citroën —the Michelin group. The holding company could thus gain control of Citroën, which Fiat by itself could not have done because its own holdings in Citroën were insufficient. This can be pictured in Fig. 2.3.

Hybrid solution IV consists of a direct exchange of shares between the two companies involved. In other words, each company purchases stock in the other. This solution was adopted in the Arbed–Roechling–Burbach case, although in a greatly modified version.[34] Because there are cross-holdings of stock, the financial ties are very strong. Unity of

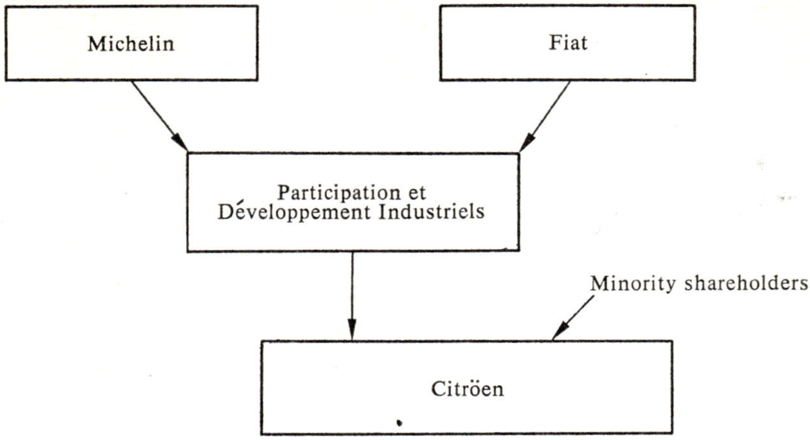

Fig. 2.3

command can be formalized through an agreement providing for a common board for the two companies. This type of operation has one major drawback. It requires that large blocks of the companies' stock be manipulated freely. This is not always feasible, particularly in large, publicly held companies where the stock is widely dispersed. In the Arbed–Roechling–Burbach case it was possible because Roechling was a family-owned company and Arbed could also count on close groups of major stockholders.

Hybrid solution V consists of the formation of a holding company to hold the shares of the original companies. The original companies become subsidiaries of the new holding company, and the stockholders of the original firms agree to exchange their shares for the shares of the new holding company. Hoesch and Hoogovens initially considered adopting this model for their union. This solution is shown in Fig. 2.4.

The principal advantage is that it formalizes hierarchy and unity of command. The holding company—which the Germans call *Obergesellschaft* (the company that is 'above')—is unequivocally the highest organ of the group. It plays the role of parent company and thus has clear responsibility for setting the strategy of the group. The principal disadvantage of this solution is, again, that it requires the cumbersome exchange of all the shares held by the public: the stockholders have to agree to convert their shares of the original founding companies into shares of the new holding company.

Hybrid VI offers a solution to the problem of manipulating stock. This solution can be referred to as the Agfa–Gevaert model. Although Royal-Dutch/Shell adopted a comparable structure as early as 1907, this set-up is referred to as the Agfa–Gevaert model because this concentration and its legal structure have been the most widely acknowledged

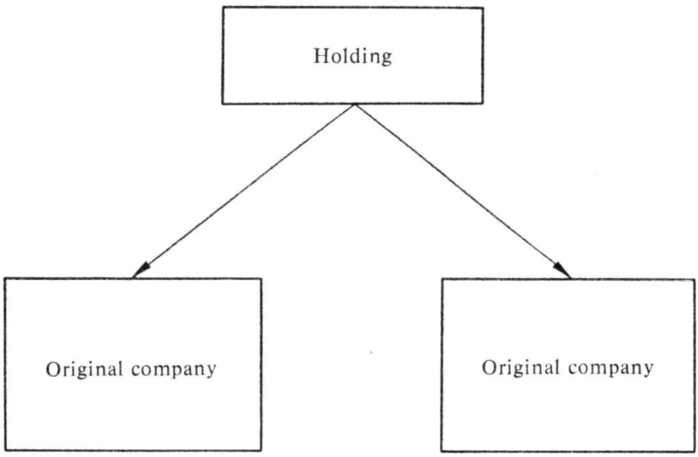

Fig. 2.4

form of international amalgamation since the emergence of the EEC. This consolidation has been described as a 'concentration of equals obtained through a double holding based on national jurisdictions'.[35] Each of the original companies sets up a wholly owned 'working company'. All the assets of the founding companies are transferred to the working companies, which take up all the activities of each of the original companies. Then, each founding company exchanges 50 per cent of the shares of its own working company for 50 per cent of the shares of the other's working company. The end product can be seen in Fig. 2.5.

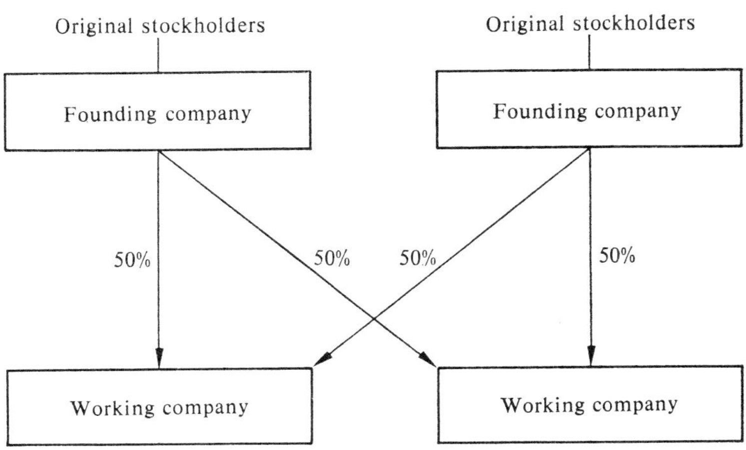

Fig. 2.5

Each founding company owns 50 per cent of the other's assets. An important advantage of this set-up is that it leaves the original stockholders' complexion unaltered, which is helpful when shares are greatly dispersed among the public. The financial links are clearly most effective. Unity of command is brought about by an agreement arranging that the two working companies have identical boards.[36]

There is one last hybrid solution—solution VII—which has been adopted, for instance, by VFW–Fokker. There is a possible drawback in the Agfa–Gevaert solution: unity of command is not formalized. Some companies feel it is not enough to have a common board and that one needs to have an explicit central decision-making unit. Thus, VFW–Fokker went a step further than Agfa–Gevaert and created a *Zentralgesellschaft*, a central company with autonomous legal personality. The concentration can be illustrated in a four-step process (Fig. 2.6).

Here, then, the common decision-making unit finds a formalization. It is the board of the *Zentralgesellschaft*.

There can be many variations of these models. For example, Dunlop and Pirelli have basically adopted hybrid solution VI.[37] However, they have created not one but several operating companies each. This was due to the complexity of the existing structures of the companies which already operated throughout the world with more than one corporate body. In particular, Pirelli was organized around two principal companies, an Italian company (Pirelli SpA) grouping Pirelli's activities in

Fig. 2.6a. Before the concentration.

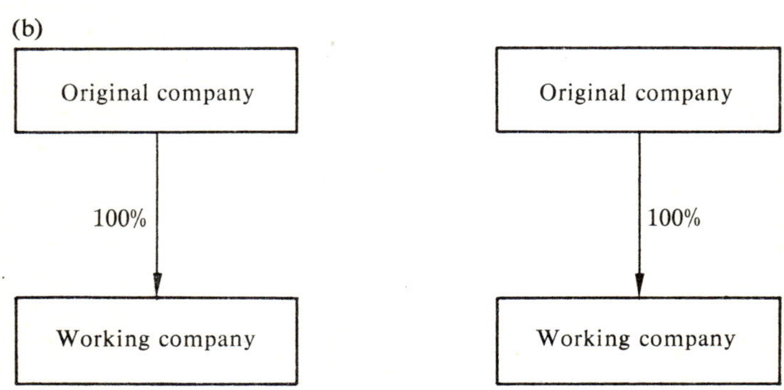

Fig. 2.6b. Creation of two working companies, fully owned by the original companies, to which all the assets and activities of each original company are transferred.

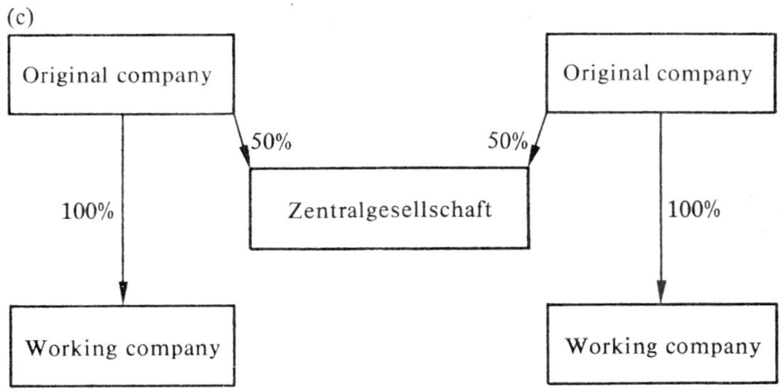

Fig. 2.6c. Creation of a Zentralgesellschaft, *owned 50 per cent by each of the partners.*

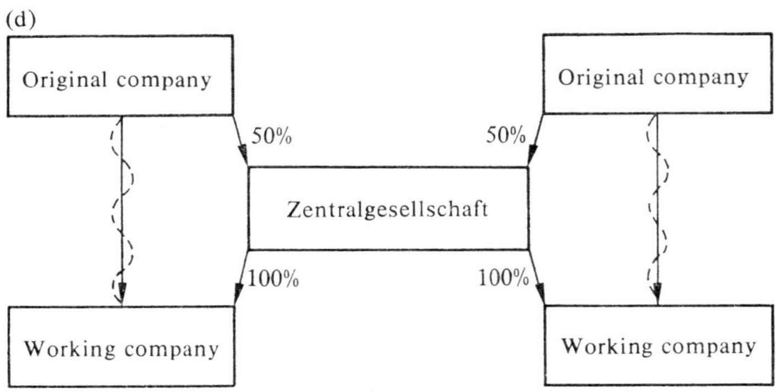

Fig. 2.6d. The stocks of the working companies are transferred to the Zentralgesellschaft *which becomes the coordinating unit of the group as it controls all the stocks of the operating companies.*

the EEC, and a Swiss company (Société Internationale Pirelli SA) grouping Pirelli's activities outside the EEC. In the Dunlop–Pirelli union each partner created several subsidiaries into which were transferred the assets of the founding company. The founding companies, then, exchanged the shares of each subsidiary.[38]

Another example of a variation of a basic hybrid model affects the adjustments required when one partner is larger than the other. Particularly in the last two models, it would be possible at first glance to alter the financial cross-holdings to reflect the actual relative importance in the proportion held by each partner. The problem, however, would be that a slightly larger size of one partner could give him majority control. For instance, if one company is worth 52 per cent of the group and the other 48 per cent, the former would be in full control of the group, although it was only slightly larger. This is clearly unacceptable for the smaller company. To avoid this, a solution is to give the more important company a direct share in the other company. This solution is adopted in the Hoesch–Hoogovens concentration, which adopts hybrid model VII. Hoogovens is somewhat larger than Hoesch.[39] The solution of proportional cross-holdings would have resulted in the pattern shown in Fig. 2.7.

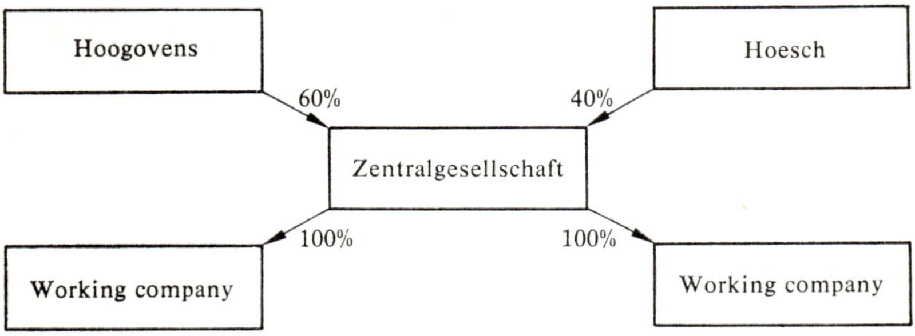

Note: The 60% and 40% are hypothetical.

Fig. 2.7

In such a solution, Hoogovens would have had full control over the *Zentralgesellschaft* which, theoretically, would have given it full control over the operations of the entire group. To obviate this unsatisfactory state of affairs, it is possible to allow the bigger company to purchase directly a percentage of the partner's stock. Then, the holdings of the two partners in the working companies can remain equal while the imbalance created by the greater importance of one over the other is compensated by the portfolio holding of the major partner in the minor partner (Fig. 2.8).

A lot more could be said about each form of concentration and far more detail could be added to the cited examples.[40] The above discussion, however, should be enough to show what surrogates to the merger can be found.

The question now becomes: what are the technical difficulties faced by the hybrid solutions? At the moment the concentration takes place, there is primarily a fiscal problem. In an Agfa–Gevaert model, taxes are levied when assets are transferred from the founding company to the newly formed operating company. It is noteworthy that these problems typically have their roots in national jurisdictions and refer to those operations which remain within national boundaries. Normally, the set-up problems are not, however, of crucial importance from a purely technical point of view, and their fiscal costs are bearable.[41]

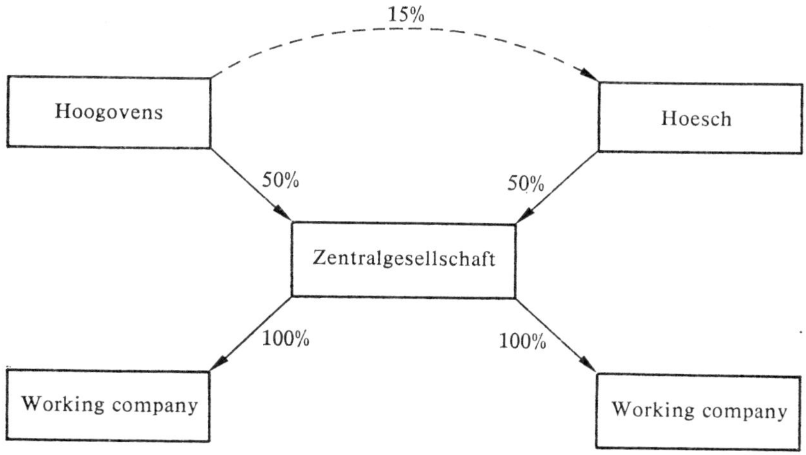

Fig. 2.8. The dotted line represents a holding of 15 per cent of Hoogoven's in Hoesch's capital.

While hybrid solutions usually encounter relatively few legal and fiscal difficulties at the moment the concentration takes place, important fiscal problems arise at the operating level, i.e., when the concentration has become a working organization.[42] The main problem is that of double taxation of companies of different nationality: 'The acquisition (or exchange) of stock between two companies is simple from the juridical point of view and generally poses no problems at the moment it takes place; the same cannot be said about what happens afterwards. Indeed, it occurs, especially in the case of international relations, that profits which have already been taxed at the subsidiary's level, are once more taxed when they are distributed to the parent. The resulting double taxation constitutes the major obstacle to this type of concentration.'[43]

Specifically, this double taxation occurs as follows. First, taxes are levied in the country where profits are earned. If the profits are transferred to a parent company based in another country, the recipient has to pay again. In the case of an Agfa–Gevaert model, a working company may earn a profit which is transferred to the holding company of the other country. Profits are taxed at the working company level and then at the holding company level as its own profit. While there are double taxation agreements to avoid this, their network is incomplete.[44] 'According to EEC figures, in 1970, out of the 30 possible bilateral relationships between the six EEC countries, double taxation on dividends is payable still in 16 cases and on interest payments in 14.'[45] Further, there are difficulties which arise with each particular case; for example, in a concentration between a German and a Belgian company. In Germany the tax rate on retained earnings is 59 per cent and approximately 35 per cent in the case of distributed profits. In Belgium the tax rate is uniformly 40 per cent. The rationale for the German law is to reduce the impact of double taxation at the corporate level first, then at the stockholders' level. The difficulties arise in an Agfa–Gevaert model, when the German working company distributes its profits to the two holding companies. Because it distributes profits, it should pay only 35 per cent taxes. But the German internal revenue raises some questions because part of the dividends go abroad to the Belgian holding company and are thus lost for Germany. The German internal revenue sees no justification here for the application of the liberal tax rate of 35 per cent on those profits distributed by the German working company to the Belgian holding company.[46] Difficulties such as these render the double taxation agreements unsatisfactory because they end up only partially eliminating double taxation.

There is also a withholding tax problem. As noted by the EEC draft directive on parent-subsidiary taxation, in most cases there is a withholding tax which a subsidiary must pay if it distributes dividends to its parent based in a different country.[47] In the case of an Agfa–Gevaert model, a working company has to pay a withholding tax when it distributes dividends to the parent company. This again constitutes a double taxation if the holding company has to pay a withholding tax when it distributes dividends to its shareholders.[48]

A final area of concern: it is impossible for an internationally consolidated group to deduct the losses of one company from the gains of the other. In other words, it is not possible, for fiscal purposes, to consolidate the income statements of the whole group. Consequently, if one part of an internationally concentrated group of companies has a loss and the other a gain, it is not possible to do 'the algebraic sum' and it is necessary to pay taxes on the total of the positive income figures, with no allowance for the losses. This is aggravated by the fact that tax credits are often unknown in European fiscal systems, thus eliminating forever any allowance a group might get for the unprofitable performance of one of its companies.[49]

These fiscal problems can be of considerable importance. Up to now companies have been able to reduce their impact either by obtaining *ad hoc* allowances from their internal revenues or by adjusting the income figures through manipulations of transfer prices. While the latter solution has been the most popular one for many years, the trend towards stricter and more sophisticated internal revenues is making this alternative more and more difficult to put into practice. While it is still feasible in countries like Italy, in others such as Holland, Great Britain, and Germany it is becoming increasingly difficult to rely on transfer prices for fiscal purposes. Instead, the trend is to negotiate an *ad hoc* solution with national tax authorities, to avoid double taxation problems. Thus, in the VFW–Fokker agreement 'a unique tax agreement was reached with the two governments, which apparently overcomes these obstacles, but the details have not been made public'.[50] It should be clear that both these solutions are temporary and that an explicit policy has to be adopted regulating these fiscal issues. There is widespread agreement among the companies interviewed that the aleatory nature of these solutions makes them unsatisfactory.

Governmental agencies' work: From businessmen's perspective

On the problems surveyed in the two preceding sections, there is work being done by governmental agencies and, in particular, by the EEC Commission. The work of the Commission is basically centred on three areas and is synthesized in three documents. First, the Commission has developed a proposed statute for a European company, designed to make mergers possible from a legal point of view. Second, it has developed a draft directive designed to eliminate the fiscal problems of setting up a merger, namely, the tax burden of the transaction itself. Third, it has developed another draft directive designed to eliminate the obstacle of double taxation between a parent company and its subsidiary, which amounts to reducing the tax barriers encountered by a concentration at the operating level.

The proposed statute for a European company 'aims at the creation of a new type of company, the *Societas Europaea* which will take exactly the same form in all the six countries of the Community. This company will co-exist in each country along with the existing companies created under the separate national laws . . .'[51]

Such a company would be supranational in character and would come into existence through a convention signed by all the member states. Work on such a project started as early as 1959, when the French government first proposed the idea of developing a new form of company designed for truly multinational European firms. At the Commission's request, in 1966 Professor Pieter Sanders, Dean of the School of Law of the University of Rotterdam, prepared a draft of a project for a European company.[52] In 1970 the Commission itself completed its own draft and submitted it to the Council of Ministers. This draft is considered the official version of the proposal for a *Societas Europaea*—hereinafter referred to as SE.[53] While the objectives of such a statute have varied over time, the most recent version of its goals is essentially to facilitate transnational mergers from a legal point of view.[54] It would be inappropriate to engage at this point in an in-depth discussion of the statute, particularly as several treatments of the subject are already available.[55] It is important to point out that this is an extremely difficult project to develop. A great deal of work has already gone into it and it is widely believed that much effort is still needed for it to become accepted. Indeed, many—like the Chairman of the Deutsche Bank, Hermann Abs—think that the project seems to have been abandoned.[56] Major stumbling blocks encountered by the statute are the question of the principal organs of the SE, the problem of the form of shares, and the issue of worker participation in management.

The question of the principal organs of the SE arises from the conflict between German company law and that of most other member states. The German system requires that a stock corporation have two separate organs: an *Aufsichtsrat* or supervisory board, the role of which is to counsel and to control the working of the other organ, the *Vorstand* or managing board, which is the real executive body of the organization. The systems of the other EEC countries are closer to the US model of a principal organ—the board of directors, responsible for the management of the company. The question is which model to choose for the SE.[57]

The problem of the form of shares comes about because in most EEC countries shares are typically to the bearer, while in Italy the law requires that they be registered. (The reason is that this provides control over the income of stockholders for fiscal purposes.) Here, the problem is to bring the Italians to accept bearer shares for the SE, which is said to be essential for the financial flexibility of the European company. The Italians feel that there will be incentive for Italian companies to become SEs in order to enable their investors to escape the control the internal revenue exerts through registered shares.[58]

The most painful problem encountered by the SE statute is worker participation in management. This is a German institution called *Mitbestimmung*, which means codetermination. It provides for the participation of labour in the decision-making processes of the firm. On the supervisory board, one-third of the members are elected by workers. Moreover,

> in the case of the coal, iron and steel companies, there is not only a 50 per cent representation in the supervisory board [instead of one-third] . . . but there is also on the *Vorstand* a labor director who is appointed by the employees. Thus, the employees are represented in both the organs of management and supervision, and their members have the same rights of voting and participating as any other member appointed by the shareholders . . .[59]

While in some countries like Holland there is talk of adopting a system similar to the German one, in most of the EEC countries there is nothing even approaching such a system.[60]

The problem of whether or not to have worker participation in the SE is a particularly difficult one to resolve because it has ideological overtones. The Germans want to have it at all costs. Worker participation has had satisfactory results in their country because it has brought about a constructive dialogue between management and labour. At the other extreme, the Italian labour forces, under strong communist pressures from unions, oppose it fiercely.[61] They, like their counterparts in France and Belgium, feel they serve worker interests better by being 'on the other side of the table', as an Italian executive stated it. This puts them in a stronger position to challenge the patronate and the propertied classes. A codetermination system would go against their doctrine of class struggle. There is thus a fundamental disagreement which has its roots in differences in social values. Indeed, even a compromise solution seems difficult to envision for the foreseeable future.

While these three problems are the most controversial issues, the SE Statute also encounters other difficulties. Among these should be mentioned the question of access to the European company and the tax problems involved, which will be discussed shortly. It should be clear from the above that the elaboration of the statute is a very complex process. It has required the commitment of considerable resources, and will require much more human talent before it becomes operational.

The second area of the Commission's work has been on the fiscal problems which arise at the moment a merger takes place. As was discussed earlier in this chapter, it is essentially capital gains taxes and transfer of assets taxes that hamper an international merger. The Commission's work in this area is summarized in the draft directive on the tax system applicable to mergers.[62] As noted by the *EEC Memorandum*, the directive aims at fiscal neutrality, i.e., taxes shall be neither an obstacle to nor an incentive for a concentration.[63] The concentration should be motivated by economic, not fiscal, reasons. The directive proposes the deferment of capital gains resulting from the merger until these capital gains are actually realized. Two conditions are placed on such a system. First, the assets of the extinguished corporate body must remain in its country of origin. They are then transferred to the accounts of a permanent establishment belonging to the new corporate body (absorbing company) in the country of the extinguished one. Second, their depreciation must take as a base the value that appeared on the accounts of the extinguished corporate body. With regard to the first condition, assets may in fact be transferred out of the country of the extinguished corporate body, as long as capital gains taxes are paid: in the event of transfer of assets, it is considered that the capital gains are realized, and they are consequently taxed. In addition, the directive provides for other set-up fiscal problems mentioned in the first section of this chapter, such as the treatment of hidden reserves or taxes on the transfer of assets. As noted by Cheris and Fischer: 'It was originally proposed that this new system of taxation of mergers be instituted no later than January 1st, 1971 . . . That date has passed with no further action having been taken by the Commission or any of the Member States.'[64] Here again, the difficulties of getting the system accepted are very great. Not only do such projects require considerable efforts for their development, but they also require considerable lobbying to gain legislative acceptance.

The third preoccupation of the EEC focuses on eliminating the barriers represented by operating fiscal problems. For present purposes one can look at the Commission's work as synthesized in the above-mentioned draft directive on merger taxation and, particularly, in the draft directive on parent-subsidiary taxation.[65] The Commission's proposals amount to the elimination of those cases of double taxation which still are in existence. Profits should be taxed in the country where they are earned. Then the parent company should receive a credit for its subsidiaries' tax contributions: it should deduct from its own taxes those taxes the subsidiaries have already paid. Likewise, there will be no withholding tax at the subsidiary's level, and a withholding tax will only be paid when the parent pays dividends out to its shareholders.

In addition, the Commission advocates a fiscal system based on taxes levied on a firm's 'consolidated profits'. Figure 2.9 shows how the scheme operates.

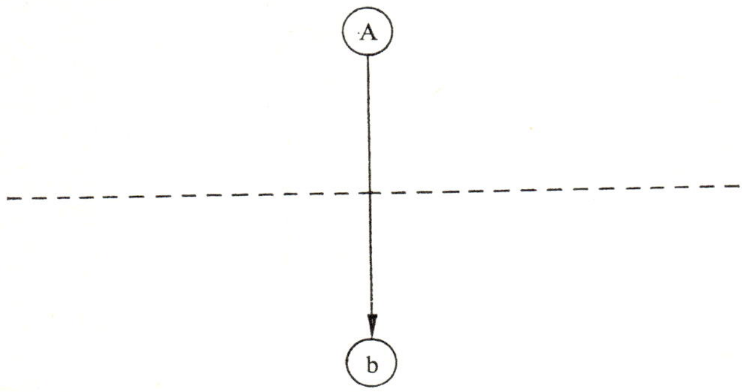

Fig. 2.9. (A) is the parent company and (b) is its subsidiary in another country.

Under the 'normal' system (as opposed to the 'consolidated profits system') in which there are double taxation agreements between each country, (b) pays taxes in its country in accordance with the local tax rate; (A) then deducts from its own taxes those taxes already paid by (b). Under such a system, if (b) incurs a loss of (x) while (A) has a profit of (y), (A) has to pay the full taxes on (y) and cannot deduct from it the loss its subsidiary has incurred. This problem is solved by the 'consolidated profits system'. Here (b) still pays its taxes locally based on its profit performance; then there is a consolidation of the pre-tax income figure of (A) and (b); on the basis of this figure, a tax figure (T) is computed, using the tax rate of (A)'s country; the taxes already paid by (b) are then subtracted from (T); this gives the final tax figure (A) has to pay. The advantage, of course, is that in case (b) has a loss (x), it is possible for (A) to deduct this loss from its own profit (y). (A) will pay taxes on (y − x).

The above has surveyed the main contribution of the EEC Commission towards the task of eliminating the fiscal and legal barriers to international concentration. It is now desirable to evaluate this work from the practitioners' point of view and, if appropriate, make recommendations. First, however, it is necessary to indicate the point of view of top management on the impossibility of merging and on the hybrid solutions.

It is safe to say that from management's perspective the present legal impossibility of merging is a trivial problem. For the vast majority of interviewees the hybrid solutions are satisfactory and the absence of a legal fusion of the corporate bodies is not an important handicap. The objective of the companies is to achieve an organizational and economic amalgamation. How the companies' lawyers comply with this is irrelevant from the administrators' point of view. As pointed out by the Unilever executives, their official organizational chart is a good illustration of this (Fig. 2.10). In this chart it is noteworthy that the only mention of a Dutch corporate body and a British corporate body is in small print within the upper rectangle. The managerial integration is complete and totally independent from the legal form. Indeed, many managers within the organization ignore the legal structure and work as if there were only one corporation.

In fact, one does not see why there should be a merger in an international concentration when there are so many domestic concentrations which leave the corporate bodies of the participating parties intact. As a Dutch executive put it: 'Who said that a merger should be a fusion of the legal bodies? We cannot do it in our national mergers and nobody would dream of saying that a merger is impossible in Holland. Why should an international merger require a legal fusion when national mergers work great with financial cross-holdings?' Indeed, there is wide agreement among European managers that technically the impossibility of a juridical merger is of minor importance. This is well summarized by the following statement of a French executive: 'All this fuss about juridical mergers is lawyers' fancy. They created the problem and try to convince practitioners that it is indeed a problem. In fact, it is nothing but a hypochondria.'

Of all the companies interviewed which had undergone a transnational concentration, only one stated that it would adopt the Commission's proposed statute for a European company, were it available. When questioned regarding what the European statute would add to its union, this company agreed it would not change much. Indeed, no change would take place in the daily operations and no benefit would derive from the managerial standpoint. It would 'simply bring things in order'—formalize the union and give it clearer public status. All the other companies said they would not adopt the statute, at least in the form of the official proposal of the EEC. One executive remarked: 'Legal integration is not necessary to have economic integration: the

Unilever structure

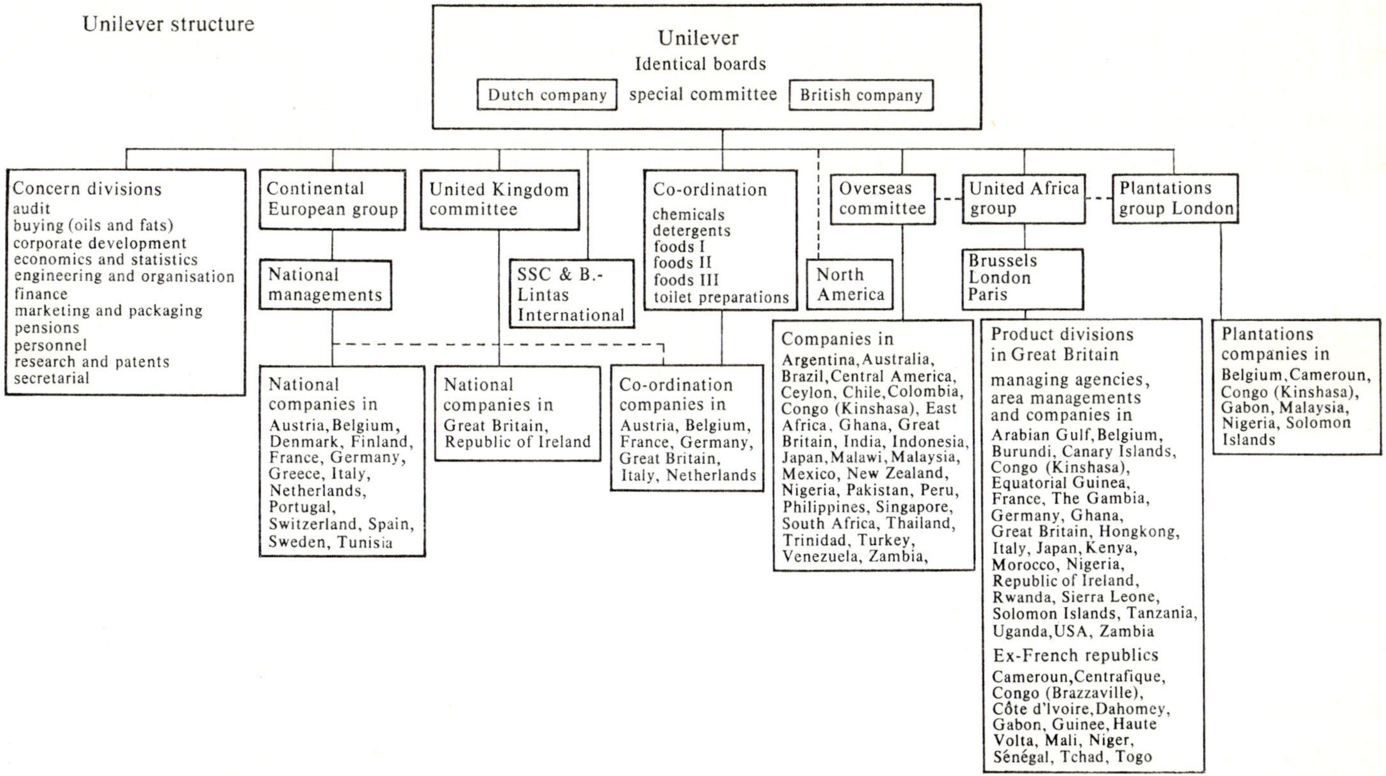

Fig. 2.10. Unilever structure

Commission is wasting its time trying to develop the Statute of a European Company.' Thus, the unimportance of the *de jure* merger practically eliminates the need for the European company statute. Indeed, such an instrument (at least in its present format) would not add much, and it is safe to predict that very few companies would adopt it, were it available.[66] A study by CREDA, of more than 500 French companies, came to a similar conclusion.[67]

This should not imply that the SE statute project is totally irrelevant. As will be seen in chapter 7, companies simply do not yet need such an instrument. The juridical merger is the final step of an amalgamation process and virtually no European company has reached the point where such a step is due. Moreover, the Commission tends to believe that the contribution of an SE would be psychological. The argument is that, by giving two organizations of different nationalities a supranational status, the problems of having to choose one nationality to the detriment of the other would be eliminated. As will be seen in chapter 6, this is also illusory: it is the physical location and the nationality of key managers that determine the perceived nationality of an organization, and not the location of its registered office. As a French executive put it: 'When Standard Oil opens up a subsidiary in Paris and gives it autonomous legal personality, this subsidiary certainly does not have French nationality.' The same type of argument also applies to the tax reforms connected with an international merger. If a merger is not necessary, there is no need to make it acceptable from the fiscal point of view. To repeat, both legally and fiscally the resources committed to making a merger possible are not allocated optimally, particularly until more urgent and necessary steps have to be taken.

The really pressing issue is to perfect the hybrid forms of concentration. These forms correspond to present-day managerial reality: no two companies consolidating internationally are ready for a juridical merger yet. Chapter 7 will describe the necessity of a transitional stage, where companies have some freedom *vis-à-vis* each other—a situation that a merger does not allow. The more flexible hybrid solutions are preferable to the merger even were the latter possible. Moreover, these forms are feasible now and can be relatively easily improved to become completely satisfactory. The EEC's efforts can be much more effective if directed towards this endeavour.

The EEC Commission's efforts designed to eliminate the operating fiscal problems of a concentration are in the right direction. Virtually all the companies interviewed agree that the objective of perfecting double taxation agreements should receive prime attention among legislators. They should, first of all, be extended to all EEC countries. The same type of attention should be given to the project of eliminating withholding taxes for subsidiaries and of levying these taxes only on the parent company. Furthermore, with regard to a 'consolidated profits' system, the ideal solution would, of course, be that of operating under a single tax system throughout the EEC. From the companies' point of view, this would simplify things a great deal because they could operate on European scale as they do on domestic scale today. While it has theoretical appeal and is logical if the Common Market is really to become a single economic entity, there are many impediments to this solution. The first one is, of course, that fiscal systems are dissimilar from country to country, and a situation could arise in which companies would all be based in the country with the most liberal tax system. In fact, this solution would require a total harmonization of the tax systems in the EEC. Moreover, internal revenues are very national in outlook, and this system would be viable only if there were political integration.

As a consequence, managers recognize the necessity of a compromise solution which preserves the individual prerogatives of each national fiscal system. However, the system of consolidated profits, as proposed by the EEC, is imperfect in the case of hybrid solutions. To illustrate this point, reference will be made to the same situation described on page 34. The Commission's proposal is satisfactory where the parent (A) wishes to deduct losses of a subsidiary (b). But the converse situation is also possible, namely that (b) has a gain and (A) a loss. Under the Commission's proposal, (b) then has to pay full taxes on its profits while no provision is made for the losses of (A). If the parent has a loss, it is not possible to deduct this loss from the taxes the group as a whole has to pay. It can even happen that while the group as a whole has a loss, the subsidiary still is expected to pay taxes. This problem is quite important in a hybrid solution where (A) and (b) are of similar size. In such circumstances the status of parent and subsidiary is somewhat arbitrary. This problem is aggravated by the fact that the Commission suggests that election for the 'consolidated profits' system by a group of companies must be made for a minimum of five years, during which presumably the status of parent and subsidiary cannot be reversed.

To overcome this problem, several interviewees proposed that the reversal of the status of parent and subsidiary be permissible every fiscal period. It would then be possible for a concentrated group to give the status of parent to that one of its companies which had a profit in a given period, i.e., to the consolidation where the profits occurred. This solution, however, would encounter administrative problems deriving from the different tax bases of the various member states.

Another possibility would be the following.[68] In a concentrated group of X companies the total income is computed. If this figure is negative, no taxes are levied at all. If this figure is positive, all the companies of the group which have had a profit should be considered. These companies will be referred to as 'A companies'. The profits of 'A companies' should then be added up. This should give the total of the incomes of all the companies of the group which had a profit, namely, the group's total profit minus the losses of the unprofitable companies. This figure will be referred to as the 'A profit'. Next, the proportional contribution of each 'A company' to the 'A profit' will be computed, namely, the percentage each 'A company' contributed to the 'A profit'. This will give a percentage figure to each 'A company'. Applying this percentage figure to the actual profit of the group, each 'A company' will be attributed a share of the group's actual profit. It is *this* figure which will be used as the tax base for taxing each 'A company' in its own country; each country of an 'A company' will use this figure as a base for taxing the company according to its own tax rate.

To clarify this, an example should help. Consider a group composed of four companies (a, b, c, and d), all in different countries. (Fig. 2.11).

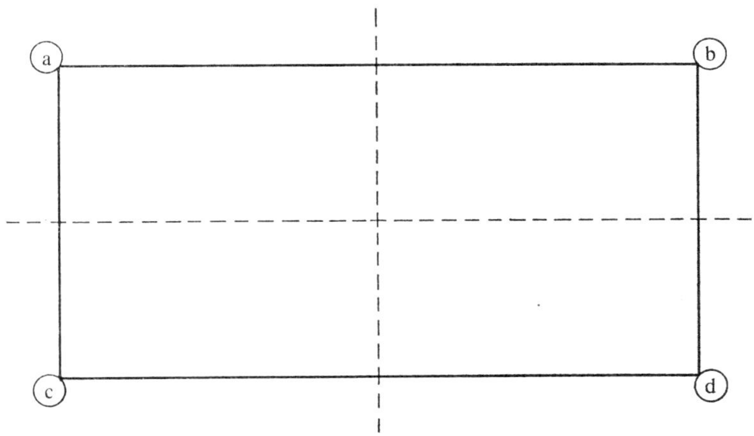

Fig. 2.11

Assume that each company has had the following performance in a given fiscal accounting period.

(a)	has had a profit of	60
(b)	has had a profit of	100
(c)	has had a profit of	40
(d)	has had a loss of	100

The total income figure of the group is positive. The group has had a profit of 100. The companies of the group which have had a profit are (a), (b), and (c). These are the 'A companies'. The total profit for the companies (the 'A profit') is 200. The proportional contribution of each 'A company' to the 'A profit' is computed as follows:

$$\text{for (a)} : \frac{60}{200} = 30 \text{ per cent}$$

$$\text{for (b)} : \frac{100}{200} = 50 \text{ per cent}$$

$$\text{for (c)} : \frac{40}{200} = 20 \text{ per cent}$$

Using these percentages each 'A company' will be attributed a share of the actual profit of the group:

(a) will be allocated 30 per cent of 100, i.e., 30
(b) will be allocated 50 per cent of 100, i.e., 50
(c) will be allocated 20 per cent of 100, i.e., 20

It is these figures which will be used by the countries of (a), (b), and (c) for taxing the companies.

The advantages of this system are that it only taxes a group when it has a profit, and permits a greater flexibility than the 'consolidated profits' system in that it does not require the election of a headquarters base for a group of companies. This is akin to the concept of a supranational European company which advocates that such a concern be a truly multinational one, in the sense that it be identified with no particular member state. It also allows the fiscal imposition to be proportionate to the actual profit of the whole group (including tax allowances for the so-called parent company). Finally, it still permits each country to retain its prerogative of levying taxes on that share of the group's profits earned on its territory.

The principal question to be raised with this system is that the countries of the 'A companies' pay for the losses of those foreign companies which are unprofitable. In other words, the country in which a profit is made gives up taxing the full profit to compensate the losses of a company of a foreign country. The answer here is that in the 'consolidated profits' system the parent company's country also ends up paying for the losses of unprofitable foreign subsidiaries. If the principle of injuring one country because of unprofitable operations in another is acceptable in the 'consolidated profits system', why should it not be equally acceptable here? Moreover, one can assume that a country's losses with one group will be compensated by gains with another. It is also possible to introduce a clause according to which a group could not continue to benefit unconditionally from such a system indefinitely. After a certain number of years it would become the group's responsibility to indemnify those countries which have paid for others' losses for too long a period.

Clearly, there are many difficulties with such a system which have not received adequate attention here. One is the problem raised in some countries like Germany by the different tax treatment for retained earnings and distributed profits. By no means is this discussion meant to be a definitive proposal. The need for a closer analysis of the problem by fiscal experts is clearly recognized. We have merely tried to point to the direction of fiscal reform which is most attractive from management's point of view.[69]

By-products of the legal format

Except for the operating fiscal barriers and although there is room for improvement in terms of legal amendments, management does not view purely technical barriers as major obstacles to transnational concentration. The operating fiscal barriers themselves are not absolute impediments. They simply reduce the attractiveness of transnational link-ups. Indeed, although they are potentially a major threat, they have, up to now, been surmountable. Apart from these barriers, international concentrations are feasible, and the legal constructs they require are not that complex. Many multinational companies (and even some national companies) have legal structures as complex or even more complex than the hybrid forms described in the second section of this chapter. There are solutions to the legal impossibility of merging which managers find satisfactory, and the difficulties implied by these solutions are bearable.

Besides the technical issues just discussed, there are a number of problems which are by-products of the legal format issue. These are not legal problems; rather, they are side effects thereof. There are three main types of by-products: the effects of differing national company laws on organizational structure; a lack of adequate information and consulting expertise whose most serious consequence is to generate misconceptions about the development of transnational consolidations; and inhibitions about the hybrid models discussed above.

DIFFERENT NATIONAL COMPANY LAWS

Each European country has different company laws. Among other things, these laws regulate the form a corporation shall take and what its organs shall be. While these laws would normally have a bearing only on the juridical format of an enterprise, they may in practice have an important effect on the internal or managerial organization of the firm. Because of the differing national laws corporations have developed and adopted organizational structures which vary from country to country and often conflict with each other.

The major difference is between German companies and other EEC companies. As mentioned previously, German corporate law requires a formal division of the directors into two separate organs, a managing board or *Vorstand*, whose task is to attend to the daily affairs of the company, and a supervisory board or *Aufsichtsrat*, which has responsibility for controlling the work of the *Vorstand*.[70] While there are differences among them, generally speaking the company laws of other EEC countries call for a board of directors (the French *Conseil d'Administration*) which is in charge of running the company. Further, the German corporate law is the only one requiring worker representation in the principal management organs. As a result the higher decision-making units of German companies differ significantly from those of other EEC companies. Top management is clearly separated in an executive group—the *Vorstand*—and in a legislative group—the *Aufsichtsrat*. In a concentration it may be difficult to integrate top management because the management organs do not correspond to each other. Thus the German managers feel that the systems of the other EEC countries do not define the top management job appropriately, and the managers in the non-German countries view the German system as restrictive and, moreover, perceive worker participation as a constraint.

This problem should not be overemphasized, however. Companies with concentration experience report that in practice the amalgamation develops quite smoothly. In the concentrated group a new hierarchy emerges anyway, as a result of the union of two independent organizations each having its higher decision-making units. The new hierarchy typically develops as a compromise solution which satisfies the needs of both parties involved. Managers nevertheless emphasize the desirability of implementing the amalgamation gradually, allowing the organizations to adapt to the partner's working habits. In fact, this is congruent with the need to implement a consolidation progressively—a topic discussed at some length in chapter 7.

LACK OF INFORMATION

The second by-product is a lack of adequate information and consulting expertise. Executives complain about inadequate sources of data on the juridical environment. To understand this, one has to bear in mind that fiscal and company laws are not simply different from country to country but that many of these are also constantly changing. Moreover, there are fundamental differences in the legal systems: the roots of the systems are often based on totally different ground principles. A good example here is the English Common Law and the Napoleonic Code of many EEC countries. In comparing the treatment each system gives to a particular issue, it is not enough to compare regulations on that issue from country to country. It is also necessary to analyse the fundamental differences in the philosophy of each legal system in order to understand the spirit of a given law. It is an important condition to grasp the true significance of a law and thus be able to tackle it. Another example is fiscal law. Not only are tax rates different from country to country, but taxes are also levied using different figures. This means that the fiscal basis is dissimilar from country to country. A good illustration is the difference between the German and the French system of taxing a corporation and its stockholders. As mentioned in the second section of this chapter, in Germany retained earnings are taxed at 59 per cent while distributed profits are taxed at 35 per cent. This is to reduce the impact of double taxation between what the company pays and what the stockholders have to pay. In France, under the system of the *avoir fiscal*, corporate profits are taxed at a uniform rate. The stockholders can then obtain a *crédit d'impôt* which enables them to deduct from their personal income taxes those taxes the company paid on the part of its profits which it distributed to the stockholders. Consider, for instance, a situation in which a company has profits of 100. If the going corporate tax rate is 50 per cent, it will pay 50, and profits after taxes will be 50. If it distributes half of this, the stockholder (assume there is only one) will receive 25. The stockholder will, however, declare 37·5 (25 + 12·5). The 12·5 corresponds to the *crédit d'impôt*. It equals the taxes paid by the company on distributed profits. The 37·5 will be taxed at the stockholder's tax rate—say 40 per cent. This gives a figure of 15. From this figure the stockholder is then able to deduct the *crédit d'impôt* of 12·5. What he actually pays is 2·5.

Besides such difficulties in the basic systems, there are major differences in the accounting methods used for fiscal purposes; accounting regulations employed for the financial statements used by the various internal revenues are different.[71] Finally, laws are implemented according to different standards. The precise Germanic interpretation contrasts sharply with the loose, indeed negotiable, Italian interpretation.

While these differences themselves do create some difficulties, it is possible to adapt to them. However, it is first necessary to learn about them, and it is this learning process which executives complain about, because there are no adequate sources of information. There are few sources of data which present comparative analysis of legislation and draw some practical normative conclusions for the firm. Managers claim that they can expect little help from published material in evaluating the difficulties of consolidations. Expressions such as 'no action-oriented literature', 'nothing but academic cogitations', and 'contemplative meditation' were used by interviewees to describe the inadequacy of the printed information available.

This information gap is reportedly aggravated by the scarcity of professional consulting in these areas. Companies are dissatisfied with lawyers' services which are ineffective in international matters. The only exceptions to this are the European offices of US law and accounting firms. Indeed, these organizations have European-wide networks and are able to service a client in his total European operations. However, these organizations are perceived by European managers as having a particular expertise in the problems involving a European country and the US—in the relationships between a US parent company and its European subsidiaries rather than in intra-European problems. Further, interviewees have pointed out that there is a psychological resistance to involving foreigners in one's financial, legal, and fiscal affairs. In the words of a French executive: 'As long as you seek assistance for an internal reorganization or a corporate policy formulation, you don't mind letting "strangers" in. But when the problem involves national institutions such as the legal system, one has the impression that a "stranger" should not be permitted to interfere.' Indeed, the fact that the majority of the clients of US law and accounting firms are US companies is consistent with this attitude.[72]

European lawyers are not, in management's view, organized to perform international services because there is no network of legal experts across national boundaries. Individuals cannot be expected to be familiar with the legislation of all countries, but it would be possible for a group of lawyers located in different countries to set up an organization in order to assist international consolidations. Moreover, management deplores the limited scope that investment banks (what the British call Merchant Banks or what the French call 'Banques d'Affaires') have beyond national frontiers. In a national merger such financial institutions offer considerable assistance to the companies, both for financial and juridical matters. They are not equipped, however, to offer similar assistance internationally. Both industry and investment banks interviewed during this study recognize that there is considerable room for improvement here. These institutions themselves should become more international in scope (particularly those on the continent). As it would be difficult for them to do so quickly through direct investment, it has been suggested by several financial executives that they themselves engage in international consolidations. Such link-ups across national boundaries would foster the development of the necessary financial services network for international, legal, and fiscal assistance.

A final source of concern is the limited amount of information available on the experiences of companies which have consolidated internationally. The solutions to technical problems are not in themselves too complex for adoption by large companies with comprehensive legal and fiscal departments. However, the search process required to develop such solutions is allegedly a painful one, especially in view of the information gap just discussed. The necessary investigation and analysis of the legal environment is a costly process. Managers believe this process can be greatly facilitated by using the experience of others. Lessons from past concentrations can be all the more valuable as the number of possible solutions adopted for solving the technical problems is relatively finite. The search for a hybrid solution typically leads to one of the seven models described earlier. The problem is that information on past consolidations is scanty. Except for companies of one's own nationality where personal contacts facilitate the search for data, management cannot easily obtain insights into the development of a consolidation. In particular, the available explanation of why one legal construct was used rather than another is inadequate; there is little accessible information on how the decision about a particular structure was reached. The available material is of limited use because it usually gives only the results of an investigation, omitting the analysis leading to these results. Consequently, the same problems are solved over and over again, and few generalizations are made which could lessen the work when the problem comes up again. As a German executive put it: 'The same models are constantly reinvented, but each individual experience is useless because no account is given of it beyond laconic press releases by the PR people.'

There are two consequences of this state of affairs. First, managers feel the development of a hybrid model is more complex than it should be. The lack of adequate information and consulting makes the search for a hybrid solution a cumbersome process. A company considering an international concentration has to develop its own comparative analysis of the legislation. Feasibility studies have to rely on simulated representations of the legal environment which are allegedly difficult to build because it is not easy to forecast precisely all the problems that will be encountered in practice. An Italian executive stated it this way: 'We have to be self-taught and, what is worse, with no books. Indeed, we have to create the material we have to teach ourselves.' The importance of this difficulty should not be exaggerated, however. While the development of the legal structure of a consolidation can clearly be simplified through better sources of information and consulting, the experience of concentrated groups has shown that the task is not as complex as most interviewees believe it is. In this connection, it is interesting that the problem was emphasized most by interviewees whose international business experience went little beyond export-import activities. As soon as an interviewee had experience either with direct foreign investments or with international partnerships, he was notably less concerned about the problem. Managers who had transnational concentration experience hardly ever mentioned the problem at all.

The second and more important consequence of the information and consulting gap follows from the preceding observations. International consolidations are perceived as more complex than they really are. Their legal structures are viewed as very intricate and hard to manage, and managers therefore have an *a priori* distrust of them. The main cause of this type of misconception, as has been noted, is the lack of adequate information and consulting expertise.[73] To repeat, the legal formats of the hybrid models described in the second section of this chapter are not overly complex. The information and consulting gap, however, 'wraps them in mystery', as a French interviewee put it. This causes management to shy away from concentrations. As a manager of a transnationally amalgamated group put it: 'The most serious consequence of the lack of information is that it has resulted in people believing concentrations are much harder to do from the juridical standpoint than they are in fact.' Furthermore, this misconception tends to focus on the development of a legal instrument designed to permit a juridical merger, which is not essential—as was seen earlier. Managers with international concentration experience often referred not only to a lack of information but to sources of misleading information. The press often discusses superficially the impossibility of merging. Moreover, the Commission is sometimes perceived as fostering such a misconception in order to justify the development of the SE statute, its objective allegedly being to develop an instrument of its own, and thereby acquire importance *vis-à-vis* national laws. 'The Commission is on an ego trip', stated a Belgian executive. 'It wishes to develop its own laws in order to assert itself, perhaps even to justify its existence.' Although this is probably an extreme view, the legal difficulties of an international concentration have clearly been exaggerated. Most of the companies with experience in international concentration stated that prior to the operation they expected more technical problems than in fact occurred, or at least that the problems encountered were easier to solve than anticipated.

INHIBITIONS

The third type of by-product will be referred to as inhibitions. These emotional biases concerning legal issues are closely related to the misconceptions just discussed and also have their roots in erroneous information management has about consolidations.

First, inhibitions pertain to the perceived effectiveness of the hybrid solutions. They are not viewed as 'real mergers' and there is an *a priori* feeling that the amalgamation cannot be complete. As stated by one of the executives of a concentrated company: 'There is a gut feel prior to the operation that these forms of concentration fall short of full integration.' It is perceived that they do not fulfil the requirement of linking two organizations completely, or lead to a harmonious interlocking of the operational side of the enterprise. There is a belief that the non-integration of the legal structure impedes the integration of the internal organizational structure. Such inhibitions are particularly strong with two categories of managers. First, Germans have expressed most concern about the impossibility of doing a juridical merger. In the second set of interviews, the reason for this concern was investigated. Managers with international business experience and interviewees in an observer's position (e.g., financial institutions' executives) believe that this is a result of the Germanic formalism and inclination for order and rigour.

Germans strive for a well-ordered structure, a corporate form which corresponds as closely as possible to the actual organizational structure. Hierarchy and division of responsibility should be formalized and should be reflected as much as possible in the juridical structure of the firm. As one of those interviewees said: 'Germans are impressed by form: for them, form has a greater bearing on the substance than for others, such as the Latin people for instance, who often are completely unaware of the form.' A corroboration of the German concern for juridical form is the fact that hybrid model VII has been used only in those concentrations involving German companies. This model offers the advantage of formalizing the central decision-making unit of the group in that the *Zentralgesellschaft* clearly sets itself up as the highest hierarchical unit of the group.

Second, such inhibitions are strong with non-lawyers, i.e., executives with no legal background. They are most impressed with the juridical difficulties, which they are often unprepared to question. It is they who tend to think that non-legal integration gets in the way of administrative integration. With a few of the more co-operative of these executives, it was possible to discuss the problem, as they perceived it, in considerable depth—to ask the 'why' questions and to require a high degree of specificity in the responses. Invariably the respondent discovered that the legal impossibility of merging was not a major stumbling block but a trivial issue.

A final aspect of inhibitions is the perceived negative connotation of adopting the expedient of a hybrid solution instead of doing a merger. The necessity of circumventing the law generates the belief that concentrations across national boundaries are not looked upon favourably. A corporate legal adviser stated it this way: 'The fact that one must adopt a surrogate form is taken to mean that the concentration is not "good", almost as if there was a moral judgment attached to the impossibility of merging. People say to themselves: "If the law does not provide for a merger, then it must mean that the law does not welcome such operations".'

To eliminate the obstacles created by these two by-products—lack of information and inhibitions—two basic recommendations can be made. The first is to improve the assistance to companies for the development of appropriate legal formats for consolidation. This can best be achieved by setting up a specialized service organization.[74] This organization should be comfortable in the various legal environments. It should build up expertise by taking advantage of the experiences of past concentrations in order to avoid the wasteful duplication of constantly having to re-invent the same models. Moreover, a body of knowledge should be developed in printed form. Here, the emphasis should be to explain clearly the legal environment in 'businessmen's language'.

The second recommendation is to inform the business community of the effectiveness of hybrid solutions. It is clear that misconceptions and inhibitions are caused by a lack of appropriate analysis of the issues involved. In view of the performance of international consolidations, such fears are unjustified (most of the problems encountered by the concentrations are not generated by their legal format). There is a need to publicize the results of such groups: to explain how they are built and how they function, and also to convince the business community that their legal structure is efficient. An effort should be made to counter the publicity concerning the complexity of these operations and to show that they represent viable juridical alternatives.

The first recommendation should probably be implemented by an independent service organization. Consulting should be organized to assist 'concentrators' with technical matters. Law firms or Merchant Banks could be used. Advice from industrial companies that have had international concentration experience would also be valuable. Indeed, such companies could put the fruits of their experience together and constitute a consulting organization. As to the second recommendation, responsibility could be given to professional associations such as the BDI or CNPF.[75] These organizations could act jointly in publishing material designed to inform managers about the possible routes leading to transnational consolidations.

NOTES

1. In addition to the work mentioned in the first section of chapter 1, one can cite:

(a) Lutter Marcus, *Empfehlen sich fuer die Zusammenfassung europaeischer Unternehmen neben oder statt der europaeischen Handelsgesellschaft und der internationalen Fusion weitere Moeglichkeiten der Gestaltung auf dem Gebeite des Gesellschaftsrechts?* Verlag C. H. Beck, Muenchen, 1970.

(b) Mario Iannuzzi, *Il diritto delle società per azioni nella Comunità Economica Europea*, Associazione fra le società italiane per azioni, Roma, 1972.

(c) Joseph Kauffman, 'Obstacles tenant au droit fiscal', Rapport, *Revue du Marché Commun*, No. 109, January–February 1968, pp. 449–66.

The reader is also referred to the bibliography, which contains extensive legal and fiscal references.

2. See: *La politique industrielle de la Communauté: Memorandum de la Commission au Conseil*, Commission des Communautés Européennes, Brussels, 1970 (hereinafter cited as *EEC Memorandum*), p. 153.

3. The Italian Law applies not only to domestic companies but also to foreign ones.

4. For a more detailed analysis of this problem, see: Guido Brosio, 'National Tax Hindrances to Cross-border Concentration in the European Economic Community', *Harvard International Law Journal*, II, 1970, pp. 311–57.

5. Aktiengesetz, paragraphs 345 and 346.

On this point, see also: Berthold Goldman, 'Obstacles tenant au droit interne des sociétés', Rapport, *Revue du Marché Commun*, No. 109, January–February 1968, p. 307.

6. From Michael B. Stewart, 'Transnational Enterprise: The European Challenge', *Columbia Journal of World Business*, July–August 1972, p. 11.

7. Article 2437 of the Italian Civil Code.

8. For a discussion of taxation in each country see Appendix 3.
9. For an analysis of the operating taxes, see the latter part of the next section.
10. This is measured 'inductively' by the internal revenue. In certain European countries, such as Italy, the internal revenue uses the 'inductive method' to determine what a taxpayer has to pay. This method calls for taxes to be determined on the basis of *presumptions* about one's wealth, derived from external signs. For instance, in the case of an individual, some of his taxes are determined not on the basis of a verified income figure but, rather, solely on the basis of his own or his family's apparent standard of living. The tax figure thus determined by the internal revenue is then subject to objection by the taxpayer; this, typically, originates a dispute and a subsequent negotiation. In the case of a concentration, the alleged capital gain created by the exchange of shares is determined 'inductively' by the internal revenue; i.e., the internal revenue intuitively establishes the amount of this capital gain.
11. For a discussion of the issue of cross-participations, see: Berthold Goldman, 'Obstacles tenant au droit interne des sociétés', p. 313.
12. See: 'Les fusions internationales de sociétés dans la Communauté Economique Européenne', Union des Industries de la Communauté Européenne (UNICE), Brussels, 1967.
13. In much of Europe, provisions are not generally made for tax credits.
14. For a similar analysis, see: William Garcin, 'Obstacles tenant au droit interne des sociétés', Communication, *Revue du Marché Commun*, No. 109, January–February 1968, p. 369.
15. 'Les fusions internationales de sociétés dans la Communauté Economique Européenne' (UNICE).
16. *EEC Memorandum*, p. 153. This quote was translated from the French text.
17. *EEC Memorandum*, p. 159. This quote was translated from the French text.
18. See: Remo Franceschelli, 'Obstacles tenant au droit interne des sociétés', Intervention, *Revue du Marché Commun*, No. 109, January–February 1968, pp. 420–25.
19. These practical difficulties will be discussed in detail in chapters 3 and 4.
20. As reviewed in Appendix 3, one has to take into account the fiscal burden imposed by the country to which the company is transferred (e.g., the German *Kapitalverkehrssteuer*, a tax on the contribution of assets).
21. The bilateral agreements between member states now in force are the following:

France–Belgium (stipulated on 6 October 1927)
France–Luxembourg (stipulated on 31 March 1930)
France–Holland (stipulated on 20 February 1933)
France–Italy (stipulated on 23 August 1951)
France–Germany (stipulated on 27 October 1956)
Italy–Germany (stipulated on 21 November 1957)
Germany–Holland (stipulated on 11 February 1907)
Belgium–Luxembourg (stipulated on 25 July 1921)
Holland–Luxembourg (stipulated on 1 April 1933)

22. 'Convenzione sul reciproco riconoscimento delle società e delle altre persone giuridiche di diritto pubblico o privato', Brussels, 29 February 1968.
23. See: Anna Bartolini, 'Reciproco riconoscimento di società giuridiche', *L'industria lombarda*, No. 9, 26 February 1972.
24. Article 14 of the agreement specifies that the agreement will become effective three months after the last member state has ratified it. While the other five member states have ratified it, to date the Netherlands has not.
25. See: Annexation to the Protocol of 27 October 1956 between West Germany and France, paragraph 3.
26. For an excellent review of these points, see: Pierre-Henri Teitgen, 'Rapport de synthèse', *Revue du Marché Commun*, No. 109, January–February 1968, pp. 539–52.

27. For a full description of this organization, see: Charles Wilson, *The History of Unilever*, Cassell, London, 1954.

28. Paul Morton Goldberg, 'The Evolution of Transnational Companies in Europe', Ph.D. Dissertation, Massachusetts Institute of Technology, Sloan School of Management, 1971, p. 112.

29. E. A. Hofman, 'The Dual Structure of the Unilever Group of Companies and the Equalization Agreement', *Journal for Companies, Associations and Foundations*, Special Number on Groups of Companies, September 1968.

30. Panavia has not reached this point. The three participating companies have formed the joint subsidiary for the purpose of pooling their efforts for only one part of their activity. For the rest, they are independent and unrelated. Consequently, Panavia, as of now, cannot be considered a concentration.

31. Outside the EEC, Scandinavian Airlines System is organized in a somewhat similar fashion. The National Airlines of Sweden, Norway, and Denmark have agreed to join forces by signing an International Consortium Agreement, thus forming a jointly owned entity pooling all the activities of the founding companies.

32. There may be some question as to whether Fiat–Citroën could ever have been regarded as a concentration. See note 39, chapter 1.

33. See the discussion in the second section of chapter 1.

34. Arbed, a Luxembourg steel and mining company, owned a subsidiary in Germany, Burbach. Roechling, a German company, bought this subsidiary, paying Arbed with part of its own shares. Arbed received additional stock from Roechling in exchange for some of its own stock. The final situation is that Arbed owns 50 per cent of Roechling; Roechling owns Arbed's old subsidiary, Burbach, plus a stock participation in Arbed.

35. Gerhard Klatt, 'Steuerliche Probleme einer sogenannten "Europaeischen Gesellschaft"', *Europaeische Steuerzeitung*, No. 47, August 1971, pp. 67–76, at p. 67. This quote was translated from the German.

36. In fact, in the case of Agfa–Gevaert, one cannot speak of a board because of the particular requirements of German law. Rather, one should talk about two principal management organs, a *Vorstand* and an *Aufsichtsrat*.

37. This is, in fact, a simplistic description. For details, see:

(a) 'The Dunlop Company Limited Union with Pirelli S.p.A. and Société Internationale Pirelli S.A., Proposed Revisions to the Trust Deeds Constituting the First and Second Debenture Stocks', Dunlop House, London, 1970.

(b) 'Proposals to Effect the Union of the Operating Activities of the Dunlop Company Limited, and Pirelli S.p.A. and Société Internationale Pirelli S.A.', Dunlop House, London, 1970.

(c) 'Dunlop–Pirelli: A European Experiment', Paper No. 442, Dunlop, London, 1971.

38. Further, Dunlop–Pirelli do not have unity of command. In view of the crisis the companies are presently facing (see the discussion in the latter part of chapter 4), this is believed to be a considerable drawback for the group to handle effectively the difficulties they encounter.

39. In fact, Hoesch is larger than Hoogovens in terms of sales. However, the concentration 'will probably not be 50–50, but on a 60–40 basis in Hoogovens' favor, because the assets it puts in are worth more'. Christopher Layton, *Cross-Frontier Mergers in Europe*, Bath University Press, 1971, p. 28.

40. For a more extensive treatment of cases of international concentration see, for example, Paul Morton Goldberg, 'The Evolution of Transnational Companies in Europe', Chapter IV.

41. Among others, this point is made by the Président-Directeur Général of Agfa–Gevaert, Bertrand Motte, in 'Obstacles tenant au droit interne des sociétés', *Revue du Marché Commun*, No. 109, January–February 1968, pp. 392–98.

42. For a discussion of the fiscal problems encountered by the most acknowledged hybrid concentration—Agfa–Gevaert—see: Gerhard Klatt, 'Steuerliche Probleme einer sogenannten "Europaeischen Gesellschaft"'. (The author of the article is a company official.)

43. 'Proposition de directive concernant le régime fiscal commun applicable aux sociétés mères et filiales d'Etats Membres différents', Commission des Communautés Européennes, COM (69) 6 final, Brussels, 15 January 1969, p. 1. This quote was translated from the French text.

44. See: *The Development of a European Capital Market*, EEC Commission, Brussels, 1966, p. 296.

45. Michael B. Stewart, 'Transnational Enterprise: The European Challenge', p. 11.

46. See: Gerhard Klatt, 'Steuerliche Probleme einer sogenannten "Europaeischen Gesellschaft"', pp. 69–70.

47. 'Proposition de directive concernant le régime fiscal commun applicable aux sociétés mères et filiales d'Etats Membres différents', p. 3.

48. On a domestic scale, this would not be the case as national fiscal law provides for exemption of one of the two withholding taxes: in a case of a domestic parent-subsidiary relationship, only one of the two companies has to pay the withholding tax, while the other receives an exemption from it.

49. For a further analysis of these operating fiscal problems, see: Guido Brosio, 'National Tax Hindrances to Cross-Border Concentration in the European Economic Community', pp. 340–44.

50. Paul Morton Goldberg, 'The Evolution of Transnational Companies in Europe', p. 171.

51. Dennis Thompson, *The Proposal for a European Company*, PEP, Chatham House, London, 1969, p. 46.

52. Pieter Sanders, *European Stock Corporation, Draft Statute with Commentary*, Commerce Clearing House, Chicago, 1969.

53. *Proposed Statute for the European Company*, Commission of the European Communities, Supplement to Bulletin 8, 1970 of the European Communities.

54. Interviews done in 1972 with EEC officials working on the elaboration of the statute revealed that the SE should be accessible only in one of the following cases:

—by a merger between two or more EEC national companies of different nationalities;

—by the creation of a holding company, which owns 100 per cent of the stock of national EEC companies of different nationalities;

—by the founding of a joint subsidiary by two or more EEC companies of different nationalities;

—by the creation of a subsidiary by another.

This shows that, apart from the last case, the SE is designed to facilitate European transnational concentration.

55. See: S. D. Cheris and E. R. Fischer, 'The European Company: Its Promise and Problems', *Stanford Journal of International Studies*, Vol. 6, Spring 1971.

Dennis Thompson, *The Proposal for a European Company*.

Jean Van Ryn, 'La société européenne II', *L'harmonization dans les Communautés*, 1968.

Jacques Roelans, *Régimes fiscaux applicables aux fusions de sociétés dans les Etats Membres de la C.E.E. et perspectives communautaires*, Bruyland, Brussels, 1970.

Mario Iannuzzi, *Il diritto delle società per azioni nella Comunità Economica Europea*, pp. 223–59.

56. This opinion was presented in a letter Mr Abs sent to the author on 6 October 1971.

57. See: Gustavo Minervini, 'Un recente progetto di società di tipo europeo', *Rassegna Economica*, No. 5, September–October 1967, pp. 1168–69.

EXETER UNIVERSITY LIBRARY

58. See: Raffaello Fornasier, 'Toward a European Company', *Columbia Journal of World Business*, September–October 1969, pp. 51–57.

59. Dennis Thompson, *The Proposal for a European Company*, p. 60.

60. While it is very doubtful that such a system will be accepted by other member states, the Germans are thinking of going even further in the co-participation direction: the Brandt administration is proposing to bring the one-third labour representation of the *Aufsichtsrat* to 50 per cent for all stock corporations (as in the coal and iron and steel companies).

61. See: P. P. Fano, 'The Italian Labor Movement and Collective Bargaining', in *Western European Labour*, Alfred Kamin (ed.), The Bureau of National Affairs, Washington, 1970, pp. 99–108.

62. 'Proposition de Directive concernant le régime fiscal commun applicable aux fusions, scissions et apports d'actifs intervenant entre sociétés d'Etats Membres différents', Commission des Communautés Européennes, COM (69) 5 final, Brussels, 15 January 1969.

63. *EEC Memorandum*, pp. 159–60.

64. S. D. Cheris and E. R. Fischer, 'The European Company: Its Promise and Problems', p. 125.

65. 'Proposition de Directive concernant le régime fiscal commun applicable aux sociétés mères et filiales d'Etats Membres différents'.

66. A similar opinion was expressed by Hermann Abs, who believes the time is not yet ripe for the creation of a European-type company (this opinion was presented in a letter Mr Abs sent to the author on 6 October 1971).

67. 'Pour une Société Européenne à responsabilité limitée', Centre de Recherche sur le Droit des Affaires de la Chambre de Commerce de Paris, Paris, 1970.

This study suggests the adoption of a legal instrument far more flexible than the SE. It recommends a *Société Européenne à responsabilité limitée*, namely, a closed limited company.

Other legal forms have been suggested which also have high flexibility such as the *Groupement d'Intérêt Economique*. These loose juridical forms might be considered as formalizations of hybrid solutions.

(For a discussion of the *Groupement d'Intérêt Economique*, see: Mario Iannuzzi, *Il diritto delle società per azioni nella Comunità Economica Europea*, pp. 118–23.)

68. This system was developed by the researcher as a result of an interview with a major oil company. Subsequently, it was corroborated through interviews with accounting specialists.

69. In addition to eliminating these operating fiscal barriers, it is desirable to facilitate the setting-up of hybrid solutions, principally from the fiscal point of view. This consists mainly in eliminating the capital gains taxes and taxes on transfer of assets within national boundaries. This really refers to a facilitation of domestic concentration.

70. See: Dennis Thompson, *The Proposal for a European Company*, Chapter II, pp. 22–36; and Charles de Hoghton, *The Company: Law, Structure and Reform in Eleven Countries*, PEP, Allen and Unwin, London, 1970.

71. See the discussion in the second section of the next chapter.

72. Further, the local clients (i.e., non-US) of American accounting and law firms in Europe normally present cases of a client's activity involving the US.

73. This analysis was primarily developed through second set interviews with executives with transnational concentration experience.

74. This idea is not entirely novel and similar proposals have been formulated elsewhere. See, for example: Christopher Layton, *Cross-Frontier Mergers in Europe*, pp. 36–53.

75. The German Bundesverband der deutschen Industrie and the French Conseil National du Patronat Français.

3.

REGULATORY OBSTACLES

This chapter focuses on regulatory obstacles which have no bearing on the legal structure of an international consolidation. In addition obstacles of a macroeconomic nature will be discussed, which, although not directly codified, are explicit public policy variables. The first part of the chapter deals specifically with antitrust problems. In the second part, regulations affecting the conduct of business will be considered: exchange controls, accounting rules, restricted mobility of human resources, disparity of technical standards, non-monetary union, and nationalized industries.

Antitrust

Several commentators consider antitrust a major obstacle to international concentration in Europe.[1] In this section it will be shown that, generally speaking, antitrust legislation *per se* presents no real barrier to international concentration, but that the confusion surrounding the issue may indeed be a stumbling block.

In the various EEC member states, antitrust regulations are less sophisticated than in the US. Historically, very few cases of antitrust action have occurred within national boundaries. Until recently, only Germany was known to have a stricter attitude towards the preservation of free competition.[2] The Cartel Office probably created the most widely publicized case of antitrust intervention in Europe when it required the splitting up of the chemical giant IG-Farbenindustrie AG into three major concerns: Bayer, BASF, and Hoechst.[3] In other countries, particularly Italy, antitrust action is virtually unknown. More recently, however, a greater awareness of the necessity of preserving free competition seems to be developing, and nations are tending to implement somewhat stricter regulations.[4]

At the Community level, efforts to maintain free competition have been expressed, at least in principle, in a more formal way. The crucial provisions in this area are Articles 85 and 86 of the Rome Treaty, which are reproduced below. Article 85 refers to 'agreements between enterprises', 'decisions by associations of enterprises', and 'concerted practices'. These all fall short of concentrations and are more akin to what was defined as co-operative agreement in chapter 1. Indeed, the Commission has made it clear that it would not pass any judgement on mergers on the basis of Article 85.[5]

The basic provision dealing with concentration is Article 86. Investigation of the effects of these laws makes it safe to say that the EEC's attitude is liberal. Indeed, up to the present, there have been no real impediments to international concentration within the EEC. Under Article 86, the only case of intervention has been the Continental Can case. In 1969 Continental Can, a US multinational company in the container business, purchased 85·5 per cent of the German company Schmalbach-Lubeca-Werke AG (SLW). In the same year Continental developed the idea of forming—together with the British Metal Box Company Ltd (MB)—a holding company the main objective of which would have been the implementation of Continental Can's strategy in Europe. Two licensees of Continental would also have participated in the deal—the Dutch Thomassen & Drijver-Verblifa NV (TDV) and the French Carnaud et Forges de Basse-Indre (Carnaud). Carnaud, however, indicated quite early that it would not go along with the venture. The idea was to set up a holding company comprising the SLW organization in Germany and its Austrian subsidiary, the TDV organization operating in the Benelux countries (TDV had a subsidiary in Belgium), the Italian subsidiary of the Metal Box Company—Super Box—as well as a plant of Metal Box in the UK.

Consistent with this idea, Continental formed a holding company on 20 February 1970, incorporating it in Delaware (USA) under the name of Europemballage. Continental transferred its holdings of SLW to Europemballage. Then—in accordance with an agreement signed with TDV on 16 February 1970—Continental made a tender offer for TDV's shares. At the time this tender was announced the EEC Commission declared that the operation 'might cause some difficulties' under Article 86. Apparently undeterred by this warning, Europemballage went ahead with its plan and acquired TDV. After the acquisition the Commission announced that it would make a formal inquiry into the European metal container industry. The result of this inquiry was that the Commission in December 1971 condemned Continental Can for having violated Article 86,[6] accusing the company of taking improper advantage of its

ARTICLE 85 OF THE ROME TREATY

1. The following shall be deemed to be incompatible with the Common Market and shall hereby be prohibited: any agreement between enterprises, any decisions by associations of enterprises and any concerted practices which are likely to affect trade between the Member States and which have as their object or result the prevention, restriction or distortion of competition within the Common Market, in particular those consisting in:
   (a) the direct or indirect fixing of purchase or selling prices or of any other trading conditions;
   (b) the limitation or control of production, markets, technical development or investment;
   (c) market-sharing or the sharing of sources of supply;
   (d) the application to parties to transactions of unequal terms in respect of equivalent supplies, thereby placing them at a competitive disadvantage;
   (e) the subjecting of the conclusion of a contract to the acceptance by a party of additional supplies which, either by their nature or according to commercial usage, have no connection with the subject of such contract.
2. Any agreements or decisions prohibited pursuant to this Article shall be null and void.
3. Nevertheless, the provisions of paragraph 1 may be declared inapplicable in the case of:

- any agreements or classes of agreements between enterprises,
- any decisions or classes of decisions by associations of enterprises, and
- any concerted practices or classes of concerted practices which contribute to the improvement of the production or distribution of goods or to the promotion of technical or economic progress while reserving to users an equitable share in the profit resulting therefrom, and which:
  (a) neither impose on the enterprises concerned any restrictions not indispensable to the attainment of the above objectives;
  (b) nor enable such enterprises to eliminate competition in respect of a substantial proportion of the goods concerned.

ARTICE 86 OF THE ROME TREATY

To the extent to which trade between any Member States may be affected thereby, action by one or more enterprises to take improper advantage of a dominant position within the Common Market or within a substantial part of it shall be deemed to be incompatible with the Common Market and shall hereby be prohibited.
Such improper practices may, in particular, consist in:

(a) the direct or indirect imposition of any inequitable purchase or selling prices or of any other inequitable trading conditions;
(b) the limitation of production, markets or technical development to the prejudice of consumers;
(c) the application to parties to transactions of unequal terms in respect of equivalent supplies, thereby placing them at a competitive disadvantage;

or,

(d) the subjecting of the conclusion of a contract to the acceptance, by a party, of additional supplies which, either by their nature or according to commercial usage, have no connection with the subject of such contract.

Source: *Treaty Establishing the European Economic Community.* Secretariat of the interim Committee for the Common Market and Euratom, Brussels, 1958, pp. 85–87.

dominant market position when it purchased TDV. The Commission requested that Continental Can put an end to this violation and that it submit proposals to the Commission before 1 July 1972 as to how it intended to do this. Continental then appealed to the European Court in Luxembourg. The Court decided in favour of Continental and against the Commission. The Commission's decision of 9 December 1972 was thus repealed.[7]

The fact that there has been only one antitrust case in the EEC seems to show that European antitrust is liberal. Indeed, the fact that this single case was finally resolved in favour of the company appears to indicate further that European antitrust is distinctly less strict than its US counterpart. Moreover, there is a feeling in the European business community that the Commission would not have taken any action against EEC companies had they been in the same position as Continental Can. The Continental Can case provided an ideal opportunity to affirm the EEC's will to preserve competition while simultaneously engaging in an action compatible with Europe's defensive posture towards the American challenge. Strong doubts are legitimate with regard to what would happen in a similar case involving only European companies. The Dunlop–Pirelli union is probably the best example of this; while many commentators expected a ruling against the consolidation, the Commission made no opposition to it. Given the choice between competition and the development of European giants through international concentration, the Commission inclines to the latter.

In fact there is serious question about whether the Commission can even use Article 86 against a concentration *per se*: can a concentration itself amount to abuse? A concentration can lead to a dominant position but until the concentration has started to operate, it cannot be said to 'take improper advantage' of its dominant position. This is in contrast with the US antitrust law which (at least since the Alcoa case) can be considered to prohibit dominant position *per se*. In other words, Article 86 appears to be a tool to monitor the behaviour of large concentrated groups, but not a tool to control the formation of such groups.

However, since there is no other antitrust provision in the Rome Treaty, the Commission has endeavoured to find ways to stretch Article 86 in order to be able to act against consolidations on the basis of this article. In the Continental Can instance the Commission argued that prior to the acquisition of TDV, Continental was already in a dominant position—which in itself did not constitute a violation of 86; there was violation at the moment when Continental, taking advantage of its dominant position, acquired TDV, thus eliminating competition. In other words, Continental was accused of abusing its dominant position when it purchased TDV.

Prior to this case it was not clear whether Article 86 could be used as a tool against concentration, and the question has been much debated.[8] Since the Continental Can case Article 86 is indeed regarded as a tool for controlling consolidations. While the European Court acquitted Continental, it admitted that the Commission was right on the theory that Article 86 was indeed to be considered as an instrument to monitor concentration in the EEC. In other words, the Court established the principle that Article 86 can be used to act against a consolidation, but in the particular instance of Continental Can it found that the Commission did not provide enough evidence to justify the use of the article.[9]

The Court's decision about the theory (i.e., the principle that Article 86 can be a tool to control concentration) has been widely criticized. The main reasoning behind these criticisms is that, had the legislators of the Rome Treaty intended to include a tool to control consolidations, they could have been more positive about the matter. Specifically, they could have included provisions similar to those of the 1951 Treaty of Paris (pertinent to the coal and steel sectors) which explicitly state that concentration *per se* can be ruled against.[10] 'Since the Treaty of Paris included clear provisions to monitor concentration, the fact that these provisions were omitted from the Rome Treaty is an indication that the legislators specifically intended to exclude such provisions from the Rome Treaty', said a corporate lawyer. Despite the questionable soundness of the Court's decision regarding 'the theory', it is generally felt that the 'principle' will be hard to implement and that it will be particularly difficult in practice to make a strong case to show that a concentration constitutes an abuse of a dominant position. In the words of an international executive: 'Even if it is possible in principle to hinder a link-up on the basis of 86, the Continental Can case shows that this is a very theoretical possibility; indeed, concentration in the EEC should not stumble over Article 86.'

While the EEC has made it clear that it will not take any action against mergers under Article 85, there are two reasons that make it desirable to analyse the implications of this article for international concentration. First, it might be debatable whether certain hybrid forms of concentration are—for antitrust purposes—to be regarded as mergers or as co-operative agreements. If they are co-operative agreements, concentration might fall under Article 85. Second, as will be shown in chapter 7, concentrations might have to be preceded by co-operative agreements. This means that the intermediate stage leading to a concentration can be viewed as falling within the scope of Article 85.[11]

With regard to the former question, it is quite clear, in view of EEC official statements, that the forms of concentration dealt with in this study are not viewed as co-operative agreements but as mergers.[12] Moreover, jurisprudence shows that the EEC's attitude is congruent with this position. There was never any serious question of considering the concentrations presented in chapter 1 as co-operative agreements.

The question of co-operative agreements as preliminary to concentration might, in appearance, create difficulties on the basis of Article 85. Co-operative agreements can be ruled against if they reduce free competition. However, the attitude of the Commission is quite liberal here, too. As discussed in the *EEC Memorandum*, the Commission has stated clearly that it does not intend to hinder co-operation among EEC firms.[13] To the contrary, it is all in favour of such co-operation.[14] There is considerable evidence to back up this position. First, Paragraph 3 of Article 85 provides that no ruling against a co-operative agreement shall occur if the agreement does not unreasonably restrict the parties and if the reduction of competition does not affect a large portion of the goods involved. It is generally accepted that this Paragraph substantially reduces the scope of Article 85. Further, the decisions of the Court of Justice and of the Commission have made it clear that Paragraph 1 is applicable only when the restriction of competition is 'sizable'. In fact, even when this *is* the case, the Commission grants the benefit of Article 85, Paragraph 3, if the agreement is necessary for economic and technological progress—provided that consumers receive some benefit from the agreement. Moreover, the *EEC Memorandum* rightly recalls that a list of types of agreements not falling under the scope of Article 85 has been adopted with the communication of July 1968.[15] The Commission is also considering the adoption of regulations which would exempt all minor agreements from Article 85. In addition, the *Memorandum*'s interpretation of Article 85, Paragraph 3, is that those agreements that would normally be ruled against under Article 85 shall not be ruled against if it appears that the positive aspects of the co-operation are greater than the negative aspects of restraint of competition. There is already a regulation in this regard for certain categories of agreements. The Commission is also at present elaborating regulations providing for a similar treatment concerning agreements on R & D specialization, common selling, and common procurement. Finally, because regulation 17 has instituted the requirements that a co-operative agreement be notified to the Commission,[16] certain exemptions from this requirement have been passed pertaining to agreements on the adoption of common norms for certain products and common research.[17] The Commission is also preparing regulations to extend these exemptions to other cases.

The preceding discussion should not give the impression that the EEC has an unconditionally *laissez-faire* attitude towards antitrust questions. In particular, under Article 85, it has taken some action against companies. For example, as noted by Werner Feld: 'In July 1969 the EEC Commission found that several chemical companies had violated the EEC antitrust regulations and imposed relatively heavy fines. Among the fined companies were giants of the European chemical industry.'[18] However, on the whole the EEC clearly has a liberal attitude towards antitrust questions, certainly more liberal than that of the US. The cases of intervention under Article 85 not only were justified but were also of limited consequence for the companies involved. This liberal attitude is in fact growing stronger as the Commission is realizing that companies perceive its policy to be more rigid than it really is. The documents the Commission has put out in recent years are often designed to temper its earlier statements, in particular Article 85 and 86 (or, more precisely, their interpretation). Earlier statements have given the impression that the Commission is stricter than it wants to appear. Now, documents like the *EEC Memorandum* attempt to correct these misinterpretations.

Faced with these facts, what is the companies' perspective on the problem? As with the legal and fiscal obstacles, there is confusion and a feeling of uncertainty about the antitrust question. The problem is misperceived by the business community, mainly because of a communication gap.

The first source of difficulty is the absence of an antitrust tradition in European countries. When the Rome Treaty was signed in 1957, European managers in general felt uncomfortable with its antitrust provisions, simply because this was a new phenomenon. During the interviewing for this study, the statement was often made (particularly by older executives) that when Articles 85 and 86 first came into existence, they had a perceived content which far exceeded their actual importance. As an Italian executive put it: 'Articles 85 and 86 took (in the late 50s) a mystical meaning for us. They intimidated us a lot!' Today there is still some emotional concern about this issue, especially for those European companies which are more national than international in scope. It is noteworthy that the executives who expressed concern about these questions, but were least articulate about them, were those from countries like Italy, which have the least antitrust regulation, or those who had limited international business experience. The explanation is that they react somewhat irrationally to EEC's antitrust regulations because they are not familiar with the antitrust concept. If pressed to say why they react as they do, they are often incapable of specifying rational reasons.

Beyond general reservations regarding international consolidations, antitrust regulations—by the mere fact that they have newly come into existence—foster the impression that the EEC has an *a priori* mistrust of consolidations. Because they are not accustomed to antitrust regulations, practitioners have read into those of the EEC more than is contained in them. On this point a German executive made an interesting observation. Management tends to associate these regulations with the information content of the impossibility of doing a merger discussed in chapter 2: not only is there no legal provision for a merger, but there is also a host of regulations against concentration. Indeed, it must really mean that international concentrations are not welcome!

A second source of problems is the unclear way in which antitrust provisions are expressed. With regard to Article 85 and particularly 86, firms perceive them as dogmatic. Businessmen find that the notion of 'abuse of dominant position' is not operational and is quite obscure. This is all the more disturbing to them because the EEC was not able to specify what it meant in more practical terms than the instances mentioned in the Article itself. Indeed, the subsequent documents designed to clarify Article 85 and 86 do not contribute a great deal from the businessmen's point of view. The following quote from the Commission's *Memorandum* of 1966 illustrates this point: '[Market domination] is primarily a matter of economic potency, or the ability to exert on the operation of the market an influence that is substantial and also, in principle, foreseeable for the dominant enterprise.'[19] If one considers that this is an attempt to clarify Article 86, it should be obvious why executives are disillusioned with any attempt to draw some practical conclusions from the EEC's declarations.

This lack of clarity is worsened by the proliferation of statements and declarations aimed at elucidating the Commission's position on the antitrust question. All such documents have in common an emphasis on questions of principle, which, again, is dogmatic in character. Such abundance of what a Belgian executive called 'existential philosophy' contrasts sharply with the need for operational regulations. Not until recently has the Commission been putting out concrete guidelines for companies to follow, indicating what is meant in practice by a given statement of principle. Many executives have complained about the scarcity of clear instructions, using expressions such as 'instructions for use', or 'cookbook recipes'. It is important to understand that such guidelines must be simple and unambiguous, since European executives feel less at ease with antitrust regulations than their US counterparts. The confusion is enhanced by the poverty of jurisprudence in the area. The effect of the lack of practical norms is aggravated by the limited number of test cases, which leaves companies with little possibility of clarifying the actual antitrust situation. Not only does the legislation appear unclear, but there is also a patent vagueness in the jurisprudence due to its as yet limited history.

The reaction to this position of the EEC is that companies feel they do not have an adequate understanding of the antitrust environment. An apparent illogicality in the regulations is often mentioned: it is necessary to obtain permission to engage in a less than complete collaborative endeavour such as co-operative agreement, while it is not necessary to have permission to create the ultimate form of collaboration such as concentration. Many managers do not understand why the Commission is stricter for the former than for the latter.[20]

It should be clear that as long as there are these misconceptions, there will be restraining forces for potential 'concentrators', if only from the psychological point of view. Because it is not clear what the EEC really wants, firms tend to be overly conservative. Indeed, obscurity here generates uncertainty, which promotes excessive caution. Executives often stated that the risk of concentrating was too great because of the uncertainty attached to the antitrust policy.

Other factors add to the uncertainty felt by management. The first arises from the way Article 86 is stated. As was discussed previously, the article condemns 'abuse' of dominant position and not dominant position *per se*. At first sight a link-up in itself cannot constitute a violation of Article 86, and the Commission has to wait until the concentration is operating before it can say that the concentrated group is 'taking improper advantage' of its position. Thus, by definition, the Commission would have to wait some time before it could take any action against two companies which have joined forces. From management's point of view this is unacceptable. It cannot afford to find out *ex post facto* that a concentration is not acceptable. While it is already painful enough to be prevented from carrying out a consolidation because of antitrust regulations, it is considerably more aggravating to have to split up a consolidation once it has been arduously constructed. Because of the particular formulation of Article 86, managers perceive a danger of antitrust action *a posteriori*: that is, they feel they cannot be sure of complying entirely with rules of competition until several years after a consolidation has occurred. As a German executive stated: 'It is a situation à la Kafka: you never know what the law is, not to mention whether you are complying with it.'

This situation is rendered even more disturbing by the feeling that EEC Antitrust has neither developed a definitive philosophy nor reached its full power. As a French interviewee put it: 'Today it may clear a particular consolidation; tomorrow it may decide to act against it.' The question of evolving philosophy is of special concern to managers. There is the impression in the business community of internal divergencies of opinion between different streams of thought within the Commission (particularly between the Industrial Policy department, which wants to create large industrial units, and the Competition department). This impression is nourished by the evolution of EEC policy over time, as can be seen from official documents. Its earlier statements, starting with the Rome Treaty itself, conveyed the impression that there was going to be a strict competition policy. Then, in the early 'sixties, more liberal declarations were put out. In 1966, however, the Commission delivered a Memorandum defining its own competition policy, which was interpreted as a return to a stricter position.[21] Then, in 1970, the *EEC Memorandum* adopted a clearly liberal attitude.

The Commission is in fact justified in making such changes of attitude. As was pointed out earlier, some of these changes were motivated by the erroneous interpretation given by outsiders to the

Commission's statements. Moreover, as the *EEC Memorandum* admits, a source of problems has been 'the uncertainties inherent in any new regulatory control.'[22] The somewhat hesitant attitude of the Commission was caused simply by its lack of experience in the area.[23] Despite these justifications, the fact remains that to an outsider there have been some contradictory statements, and the firms' reactions are also quite legitimate.

A further source of difficulty is the perception managers have of the requirement to obtain a clearing for a co-operative agreement. (In fact, since managers do not always distinguish properly between co-operative agreements and concentrations, they often tend to believe that the requirement of obtaining a clearance also applies to concentrations; in consequence, this discussion applies to concentrations as well as to co-operative agreements.) Several interviewees reported that the process of applying for permission to make a co-operative agreement is an inhibition for many managers who shy away from the bureaucracy involved. The Italians are the most representative of this attitude. In the second set of interviews it was established that there were two reasons for this. First, that Italy has the most limited tradition of antitrust legislation of all the EEC countries, and managers are not prepared to cope with applying for something with which they are not fully familiar. Second, that Italians have a conditioned reflex against public administration. Because they are used to an inefficient national public administration, they tend to believe that all public administrations are cumbersome and inefficient. Indeed, Italians have developed a pattern of negative response to any kind of public bureaucracy. Although this problem should not be overemphasized, it is noteworthy that the mere mention of the necessity of filing an application with the EEC for a co-operative agreement is a psychological barrier. An Italian executive who had lived for many years abroad observed: 'Italians have so much the nightmare of bureaucracy, that they sometimes prefer to give up a deal rather than even having to find out what the bureaucratic requirements are, if this alone necessitates any face to face contact with the bureaucrats.'

A final source of difficulty is the poor communication channels between the Commission and the business community. A number of executives stated that they had tried to obtain some guidance from the EEC. In particular, middle managers and staff specialists of companies had been sent to the EEC to get answers to antitrust questions. While they encountered genuine interest, the help received was largely academic. Managers complained that the Commission's orientation was neither realistic nor practical. As one executive said: 'We had a here and now question; they answered with philosophical maxims. The most down-to-earth answer we were able to obtain is that they would let us know after having given proper attention to the question. This took eighteen months.' Obviously this state of affairs could only contribute to the existing confusion.

To overcome this problem of inadequate communication, the Commission should recognize the needs of practitioners and attempt to talk 'businessmen's language'. It should prepare a final document stating its position in operational form. This document should be 'applications-oriented'—pragmatic rather than dogmatic. A step in this direction has been taken with some of the regulations discussed earlier. However, the task would be far simpler if the EEC put out an integrated statement containing all the relevant regulations and thus clarifying its antitrust policy for management. Moreover, the Commission should think seriously of developing a communications bureau to serve as a link between the business community and the EEC legislators. This bureau should have a practical orientation geared to eliminating the misunderstandings discussed above and should be staffed, at least in part, with businessmen.

The business community should also make an effort to bridge the communication gap. It should participate in the setting up of the communications bureau and also become better acquainted with the European antitrust policy. While an international effort should be made in this direction, business confederations might carry out this task.

The discussion of the practical difficulties created by antitrust policy has, up to now, focused on non-technical questions (i.e., by-products of the central question of antitrust legislation). There is a technical hindrance that should be mentioned. This is the conflict between national and EEC antitrust regulations. In certain countries, businessmen report that national antitrust authorities extend their powers over international concentration involving a national company. The problem, in management's opinion, is that national authorities tend to be shortsighted and to reason in terms of domestic competition, which is not congruent with the notion of competition on a European scale. Moreover, it often happens that an international concentration falls under the jurisdiction of national and EEC antitrust regulatory agents that have different objectives. Reportedly, what is acceptable for one may not be for the other. As Germany has the most elaborate national antitrust, it is not surprising that German management is the most articulate about this issue. This is especially so since German antitrust authorities are believed to deem European competition policy too liberal. German firms believe their national authorities have set as a more or less explicit goal for themselves to become the ambassadors of free competition in the EEC. German executives feel they are under particular antitrust pressure, even beyond national boundaries.

In fact, a concentration involving two parties of different countries may run up against four autonomous regulatory agencies, all of which have different demands and expectations: the EEC antitrust, the two national Antitrust commissions, and the US Antitrust Commission. The last cannot be dismissed lightly, particularly when one of the objectives of a concentration is the joining of forces in the American market—as demonstrated by the Ciba–Geigy case.[24]

The solution to this problem of conflict between various antitrust agencies is almost unanimously seen as the delegation of all the power to the EEC Antitrust Commission, to the detriment of national legislators. Many managers are often of the opinion that the EEC legislators, once they have clarified their policy, should also rule on domestic competition issues. There would be several advantages to such centralization of powers. First, conflicts would be avoided and the situation would be clearer. Companies would not run the risk of facing multiple, confusing antitrust pressures. Second, this would provide a viable *alter ego* to the American antitrust authorities, which certainly are not encouraged to resolve European competition questions. The argument here is that a strong EEC Antitrust would be able to monitor free competition without needing the help of US authorities; today, unfortunately, this is not the case. Moreover, EEC authorities would be able to conduct a dialogue with the US on a comparable stance. The EEC would be able to retaliate towards US firms in Europe. Third, it seems logical to delegate power over competition to the EEC, if a United Europe is to come into existence. In that event national antitrust would represent a myopic attitude. Moreover, if European industry is to become competitive on a global basis, the least that can be done is to delegate antitrust power to the geographically broadest authority.

Other regulations affecting the conduct of business

This section examines the obstacles to consolidations which have their roots in public policies and regulations. The first of these is exchange controls, which exist in most countries in Europe.[25] Even where such controls are not rigid, a firm wishing to invest large amounts of capital abroad has to obtain a clearing from its national authorities. This can be a hindrance both at the moment of construction of the concentration and at the operational level.

In forming a concentration, the first difficulty arises when there is a unilateral acquisition of stock by one of the companies (hybrid solution 3). Management in the country of the acquiring company runs into a barrier when it has to export capital to pay for the acquired company. Here, however—as in Fiat's purchase of Citroën's stock—management believes it is relatively easy for the company to obtain permission from its government to go ahead with the acquisition. A government makes few difficulties when one of its country's companies buys a foreign one. But in the converse situation serious problems may arise, as interviewees reported. The government of the acquired company may not allow the export of shares of that company. The acquiring company can then found a holding company in the country of the acquired company and thereby hold the shares of and control the latter.

Where the partners are of equal size, again the potential problem faced by managers is that a country may oppose the export of shares. This is a hindrance in the exchange of shares, say, under an Agfa–Gevaert model. However, if the government has agreed to the concentration, an *ad hoc* solution will be found. The question of government agreement is of the greatest importance and will be discussed in detail in the next chapter.

At the operating level, exchange controls reportedly may create some difficulties in that they hinder the free flow of funds between companies located in different countries. Here, too, an *ad hoc* clearance from national authorities is the typical solution. Companies arrange with their respective finance ministries to obtain an exemption from exchange controls. Moreover, exchange controls can be bypassed, to a certain extent, through transfer prices. As with operating fiscal problems, a transfer price mechanism can neutralize exchange controls or, at least, minimize their effect.

Thus exchange controls do not represent an insurmountable stumbling block to international concentration. Executives often express the hope that the *ad hoc* type of arrangements between firms and governmental authorities will be replaced by some sort of formal provision allowing internationally concentrated groups a certain degree of freedom from exchange controls.[26] This is because there is always a risk element attached to *ad hoc* solutions, which can be of a temporary nature. Particularly in southern European countries where *ad hoc* clearances can take the form of a tacit agreement (i.e., national authorities may decide to turn a blind eye to the flow of funds), there is no guarantee that some years later a stricter policy may not be enacted. Management advocates an explicit provision of general application specifying the flow of funds a transnationally consolidated group can make across national boundaries. As a Belgian executive stated: 'Transnationally concentrated groups today can obtain a certain immunity from exchange controls; this immunity, however, has to rely on *ad hoc* permissions. What is most urgent is a formal rule in lieu of these *ad hoc* permissions, which are always contingent. We insist less on increased immunity from exchange controls than on a reduction of the uncertainty of the immunity we are granted now.'

The second obstacle is accounting problems.[27] It has, in fact, two aspects. On one hand, problems are created by conflicting legal regulations; on the other, problems are created by different accounting practices in the various countries—quite apart from legal requirements. In this chapter, attention will be given to the former only. The latter will be discussed in chapter 5.

In the various member states there are different regulations on what information should be given to outsiders.[28] The sharpest contrast is probably between Germany and Italy. In Germany, disclosure requirements are stringent. In Italy, a company must publish only a few sketchy financial statements of the simplest form: the financial statements of the largest companies can be presented in less than a page. In addition, different treatment is given to virtually all accounts. The most marked differences are probably in the treatment of inventory valuation, depreciation, and reserves. For example, some countries require the LIFO method, some the FIFO method, while others allow both. Such requirements for external reporting also have a bearing on the data firms keep record of internally and on the performance standards employed.

The result is an incompatibility of figures between firms. At the moment an evaluation takes place with the prospect of a consolidation, the net worth of one company cannot be compared with that of another.[29] Indeed, financial analysis aimed at evaluating one company relative to the other is often not possible. Moreover, at the operational level of a concentration (i.e., when a consolidated group has come into existence and is functioning), the necessity of keeping separate books to satisfy the various national regulations adds to the administrative costs. While the long-run design of the EEC is to bring about harmonization in this area, companies meanwhile have devised methods to cope with the accounting differences. Probably the most experienced in this field are now Dunlop–Pirelli. The evaluation problems they encountered were quite complex, and the effort to bring about internal harmonization required the commitment of considerable resources. They called in a specialized consulting firm for help. Its task was to spell out common standards acceptable to both parties. As this company happened to be American, it was able to generate 'neutral' standards (i.e., not particularly favourable to one party) more easily than if it had been of the same nationality as one of the two parties.

Whereas this process is painful, it is so for specialists only. Top management is not directly involved, and, as an executive of an internationally consolidated group expressed it: 'We let the accountants tackle it; we only had to pay the bill.' Indeed, the importance of this barrier is overemphasized and, while the bill can be high, the problem is not insurmountable for a major concentration.

The most effective method of facilitating this process would be for a consulting organization to develop multilingual accounting expertise. In Europe, the so-called *Banques d'Affaires* could take advantage of this opportunity, if such organizations would accept the challenge of internationalizing their scope.[30]

The third obstacle is restriction on the free flow of human resources across national boundaries.[31] There are no explicit regulations against the free flow of people within the EEC. The member states have agreed not to hinder such flows and have eliminated any 'quotas' on human resources. However, it is management's experience that public authorities can control the flow of immigration by indirect regulations. They can refuse to grant work permits to foreign workers, and can also create bureaucratic difficulties which delay the permission for a foreign national to exercise his profession. In addition, unions can oppose the import of foreign workers. Three sets of difficulties, mentioned by interviewees, result from such limitations, First, the transnational group cannot benefit from the possible synergies arising when one of the participating partners is from a country in which there is an abundant labour supply which could otherwise be directed to a country where labour is scarce. Second, these restrictions do not permit integration of labour policies in a transnational group: separate administrative units in charge of the labour forces in each country must be maintained. Third the restrictions give rise to bureaucratic red tape. For management to negotiate the limitations to the free flow of its workers can be a time-consuming process because of cumbersome bureaucracies, as chapter 4 will show. The first difficulty reduces the possible attractiveness of international concentrations, and the other two add to administrative costs.

The fourth obstacle is the disparity in technical standards for goods and services—the characteristics they must have in order to comply with the requirements of national regulations. This study found that the major product disparities were in the automotive, food, chemical, and pharmaceutical industries.[32] The most striking problems in the automotive industry are those reported by Saviem and MAN (a French and a German firm having a close co-operative agreement). These two companies produce trucks; each is responsible for certain parts which are then assembled in a common product. Their problem is that the product cannot be a single one for the French and German markets because of differing technical standards—often concerning trivial details such as the shape of the lights or the height of the step for entering the driver's cabin. Such regulations are extremely detailed, and the French *Bureau des Mines*, in particular, is very strict in enforcing such standards. Further, managers report there is often no recognition of quality standards from country to country: even when the standards for a particular product are the same, the authorities of one country may not recognize the clearance of that product by the authorities of the other. The product then has to be cleared by the authorities of both countries, and executives often complain that what is satisfactory for one country is not for the other, despite the fact that the requirements are the same! In addition, there can be differences in regulations which have a bearing on the marketing of a product. Thus in the food industry, there are differences which have nothing to do with the product itself but with its packaging. For instance, margarine in Belgium has to come in a different shape than in Holland.

Management sees such disparities as preventing a total integration of production, thus precluding a full reaping of the economies of scale that could derive from a concentration. It is necessary to tailor the product to each national market, which is a costly process. Several executives felt that the persistence of these disparities is motivated by protectionist attitudes of the different member states. The elimination of tariffs and quotas within the EEC presents a threat to many national firms, and the maintenance of different standards for products is a convenient surrogate for such tariffs and quotas.[33] Indeed, one can see no other reason for the maintenance of such technical disparities as those regulating the shape of a blinker, particularly as the Commission has elaborated directives for technical harmonization. Such directives have not been implemented because of the ill-will of national governments. It is interesting that the matter of standards was mentioned particularly by companies which have had direct experience in collaborative endeavours, indicating that the problem was not sufficiently considered prior to a concentration. Companies with collaboration experience in fact acknowledge they have underestimated it.

As to disparities in standards in services, the best example is provided by the banking sector. There are substantial differences from country to country in what a bank can and cannot do, particularly the type of credits a bank can have. For example, in Italy banks are not allowed to grant medium- and long-term loans,[34] while in other European countries this is quite customary. In Germany, banks typically have substantial stock participation in industrial companies, while this is forbidden in other countries. Further, the amount and composition of reserves vary from country to country. Finally, the marketing of the banking sector has to be different in each nation (e.g., different interest rates are allowed on current accounts).

These disparities are believed by management to have their roots in the historical development of business in each country. Harmonization is much harder to bring about in this sector because the banking field has an impact on the entire entrepreneurial life of a nation, and a change here has an effect on a multitude of economic variables. These differences are far from being absolute barriers to international concentration; US banks have demonstrated the possibility of operating across national boundaries with a single policy. However, integration of operations cannot be complete because of these disparities, and in management's view they do reduce the advantages of an international consolidation and thus constitute obstacles.

The fifth obstacle, related to harmonization in the banking sector, is the absence of monetary union in the EEC. This problem has two aspects: the first is specific to the banking sector; the second is more general in character. With respect to the banking sector, it is almost unanimously felt by management that as long as there is no monetary union it will not be possible to have a concentration across national boundaries. The reason is that banks are perceived as 'money makers' and as instruments for macroeconomic policy. Because each country has its own autonomous economic policy, central banks will not permit major banks to consolidate, since they fear loss of some of their freedom. As one banker expressed it, 'Printing money is the prerogative of the nation and banks are its bearers'. International banking and international speculation are disruptive enough for the macro-finance equilibrium; therefore, a central bank is hesitant to permit its own financial institutions to concentrate across frontiers. Indeed, it is generally felt that, as long as there is no European central bank, collaboration among banks will be restricted to co-operative agreements.[35]

A legitimate question would be whether monetary union *per se* should be treated as an obstacle rather than a cause of an obstacle, which might be labelled 'opposition to banking consolidations by central banks'. While, strictly speaking, this might be more logical, to talk about monetary union as an obstacle seems more realistic since it emphasizes the nucleus of the problem.

Monetary union, or rather the absence of it, also creates more general problems, which have been raised by interviewees.[36] The necessity of having to control an organization in different units of account can be a difficult process. Multinational firms are familiar with this problem. Not only have they learned to live with it, but they have also been able to turn it into an advantage via international speculation. However, it should be noted that, for multinational firms, the risk of monetary fluctuations can be much more spread out than for an internationally consolidated group. A multinational firm operating in many countries can draw up its financial policy selecting opportunities from many countries. Moreover, it can diversify its risk by investing and raising funds in several countries at a time. A consolidated group is dependent upon the relationship between national currencies of its participating companies. It has a vital stake in that single monetary relationship. Also, it does not have the option of choosing this relationship.

Further, non-monetary union leads to a compartmentalization of capital markets.[37] As will be discussed in chapter 5, companies complain about the ethnocentrism of national capital markets. Investors refrain from investing cross-nationally, mainly because of the risk of exchange rate fluctuations. The companies also refrain from raising money on foreign capital markets because of the risk that exchange rate fluctuations may oblige them to repay a foreign debt at a more costly rate. Monetary union would bring about a greater integration of European capital markets which, in turn, would reduce the financial difficulties encountered by large internationally consolidated groups.

Monetary union would reduce the financial uncertainty of internationally concentrated groups. Financial managers emphasize that this would come about from the elimination of the risk of units of account changing their parities. The need for monetary union has been felt particularly in recent times of unrest in international finance, when some European currencies have been freely fluctuating. Besides, the reduction in uncertainty could come from the second-order effects of monetary union:[38] it would entail the co-ordination of economic policies (thus furthering the harmonization of monetary and fiscal policies), reducing the risk of conflicting policies, which in the long run are always disruptive for business. Also, it would virtually eliminate the risk of exchange controls becoming stricter over time—a very real possibility, as was discussed above.

Last but certainly not least, monetary union would serve as a psychological motivation for international concentration. The next chapter will deal with the lack of incentive to international collaboration from the institutional environment. Firms complain that they see no progress towards a United Europe at the macro-level and thus they feel less inclined to adopt a European strategy. In this connection, European monetary integration would have a strong psychological impact in that it would make the business community more aware of the trend towards European integration. Indeed, the psychological role of monetary union as a catalyst cannot be overemphasized.

The sixth obstacle is that created by the ownership of certain firms by national states.[39] While the trend towards the so-called mixed economies with strong state ownership in industry started in Italy, the phenomenon has spread. Today, governmental participation in industry is substantial in all the EEC countries. (Even in Germany the Brandt administration is perceived as intending to increase the government's stake in the economy.) This creates some difficulties for international concentrations, which can be thought of in two ways: real tangible impediments inherent to such ownership and second-order psychological hindrances.

State-owned companies often have objectives that are in conflict with those of a privately owned company.[40] They go back to the motivation of the government in nationalizing the particular company. A prime motivation is that of taking over unprofitable industries that would otherwise fail. The motivation can be either avoiding disruptive lay-offs or maintaining the production of the goods or services that the firm provides. It may be thought socially desirable not to discontinue such production (e.g., railways, although often unprofitable, provide a useful service whose discontinuation would be undesirable). This objective was the original design of IRI (Istituto per la Ricostruzione Industriale), the Italian state-owned holding company under whose control the government has brought most of its industrial and financial interests. IRI was originally designed as a 'hospital for sick companies'. It should be clear that a private enterprise cannot be expected to accept a concentration with a partner that consciously operates in unprofitable activities. The same problem is encountered when the state-owned company is active in a business for prestige reasons. An example here is the transatlantic liner business; a private organization would divest itself from such a patently unprofitable operation. The same difficulties arise when a state-owned company has as one of its major objectives investing in less developed areas of its country. Italy is the best example here, where state-owned companies have an explicit objective to invest in the Mezzogiorno—the less developed area of the south. Such an objective is not compatible with the profit maximizing behaviour of a private concern.

While the above discussion takes the point of view of the potential private partner, there are some important reasons which make it difficult as well for the state-owned company to accept a collaboration with a foreign private firm. There is a general belief that it is difficult for a government to sell shares of one of its companies to foreign hands, as an international concentration normally requires. A government feels that it is selling part of itself to foreigners. This is one of the most important alleged reasons why the agreement between Commerzbank, Crédit Lyonnais, and Banco di Roma is not a concentration with financial ties.[41] On this point, however, it is not clear that state ownership really prevents a concentration with financial links. A possibility is the founding of a new common subsidiary, jointly owned by the private and the state-owned partners (hybrid solution II).[42] But, even beyond this, a great number of nationalized companies' executives stated that they were not averse to direct financial cross-holdings. Specifically, in the Italian case, if an IRI company agrees to concentrate with a foreign partner, it would be conceivable that there would be an exchange of shares between the two companies. What would probably not be possible is an exchange of shares involving IRI's own shares, namely, the holding company itself. But this is of secondary importance since IRI's companies are not only quite autonomous but also of a more appropriate size for a concentration than IRI itself. IRI is probably too big and complex to amalgamate with a group of similar size.

Management sees more significant problems than the mere reluctance of a government to give up shares of one of its companies. First, state-owned companies are national in outlook. As an executive of one of these companies said: 'Our vocation is national, because the government, by definition, has a national mission'. Usually the goals of a state-owned company are to build up the government's economic power in the government's area of competence, which is within national boundaries. (Thus, the government may take firms under its wing to avoid their becoming involved in an international concentration: to maintain their national identity, the government nationalizes them.) Consequently, it is not surprising that state-owned companies are reluctant to consolidate internationally; they wish to avoid a dilution of their national character.

A final problem in this area is the fact that state-owned companies do not recognize the necessity of an international consolidation so strongly as private firms do. It was often mentioned during interviews that, particularly from the financial point of view, public companies can rely on greater resources for raising funds. Also, it is possible for them to obtain government subsidies to support R & D investments, even if these are not economically viable. Finally, they can charge expenses to the government in a liberal fashion. For example, airlines can charge certain training expenses for their pilots to the military airforce. The result is that public companies have a less immediate need to enter a consolidation, because they have the feeling they can succeed on their own. However, nationalization often only postpones the problem, which, in fact, makes it worse. A nationalized company can, for some time, benefit from the government's help, but this too often turns out to be insufficient in the long run.

The second set of problems deriving from state ownership in industry is psychological in nature. While these problems were mentioned by interviewees throughout Europe, they were really serious areas of concern only for southern European countries and Italy in particular. Private sector interviewees stated that, from their point of view, a collaboration with a state-owned company is considered threatening. First, the private partner perceives the state-owned company as ill managed; there is a fundamental mistrust in the private sector, of both the administrative capabilities and the achievement motivation of the executives of state-owned companies. The reason is that state-owned companies are deemed unable to attract the best people, who prefer to go to the more rewarding, challenging, and individualized jobs offered by the private sector. Often the manager of the public company is considered less ambitious and more concerned with his job security than his counterpart in the private sector. He is attracted to public companies because the rate of lay-offs is extremely low. As an Italian manager put it: 'Once you have the job you are O.K. for life. Why should you worry to work hard as it will not do you any good anyway?' Moreover, the political overtones of these organizations distract management from its business objectives. Private sector managers believe a great deal of political dabbling occurs internally, and state-owned companies often are seen as becoming political instruments. Most important of all, however, the private sector perceives much less competitive pressure on individuals in public organizations. The incentive for an individual to perform in a superior fashion is just not there. The fact that profit maximization is often not the prime objective of state-owned companies permeates the whole organization. An individual is not believed to be motivated by tangible financial incentives. Further, in the eyes of private firms, the bureaucracy of public organizations destroys the non-monetary motivations an individual may have. A man who joins a public company in the belief that he is behaving 'socially' (in the public interest) allegedly is quickly frustrated by the apathy of the organization.

The second difficulty resides in the fear the public sector inspires: it is perceived as having a far greater bargaining power because it has political backing. Private companies feel that if a dispute should occur between one of them and a public company, the latter would invariably win. This is particularly so in those sectors where the prime customer is the government. If a private company often hesitates to engage in a collaborative endeavour with a public company of its own nationality, its reservations *vis-à-vis* a foreign public partner are even greater because it is under the impression that it has no influence on the behaviour of the public partner.

It should be clear that this last psychological difficulty is exaggerated. In the second set of interviews it was ascertained that those private companies which have had co-operative experience with the public sector have had no complaints that the public partner takes improper advantage of his political back-up. Such companies report that, while the inefficiency problem is real enough to justify reservations about an amalgamation with a public partner, the fear of a public company abusing its political ties is unwarranted.

While state ownership does not in itself preclude an international concentration, there are serious difficulties nonetheless. These have to do not only with the problems pertinent to the international dimension, but also with the problems of co-operation between public and private sector. As was seen, the objectives are different between public and private enterprises, quite apart from the nationality question. It is tempting to conclude that international concentrations should take place among public companies. Indeed, the idea of a European IRI carries with it, in principle, a lot of appeal. The problems involved, however, are immense and can only be outlined here. First, from an administrative point of view, diseconomies of scale would probably be unbearable; the groups are often too big. Second, such concentrations are difficult to envision without political integration. Here again, theoretically, this is not a *sine qua non* condition: governments could pool their resources in a jointly owned organization. However, the problems encountered by Euratom cast considerable doubt on this.[43] Indeed, it is hard to imagine anything beyond international co-operative agreements between various public companies, as well as between private and public organizations.

This problem is more important on the European scene than it may at first appear. Government participation is quite extensive and covers many sectors which would benefit most from international concentration. Examples are high-technology industries such as aircraft companies or industries requiring a strong marketing commitment such as automobile builders. Often, however, state ownership hampers this. An executive of a public company complained that 'Governments are shortsighted when they nationalize some companies which patently cannot make it on their own because they preclude their salvation which lies in a cross-national link-up'.

Finally, the interviews have raised a number of miscellaneous difficulties having to do with legal requirements in the different countries. For example, contract law varies substantially, particularly between Great Britain and the EEC countries. There is no uniform patent law.[44] In particular, Italy has little patent protection—a major complaint of foreign chemical companies. However, these are not obstacles *per se*, as it is always possible to find common ground for mutually satisfactory agreements. The true difficulties are more on the administrative side. Transnational contracts have to be drawn up with greater care because each party's lawyer has to cope with foreign requirements with which he may be unfamiliar. These difficulties are really an impediment only in the early stages of a collaboration; they involve a relatively high start-up cost, until each party has learned the other's needs.

The questions discussed in this section are, clearly, not major hindrances taken individually. Apart from the question of nationalized companies (a problem only in specific cases), each of the other issues merely adds to the administrative costs of a consolidated group. Disparities in technical standards reduce the benefits of international concentrations. Differences in areas like accounting increase the administrative costs of internationally consolidated groups. While each single difficulty is not a major stumbling block, all of them together create a set of complications, which are especially aggravating for businessmen in situations where it should be relatively easy for public agents to settle the question. This is certainly true of the differences in technical standards. Here, harmonization is doubly necessary as 'non-harmonization is'—in a French executive's words—'an insult to the wisdom of civilized nations'. Indeed, the message which many businessmen read in matters like 'non-harmonization' is far-reaching: there is no political will to create a United Europe.

While harmonization is the most effective solution in some instances, the business community recognizes that in other instances it is the business community's responsibility to adapt to the environment. This is particularly true for the differences in corporate administrative regulations. Here, the fact that a learning phenomenon takes place, which quickly renders complicated matters routine, suggests that formal training is the answer. It would seem feasible to insert in a management training programme a course in areas such as the financial implications of exchange controls. While the existing management courses are still too often national in outlook (as opposed to European), the problem is really the scarcity of management education opportunities. This is a question of fundamental importance going well beyond the scope of this discussion. Indeed, it will be taken up in greater detail in chapter 6.

NOTES

1. See, for example:
(a) Paul M. Goldberg, 'The Evolution of Transnational Companies in Europe', Ph.D. Dissertation, Massachusetts Institute of Technology, Sloan School of Management, 1971, pp. 61–72.
(b) D. Brault, 'Les vues françaises sur la coopération des entreprises au regard du Traité de Rome', *Revue du Marché Commun*, No. 126, September 1969.
(c) Peter C. Cannellos and Horst S. Silber, 'Concentration in the Common Market', *Common Market Law Review*, Vol. 7, No. 1, January 1970, pp. 5–35 and Vol. 7, No. 2, April 1970, pp. 138–66.
2. The British Monopolies Commission is also stricter than the average national antitrust authorities of the EEC.
3. Barbara Gramberg, 'Die Konzentration im Bereich der Chemischen Industrie (Historische Entwicklung)', Verband der Chemischen Industrie (unpublished study), Frankfurt, 1962.
4. For an analysis of the antitrust policy of the individual EEC member states, see: *Grenzueberschreitende Unternehmenskooperation in der EWG*, Comité Européen pour le Progrès Economique et Social (CEPES), Stuttgart, Forkel Verlag, 1968, pp. 163–79.
5. See: Peter C. Cannellos and Horst S. Silber, 'Concentration in the Common Market'; and Kurt Markert, 'Mitteilung', *Revue du Marché Commun*, No. 109, January–February 1968, p. 254.
6. See: 'Décision de la Commission du 9 décembre 1971 relative à une procédure d'application de l'article 86 du traité CEE', *Journal Officiel des Communautés Européennes*, Brussels, 8 January 1972.
7. See: Arrêt du 21 février 1973 de la Cour de Justice des Communautés Européennes du Luxembourg dans l'affaire 6/72: Continental Can Company Inc., USA, et Europemballage Corporation contre Commission des Communautés Européennes.
8. See: *Revue du Marché Commun*, No. 109, January–February 1968, pp. 183–292.
9. The Court essentially felt the Commission had failed to prove that competition had actually been jeopardized. For details see: Arrêt du 21 février 1973 de la Cour de Justice des Communautés Européennes du Luxembourg dans l'affaire 6/72.
10. See: Articles 65 and 66 of the Treaty Establishing the European Coal and Steel Community (the so-called Treaty of Paris), Paris, 1951.
11. The same point is made by André Marchal in 'Nécessité économique des fusions et concentrations intracommunautaires', *Revue du Marché Commun*, No. 109, January–February 1968, p. 27.
12. See: Jochen Thiesing, 'Diskussionsbeitrag', *Revue du Marché Commun*, No. 109, January–February 1968, pp. 292–93.
13. *La politique industrielle de la Communauté: Memorandum de la Commission au Conseil*, Commission des Communautés Européennes, Brussels, 1970, p. 143 (hereinafter cited as *EEC Memorandum*).
14. Communication officielle, *Journal officiel*, No. C75, 29 July 1968, Commission des Communautés Européennes.
15. *EEC Memorandum*, p. 144.

16. Regulation 17 (1962), *Journal officiel*, No. 204, Commission des Communautés Européennes.

17. Regulation 19 (1965), *Journal officiel*, No. 533, Commission des Communautés Européennes.

18. Werner Feld, *Transnational Business Collaboration among Common Market Countries*, New York, Praeger Publishers, 1970, p. 72.

19. *Concentration d'entreprises dans le Marché Commun, Memorandum de la Commission de la CEE*, Service Concurrence, Cahier 3 (Brussels, 1966), Paragraph 63. An unofficial English translation is available in Common Market Reports, No. 26, 17 March 1966, published by the Commerce Clearing House.

20. As of now there is no correspondent to Regulation 17, for Article 86 (see supra note 16). The Commission, however, is presently preparing a proposal for a regulation requiring that, for certain types of consolidations, the companies involved ask for the Commission's approval prior to the concentration.

21. *Concentration d'entreprises dans le Marché Commun, Memorandum de la Commission de la CEE.*

22. *EEC Memorandum*, p. 143, translated from the French.

23. On this issue, see: G. Melodia, 'Evoluzione della politica comunitaria di concorrenza' in *Orientamenti della Giurisprudenza della Comunita Economica Europea in tema di applicazione delle norme di concorrenza del Trattato di Roma*, Confederazione Generale dell'Industria Italiana, Roma, November 1971, pp. 1–18.

24. Ciba and Geigy, two Swiss chemical companies, merged, and the US Antitrust required that they not pool their resources in the US, which apparently was a major goal of the consolidation. This example is cited here, although it is a national merger and one outside the EEC, because it is the most sensational example to date, often referred to within the sphere of the EEC itself.

25. See: Werner Feld, *Transnational Business Collaboration among Common Market Countries*, pp. 64–66.

26. It is recognized that any such formal provision may encounter resistance in political spheres on the grounds of the potential disruption it could cause on the monetary scene. Consequently, managers would settle for a temporary compromise solution in which transnationally concentrated groups could receive some sort of preferential treatment designed to minimize the red tape involved in international flows of capital.

27. The following discussion was developed principally from the comments of corporate staff specialists and specialized consulting organizations.

28. See: Michael B. Stewart, 'Transnational Enterprise: The European Challenge', *Columbia Journal of World Business*, July–August 1972, pp. 5–13, at p. 12.

29. See: William P. Barsanti, 'Accounting Pitfalls in Foreign Acquisitions', Speech by an officer of Arthur Anderson & Co., New York, 23 May 1968.

30. The *Banque d'Affaires* can be thought of as an investment bank.

31. For a discussion of the free flow of labour in the EEC, see: George N. Yannopoulos, 'Economic Integration and Labour Movements with reference to the EEC countries', in G. R. Denton, *Economic Integration in Europe*, Weidenfeld & Nicolson, London, 1969, pp. 220–45.

32. This is a partial confirmation of Werner Feld's data in *Transnational Business Collaboration among Common Market Countries*, pp. 69–70.

33. A similar point is made in *Agency Europe Bulletin*, 30 September 1969.

34. *EEC Memorandum*, p. 193.

35. The foremost example here is the agreement between Commerzbank, Crédit Lyonnais, and Banco di Roma, which falls short of a concentration in that it has neither organic financial ties nor an integrated group of corporate strategists.

36. See: Norman N. Mintz, 'Toward a Common European Currency', in *Columbia Journal of World Business*, January–February 1971, p. 20.

37. See: Fernand Collin, 'The Formation of a European Capital Market', lecture delivered by the Chairman of Kredietbank, Brussels, 1962, pp. 6–10.

38. These observations as well as those of the next paragraph were made more frequently by general managers as opposed to financial managers.

39. For more details on state-owned companies, see: Bernard Chenot, *Les entreprises nationalisées,* Presse Universitaire de France, Paris, 1963; and Jacques Chevrier, 'Les entreprises publiques dans une société libre: expérience d'Electricité de France', VII Congrès de l'Economie collective, 1965.

40. This discussion was facilitated, in particular, by the comments of Italian state-owned corporations.

41. The Italian and the French parties are nationalized.

42. In fact, outside of the EEC, SAS (Scandinavian Airlines System) is organized under a comparable format. The national (50 per cent state-owned) airlines of Sweden, Norway, and Denmark have formed an international consortium, thus creating a jointly owned entity which groups the activities of the partners.

For a description of SAS, see: Paul M. Goldberg, 'The Evolution of Transnational Companies in Europe', pp. 113–33.

43. Euratom is the European organization representing a pooling of efforts towards the development of a common atomic energy programme.

44. See: W. Feld, *Transnational Business Collaboration among Common Market Countries*, p. 70.

4.

BUREAUCRATIC OBSTACLES

In this chapter we turn to obstacles which derive from the institutional environment but which are not explicit: they are neither codified in laws or regulations nor part of an overt governmental policy. They are implicit and unofficial impediments which have their origins in the informal behaviour of public agencies. One of the most important obstacles to international concentration will be analysed here: the negative attitude of governments. In the last section four other non-explicit obstacles will be discussed.

The negative attitude of national governments

Most European national governments officially claim they have a 'European policy'.[1] General de Gaulle probably represented the last bastion of outspoken governmental nationalism. Today, most EEC government heads are eager to picture themselves as Europeans. In particular, they officially foster the creation of European business firms. As Nicholas Stacey wrote: 'The idea of aiding international corporate mergers was inherent in the original planning of the Common Market, and exhortations to put it into practice have been uttered at frequent intervals by politicians.'[2] The following statement by British Prime Minister Edward Heath illustrates this point: [a basic element in economic union is industrial policy]; 'this means having a basis on which European firms, not particular national firms or co-operative arrangements between national firms, but European firms, can develop on a scale which will enable them to compete with the United States or Japanese firms.'[3] Official declarations notwithstanding, it appears that the actual attitude of national governments about Europe is much less enthusiastic. At least from the businessmen's point of view, governments resist giving up national sovereignty and power.[4] If it is true that industrial integration is the driving force towards sociopolitical integration, one may conclude that politicians resist Europe.

Governments' opposition to international concentration is quite strong,[5] and was found to be of major concern to management. Indeed to several interviewees it is the most serious hindrance to international concentration. It is allegedly the culprit for the most famous failure of a concentration plan: the CFP–GBAG consolidation (which will be described shortly). It was also the major difficulty at the moment Fiat and Citroën pooled their resources.[6] Moreover, interviewees described cases of government opposition which have not otherwise been made public and cannot be cited here for obvious reasons of confidentiality.[7] It is nevertheless important to note that there have been more cases of government intervention than is commonly believed. While the problem exists in all countries, it appears greatest in France. As Robert Mattson wrote: 'France in particular has shown a definite preference for reorganizing its industries in a national context and has applied pressure to prevent multinational arrangements.'[8] On the other hand, Holland seems to have the least militant governmental opposition to international concentration. This section examines the specific obstacles that management sees governments placing in the way of transnational amalgamations; then the discussion turns to the motivations executives see for governmental officials to adopt such an attitude.

In principle, member states have agreed not to pose a direct veto to international concentrations within the Common Market. Consequently, governments use a number of disguised methods to manifest their negative position on international consolidations. Management's comments on these methods can be grouped in five sets.

GOVERNMENT PRESSURES AGAINST TRANSNATIONAL CONCENTRATIONS

The first set of methods is direct influence on the decision-making units of the firm: governmental agents exert direct pressure on management against a concentration. This method, which is the most important, has been described by interviewees in a variety of forms. First, the state may have a direct stake in a company. Even if the company is not nationalized, the government may have an equity participation in it. This is quite common in Italy. The government may use the power its ownership confers to act against a concentration. A government does not need to have majority control to exert this influence. If it has some share of the company, it can succeed in placing its own people in key positions. According to several Italian interviewees, the other stockholders often welcome this, as they know that this will give the firm many advantages such as strongly simplified bureaucracy. In fact, several firms have politicians at their head even when the government owns no stock in the firm. For example, the president of the Italian chemical giant Montedison was Cesare Merzagora, the former President of the Senate. (This was before the government became a stockholder of the company.)

Further, government may influence management through financial intermediaries. A situation of this type was often described by German managers talking about their own country. Banks have equity participations in industry. These banks, although usually private, are under the supervision of the Central Bank. The government, then, may exert pressure through the Central Bank, which in turn pressures the private banks. This was allegedly the way the concentration between CFP and GBAG was stopped. Specifically, in late 1968–early 1969, the French oil company Compagnie Française des Pétroles (CFP) intended to concentrate with the German company Gelsenkirchener Bergwerks AG (GBAG). The French company intended to purchase GBAG shares held by two German banks, the Dresdner Bank (approximately 32 per cent) and the Deutsche Bank (approximately 12 per cent). Although the details have not been made public, it is clear that the German government stopped the deal. (The German company was finally combined with another German group, the Rheinisch–Westfalisches Elektrizitaetswerk.)[9]

Finally, pressure can be exerted by public agencies through social links between public and private administration. French managers reported this is most common in France where such ties are quite strong because of the particular structure of the society.[10] Public and private administrators traditionally come from the same social strata. They tend to know each other because they have been raised together and have received the same education (typically, the Grandes Ecoles such as Polytechnique, ENA, Centrale, etc.). Also, family ties often exist between private and public administrators. Moreover, in France it is customary for an executive to spend some time in the *Administration Publique*, and for a public servant to spend some time in business. Indeed, people go back and forth from business to public administration. This reinforces the personal relationship between the two. Finally, because French industry is directed centrally by elaborate economic programmes (le Plan), the interaction between industry and government is very great. As a result government can exert a very strong influence on business strategies.[11] Most of the executives interviewed said that it is not really possible to go against the government's will because the relationship with the public administrators would deteriorate, something they could not afford.[12]

The second set of methods discussed by managers involves the government's helping purely national companies. It can favour a national company for government procurement. For example, it may, other things being equal, prefer to purchase military aircraft from a 100 per cent national company than from a transnational group composed of several companies only one of which belongs to its own country. Moreover, the government can help national companies by granting them favourable financial terms. In high-technology industry, it can finance R & D projects, applying very low interest rates on long-term debt so that repayment is strongly reduced through inflation. The government can even forego repayment altogether either by expensing the R & D costs on its own budget (i.e., the company receives a grant) or by commissioning a project (i.e., the government orders the development of a project which it pays for). If the government decides to oppose an international concentration, it can do so by promising to reduce its help to the company if it concentrates, and/or by promising more help if the company does not concentrate.

The third set of methods is to encourage domestic concentration. It was found that a government may often prefer a national solution to the problem of a company's insufficient size, and decide it would be best for a domestic concentration to take place. It can then encourage management to do so through specialized organizations, as in Great Britain with the IRC (Industrial Reorganization Corporation). A government can also directly operate a concentration by acquiring the shares of the company and consolidating it with another. In fact, it can also nationalize a company which otherwise would do an international concentration. Interviewees added, however, that nationalization is used more as a threat to dissuade the business community from doing an international concentration than as an actual means of blocking such an operation.

Another effective way of promoting national mergers is for the government to promise to reduce the red tape involved. If the government is committed to the concentration, the attractiveness of the operation is greatly enhanced. This was reported particularly in the southern European countries where the interpretation of the laws can vary considerably according to governmental back-up. 'Things are easy if the government is behind you', said a French executive. Moreover, if the government has committed itself to a given concentration, management can also rely on government's support for the future operation of the concentration, which makes it even more attractive; and this, in turn, further reduces the interest of doing an international concentration.

The fourth set of methods described by interviewees is for the government to render the bureaucracy more difficult to companies. Although a government has, in principle, no way of directly blocking a concentration, it has a range of discretionary tools for making an international consolidation quite impractical for companies. First, it can refuse to grant the special *ad hoc* permission for fiscal immunity both for the setting-up of the consolidation and for its subsequent operations. As was seen in chapter 2, consolidated groups are heavily dependent upon such arrangements. Second, the government can adopt a stricter policy for exchange controls. In the preceding chapter it was noted that the exchange control barrier can be circumvented either by more or less explicit *ad hoc* arrangements or by the national authorities turning a blind eye on transfer prices. Both of these methods require governmental collaboration. Third, public administrators can become more meticulous and picky. For example, they can order an in-depth inspection of the accounting books. This may mean that public bureaucrats come into the company and paralyse part of the organization. It is management's experience that in such instances, even if a company is law-abiding, the mere fact of having to endure a detailed inspection by public agents is a serious handicap, if only because of the time involved. Moreover, the psychological impact of such an inspection can be considerable.

The last aspect is of special concern to Italian executives. In Italy, particularly in view of the present sociopolitical crisis, enforcement of the law is not strict at all. In fact, laws are designed in such a way that it is often impossible to comply with them. Thus a profitable company can be expected—'if it declared the truth'—to pay more than 100 per cent of its income in taxes.[13] It is obvious, therefore, that no company fully complies with the law. The same is true for the fiscal position of individuals. It is no overstatement that very few companies and managers are completely law-abiding. Interviewees believe public authorities are not only aware of this, but even tend to encourage it: this gives them discretionary power over private individuals. As an Italian executive said: 'We are all released on bail'. Indeed, government has considerable leverage over managers because it can always threaten to enforce the law in a stricter fashion if the manager does not comply with its will. The following quote expresses one of the many opinions Italian executives gave on the subject: 'The law is impossible to abide. The government does not want to see that nobody complies with it and tacitly allows everybody to be an outlaw. This is fine as long as you do as you are told. But as soon as you face up to politicians on anything, they pull out any irregularity you have lived with for years and you are in for disaster.' Managers feel that in case of government's opposition to a concentration, it can threaten to use this type of expedient to dissuade management from doing a concentration. Even without striking the whole company, it can make one or a few key executives the object of its attack by ordering an investigation of their private fiscal position. This is reportedly one of the most powerful tools governmental authorities have at their disposal to enforce their will on industry.

Fifth, the government can exert pressure on management in an indirect fashion in two ways. First, the government can arouse public opinion against the international concentration. Because European governments have considerable say in the press and other mass media (radio and television are typically nationalized), they have strong influence on public opinion. If the government casts a negative shadow over an international consolidation, the goodwill of the company will suffer. This may have a negative impact in the financial community. It may also adversely influence the market, namely, the company's customers. Finally, the 'social standing' of a company may suffer on the grounds, for instance, of perceived 'unpatriotic behaviour' of the firm. Second, the government can influence the labour forces to actively oppose the concentration. Specifically, where unions are heavily politicized, as in Belgium, France or Italy, a leftist government may cause unions to order a strike against the concentration.

Beyond the five methods just described, management believes it is often not possible to know what a government would do if a company went ahead with an international concentration against political will. Many executives emphasized the fact that it is not wise in Europe to operate in disagreement with the government. Often, if the government merely lets management know it does not approve of a concentration, the management will abandon the whole project. In the words of a Belgian executive: 'The strings a government has at its disposal to pull a company in one direction rather than in another are innumerable. Without having to find out what machinations politics will otherwise use to make him see reason again, a manager merely needs to know the government's inclinations to comply with them.'

REASONS FOR GOVERNMENT OPPOSITION

The question still to be asked is, why should government oppose international concentrations? The motivations of politicians are many and complex. Management's views on this issue can be classified in three categories. First, 'economic' reasons—rational reasons a government genuinely believes in for the preservation of the economic and social welfare of the country; second, 'emotional' reasons—reasons which satisfy a psychological need such as the prestige attached to the national image of certain traditional industries; third, 'personal' reasons—reasons originating in the personal interest of individual politicians.

The first economic reason cited by management is that governments fear that an international concentration will slow down the economic development of the country. National governments are anxious not to lose the opportunity of an investment on their territory. They believe that an international concentration may cause a national company to invest less domestically. In this respect, underdeveloped regions are a cause of particular concern to national governments.[14] They believe that if a company is transnational, it will have a reduced incentive to invest in areas like the Italian South, the so-called Mezzogiorno. Moreover, governments fear that concentrations will entail rationalizations and that this often means lay-offs. In recent years, most European countries have experienced an economic recession with rising unemployment. The possibility of rationalization is perceived as a particular threat under these circumstances. While this possibility also exists in domestic concentration, governments can control national companies much more closely and can force them to be progressive in their rationalizations.

A second economic reason discussed by interviewees is that of trying to protect some companies for so-called 'national strategic reasons'.[15] These are typically in industries where it is considered desirable to maintain national autonomy. In a political or military crisis, it is allegedly important to have a self-sufficient industry in the more vital sectors of the economy. For example, in military equipment construction, governments try to maintain a strong autonomous industry. The same can be said for many high-technology sectors where it is considered part of the national patrimony to have advanced know-how. Beyond prestige reasons, such companies are perceived as affecting the rest of the economic and technological progress of the country. They also create an intellectual stimulus for scientific work. Finally, in the energy and power sectors, it is considered desirable for a country to be independent. For example, an important consideration of the German government's disapproval of the CFP–GBAG concentration was that of maintaining the national identity of the German firm in a sector considered to be of national interest in which purely national companies were rare.[16] In Germany, at the time of the concentration talks, 75 per cent of the sales of oil refineries and 80 per cent of crude oil sales were made by foreign-owned companies, and GBAG represented the vast majority of the remaining 25 per cent and 20 per cent.

A third economic reason is that governments tend to see in an international concentration a dilution of the national economic and scientific strength. Management believes that governments perceive that a national company becoming transnational represents a loss for the country. 'They do not value the benefit to Europe because they do not identify themselves with Europe', said a French interviewee. The loss for the country consists in renouncing the company's present economic and scientific assets (namely, know-how) which have been built up using national resources. Further, there is also an opportunity loss. The government feels exploited in being deprived of the benefits it considers the country is entitled to. Individual governments see that the internationalization of a national company puts them at a comparative disadvantage *vis-à-vis* those countries which preserve their national firms. They feel they are contributing to Europe, while the others are getting what a British executive called a 'free ride'.

A fourth economic reason is that governments have adopted the policy of becoming as strong as possible nationally before increasing their commitment to Europe, using the time left before a political integration of the EEC to build up their individual position. Executives feel the objective of national governments is to enter Europe in as strong a position as possible, 'by the front door with full honors', as a German executive put it; or, as a Belgian executive said, 'in order to be able to play the prima donna role'. Governments are afraid of losing ground in the European race if they allow too much internationalization when other countries reinforce their own national positions. It is a vicious circle: if all do not agree to a multilateral Europeanization of national economies, then no one country alone will accept an exodus of industrial units which weakens the national economy. While this attitude exists in every country, it is most pronounced in France. The French would like to build an optimal microcosm with its economic independence, an ideal autonomous economic system which would be able to live in autarchy. As a French executive said: 'It is as if there were to be quotas in tomorrow's Europe. Countries want to be as powerful as possible in order to have the largest share of the pie.' Such a policy calls for an ordering and reinforcement of national industry before considering collaboration with foreign partners. This attitude contradicts the aim of bringing about a reorganization and rationalization of European industry on a community scale. What economic justification can be offered for reorganizing first nationally and then on a European level? Not only may there be duplication of efforts, but the national reorganization may call for some actions that are not congruent with that on the European level. It would be far more logical to aim at European industrial reorganization at the outset.

It should be obvious that the above 'economic' reasons are ill-founded from management's point of view. Two fundamental explanations for the attitude of governments are given. First, in the words of a Belgian executive: 'Politicians do not believe in Europe.' Economic plans are national in outlook, and Europe is not the governing principle. If Europe were indeed a goal to which politicians were committed, the notion of trying to reinforce the national economy would be meaningless. As a French executive said: 'If we were all Europeans, what would it mean to try and reap the largest piece of the pie? We should all be equal.' Attitudes such as trying to preserve national autonomy, building up national economic strength, holding one's own against other EEC countries, all contradict the advocated policy of gradual co-operation across national frontiers. There is still too much internal competition in the Common Market and too little pooling of efforts is being done to co-operate against Europe's economic challengers.

Second, governments are shortsighted in their economic planning. They do not see that even if international concentration is not essential today, it will be in a few years. The need for large industrial units might well, in today's business conditions, find solution within national boundaries, but this holds little hope for the future. History confirms the evidence of this shortsightedness. A few decades ago governments did not see the importance of co-operative agreements. Now they have resigned themselves to the necessity of joint efforts, but companies say they have waited too long—to the point where it really was impossible to do otherwise. The necessity for international concentrations today is often not entirely obvious, unless one projects business conditions a few years hence. Only then can one see that international concentrations are needed. However, preparations must be well in advance because of the time required for an international consolidation to become operational. Governments do not appreciate this and prefer to postpone international link-ups so as to develop national economic potency. This, in a French executive's words, is 'a cannibalization process'. It would be most desirable to collaborate today, not only in order to start a concerted action toward the outside immediately, but also to lay the groundwork for tomorrow's integration.

Turning now to the 'emotional reasons', the first is the prestige attached to the maintenance of the national identity of industrial units. Managers affirm that governments seem to believe it part of their duty to maintain the national identity of domestic firms. As an executive from one of the smaller EEC countries put it: 'It seems that there is something magic or at least mystical about the nationality of companies.' Another executive said: 'Governments want to put their flag on anything they can.' Governments do not oppose consolidations when the group can be identified as a national company or at least as a multinational company based in their country. But they do oppose the converse case, a take-over of a domestic company by a foreign one. Even in a consolidation where the parties are of equal size, governments resist the idea of one of their companies becoming supranational. As a German executive said: 'There are, in the eyes of the government, some *heilige Kühe* [sacred cows] which foreign hands should never be allowed to touch.'

This attitude is perceived by European managers as most pronounced in France.[17] General de Gaulle's policy of national 'grandeur' (also called *politique de prestige*) is still alive. The French are considered the least committed to European integration (although more recently this has been changing). They are perceived as trying to manipulate the EEC in their favour. Many non-French executives are of the opinion that the French are attempting to create a French or quasi-French EEC: the French government tends to oppose concentrations in which a French company is not dominant. The best example here is the difficulty encountered by Fiat–Citroën in 1968 in their marriage negotiations. The French administration initially prevented the Italian company from purchasing a large share of Citroën's stock. Only after several private and official interventions was a compromise reached by which Fiat would have 49 per cent of a holding company, which itself had majority control of Citroën. It should be emphasized that the motivations of the French government were virtually all based on prestige arguments alone.

To a lesser degree, management feels that the British government is concerned with maintaining autonomy. The country's traditional insularity still makes itself felt. The recollection of the glorious past of British economic superiority unconsciously hinders the acceptance of collaborative endeavours in which the British partner does not enjoy a dominant position.

The second emotional reason discussed by executives is governments' negative preconceptions about multinational companies. Governments fear multinational companies because they do not have full control over them. A national company can be more or less compelled to comply with government's will, but a multinational company can threaten to divest itself and leave the country.[18] If this entails massive lay-offs, the government may prefer not to impose its will rather than face social disruption. As a British executive said: 'The fact that Henry Ford can shut down his plants in the UK overnight gives him more leverage than the government would like him to have.' Although a company rarely reaches the point of massive disinvestment, a government feels quite uncomfortable about this possibility. Moreover, insensitive behaviour by large multinational companies has produced negative governmental reactions. In the past large multinational concerns have sometimes behaved in a socially irresponsible way, according to European standards. For example, hiring and firing practices of some US international companies have been widely criticized.[19] This has aggravated the opinion government officials have of multinational groups.

This reportedly has had three negative consequences for international concentrations. First, governments are suspicious of international consolidations simply because they tend to associate them with multinational companies. As a Dutch executive stated, they tend to perceive international consolidations as 'one of those bad multinational giants'. Second, governments do not want to increase the number of international groups in their economy; a concentration would, they feel, worsen the problem of controlling international groups. Third, they wish to maintain national companies as such in order to counteract the weight of multinational firms. The reasoning here is that the less industrial power the state has nationally, the more it is dependent upon multinational groups.

Another facet of this issue was determined during the second set of interviews: a government's fear of losing part of its sovereignty when a domestic company becomes transnational. A government has less leverage over a transnational firm because such a firm is more independent. It acquires some of the flexibility of the multinational firm; it can invest abroad and tap resources beyond national frontiers. Since such an organization has social responsibilities towards other states, it is less likely to comply with the requirements of the socioeconomic development programme of the national state. This reduced power of the state over a concentrated group is more of a problem for European governments because their economies are more planned than in the US. It is interesting to note that in Germany, where the government has been quite liberal up to now, this problem was rarely mentioned by interviewees; but in France it was mentioned often. It is in the UK, however, that it was the cause of most concern to interviewees: not only is government intervention in the economy strong (especially when the Labour Party is in power), but US investment is also particularly high, thus increasing awareness of the problem created by multinational companies.

The third emotional reason is an inferiority complex certain governments have about their economic efficiency. According to management, certain governments believe that their national firms are inferior to foreign ones and that in a consolidation they will invariably be dominated by the foreign party. Because they also believe that this inferiority is temporary, owing to particular economic circumstances, they resist international concentration until the business trend will be more favourable for their own national companies.

This inferiority complex is most noticeable in France, especially *vis-à-vis* Germany.[20] France has had a splendid past and its dominance of continental Europe is still very much alive in the minds of its people. The country has been accustomed to cultural and political leadership since at least the seventeenth century, and this permeates the whole of French education. The political leaders of the country appear to want to build on 'the heritage of rulers of the world', as one interviewee said. Moreover, the French tend to perceive the Germans as unpolished and somewhat 'heavy', without French refinement and prestige. In addition, having first suffered defeat in the Second World War and then victory, the French have the feeling of being somehow entitled to dominance—or at least to a stronger bargaining power over other European countries, particularly Germany. At the same time, there is the insolent postwar German industrial comeback, to which the French can but contrast their own hesitant economic development. While their situation has changed in recent times, during most of the postwar period the French resented this imbalance. Particularly in the last decade, the French administration tried hard to reorganize its industry and return to the front row.[21] As a consequence French public administrators tend to impede international concentrations, particularly those with Germans. They want to wait until the equilibrium between the industries of the two nations has reached what appears to them a more realistic level, lest the Germans end up dominating a concentrated group because they are currently in a more favourable economic phase; currently the Germans would benefit from the economic, technical, and human resources of the French partner upon which the French alone cannot, for the moment, capitalize. French officials believe that the French are poorer administrators and that, in an international concentration, the foreign partner would unduly benefit from the potential of the French company (in particular, technical know-how), 'simply because', as a German executive said, 'we have better bookkeeping.'

A similar attitude, though less pronounced, was found in Great Britain and Italy. In Great Britain, its glorious past contrasts with its slow post war economic growth. This generates a certain resentment which might lead to unhealthy, impulsive isolationism. However, British administrators are seen as pragmatic, facing the situation with 'splendid wisdom', as an admirative French executive said. In Italy, the attitude is a more recent phenomenon, motivated by the present severe economic and political crisis. Italy has been used to being the EEC country with the lowest per capita income, and until the present recession was quite content with its spectacular economic growth (often referred to as 'the Italian miracle'). However, in recent years, the situation has deteriorated, and the government wishes to protect its industry which in any collaborative endeavour has a dramatically reduced bargaining power relative to its perceived potential. Here, as in France, the reasoning is that Italian industry is operating below its potential, that it is 'undervalued'. The government wishes to postpone any international concentration until the economy has recovered the position it deserves.

The fourth emotional reason reported is that international concentration may serve to export capital out of those countries that have strict exchange controls. A hybrid concentration involves cross-holdings of shares which bypass exchange controls. As was seen previously, the government usually waives the requirement of exchange controls for international consolidations, thereby enabling the owners of a company to export a large portion of its shares, which corresponds to an export of capital. This fear is prevalent in Italy[22]—first, because the country has particularly stringent exchange control rules, and second, because the present crisis increases the incentive to export capital. There is strong motivation to hold money or securities in foreign currencies. Moreover, since the leftist pressures are increasing, the propertied classes try to hedge against the risk of seeing their patrimony seized by governmental authorities—another incentive to export capital. In addition, Italian companies are often still closely held by families. The incentive is high for a family to do a concentration and thus export in one stroke half of its patrimony, as may be the case in a 50–50 concentration. Several Italian managers reported that at the moment of the Dunlop–Pirelli union there was some speculation in business circles that the Pirelli family was at least partly motivated by this desire. In fact, this is all the more plausible if one considers that a national government is much less likely to nationalize a company which is partly owned by foreigners. In the Dunlop–Pirelli case, the Italian government is less likely to nationalize Pirelli now that Dunlop is a major stockholder. Consequently, not only does a concentration allow the export of half of the shares, but it also reduces the risk of seeing the other half of the patrimony nationalized. Knowing that a concentration has these effects, the government tends to be suspicious of international consolidations.

The fifth emotional reason is ideological. There are in Europe strong leftist political movements, ranging from communist to more moderate socialist parties. Three reasons have been reported as to why these leftist parties oppose international consolidations. First, they see in them a strengthening of capitalism. This is of particular concern to the more extreme leftist parties. Communist doctrine calls for the destruction of private enterprise, and international consolidations presumably reinforce the economic power of the private parties involved. Second, beyond the mere fact that a consolidation is beneficial to capitalism, international concentration renders the companies involved more flexible and free from governmental tutelage. The possibility of future nationalization is diminished because in the so-called developed countries, governments have generally adopted the policy of not nationalizing foreign investments. Third, leftist parties tend to want a greater control over industry than right-wing parties, which are more inclined to a *laissez-faire* attitude. Because political integration is lagging behind economic integration, leftist governments are preoccupied by the fact that internationalization of industry allows it to free itself from governmental control. There is not yet a strong enough political authority to police industry on a European scale the way that national governments are doing domestically. Consequently, leftist governments are concerned that the Europeanization of industry is occurring without control by political authority. Such Europeanization is, in their view, increasing *laissez-faire*, which is counter to their doctrine. In virtually all EEC countries it was stated that governmental opposition to concentrations tends to be stronger when a leftist government is in power. This is also true in Great Britain, where the Labour Party tends to oppose international consolidations more than the Conservative Party does.

These five reasons tend to indicate that the European concept is not an overriding goal of politicians. The concept certainly has theoretical appeal, but in practice governments are still preoccupied with national problems. Many businessmen are of the opinion that this is because politicians are still responsible to national electorates. Further, the European concept is not operational, i.e., it is not a concrete reality. The mentality of governments is built around national horizons and, in the words of an executive of a multinational company, 'The new European ideal is still an intellectual chimera'.

The last set of reasons given by interviewees for governments' negative attitude to international concentration consist of personal motives of politicians. The first reason is demagogy. While Europeanism is gradually becoming an asset for a politician *vis-à-vis* his electorate, there are still exceptions to this. Particularly in France and Great Britain, the notion of a politician being a 'great defender of his country' carries with it some appeal. Although this behaviour is gradually losing its demagogical effectiveness, some politicians—with the objective of receiving votes—still oppose an international consolidation, using arguments similar to that of 'protecting the workers' interests'.

The second personal reason is that some politicians oppose international concentration because it brings about European integration faster than they would like. In Europe, many politicians are career politicians, and 'have no other way of making a living', as one interviewee said. They feel threatened by European integration because they fear that their services may be dispensed with in a politically united Europe in which human resources at the so-called service of the state would be rationalized. In a united Europe, presumably there would be fewer posts for politicians than in today's fragmented Europe. Indeed, some politicians fear becoming superfluous. One would expect this attitude to be most common in smaller countries. In fact, it so happens that the smaller countries of the EEC have relatively effective political classes which, in addition, are proportionally smaller than in other European countries. The attitude is most widespread in Italy. It is here that the political class is not only proportionally the largest in any EEC country but is also patently the most ineffective. In view of the present political crisis of the country, it is unanimously felt that Italian politicians have not done their job properly. It is the belief of managers that such politicians have a lot to lose personally in a European integration because they fear comparison with their foreign counterparts.[23]

The third personal reason is that of politicians' loss of personal leverage when a national company engages in a transnational concentration. The increase in flexibility of a company when it engages in an international concentration has consequences for the individual power of politicians. When the company is more independent, its management has less need to comply with the will of politicians. This issue takes a special form in Italy, where it is also most important. Here, corruption is substantial. National companies cannot but comply with the requirements of corruption if they want to operate in peace. 'For a foreigner it is hard to imagine what corruption is in this country', said an Italian executive. 'It is no overstatement to say that virtually all politicians are implicated in it.' Beyond politicians, corruption reaches down to all levels of public servants. Indeed, as illustrated by the article reproduced in Fig. 4.1, bribery is so widespread in the country that it has become, in the words of one executive, 'an accepted and nearly official fact of life, which everyone talks about with no sign of surprise whatsoever.'

Bustarella—Italian Officials Begin Crack Down

ROME (AP-DJ).—To do business in Italy, a little bustarella comes in handy.

Bustarella, bluntly, is bribery. The word comes from busta, meaning envelope. Typically, a top corporate executive keeps a stack of plain white envelopes stuffed with varying amounts of 10,000-lire notes (about $17) in his desk. When his company needs a favorable tax ruling, a government contract, a building permit, or payment for services rendered the government, the executive calls in an intermediary, or "consultant," and hands him an envelope. If it is not heavy enough, the consultant shakes his head, and the executive fishes for another.

Widespread but rarely publicized, bustarella has been drawing some unusual attention lately. In Rome, a state prosecutor has filed charges in order to instigate a court investigation into contracts awarded by the government's national highway board; allegedly, contracts went to companies that agreed to kickbacks funneled to political parties.

"In Italy," says one observer, "a politician is expected to get about 10 percent of every contract for the party. He's considered honest if he gives all the money to the party."

Another case that has come to light involves the giant chemical concern, Montecatini Edison, accused of juggling its books to conceal a slush fund for payoffs.

Corruption in business, of course, is not an Italian monopoly. "It's just so much more prevalent and less frowned upon here," says Oleg P. Petroff, an American lawyer who lives here. "The big difference between graft in Italy and elsewhere is that there's never any outraged uprising."

Well, hardly ever. A major reason for it is the implication of nearly all the country's politicians and parties. Although members of parliament are well paid by most standards—$2,000 a month—many must kick in as much as 50 percent of their pay to their party. To reimburse themselves, the politicians put the arm on businessmen.

Bustarella is encouraged, too, by the legal complexities of doing business. "The bureaucratic channels through which a request for payment on a firm, signed contract must pass in the Italian government, strain the imagination of an American businessman," says a confidential letter sent by a U.S. concern to its home office. "Couple with this abominable situation the corruption which has infiltrated every level of the processing route and you have the full impact of the problem of Italy. But there's no solution but to ride with it, hoping that constant follow-up and the liberal application of lire will keep things moving."

The Taxman Collects

Italian taxation is particularly complex—and, for collectors of bustarella, particularly rewarding as tax officials have enormous discretion in applying the laws.

An accountant offers a hypothetical but realistic example: A chemical company with about $5 million in sales reports a loss of $100,000. In the U.S., the company would pay no income tax. Here, should a tax official find that chemical companies of similar size were profitable, he could legally assume that the company was trying to avoid taxation and assess it, say $200,000. Typically, a $10,000 bribe would cut the bill in half.

Such payoffs are made in the form of fees to registered fiscal consultants. As long as he gets results, what the consultant does with his fees is nobody's business but his own. And a corporate executive might or might not siphon off for his own use some of the money he tells his company is going for bribes.

Montedison Slush Fund

Italian businessmen—because they are so much more concerned with politics—say they are squeezed harder than foreigners. In the Montecatini case, Cesare Merzagora, a former senator, resigned after only eight months as chairman, citing his discovery of "billions of lire" in secret company accounts. A company spokesman confirms the existence of a secret political slush fund. "Apparently, this money went to political parties and newspapers," he says. But he describes the payments as "illicit" and says they have been discontinued.

Montecatini's payments, according to one man who had a hand in them, were paid through a special "riserva" known only to a few executives. It was hidden from shareholders and tax officials by a complicated accounting procedure involving the shifting of cash between the parent company and its subsidiaries—which number about 300.

Fig. 4.1. International Herald Tribune, *Paris, 5 April 1972, p. 7.* *(Reprinted by permission.)*

Particularly from the fiscal point of view, bribery is a *sine qua non* of doing business in Italy.[24] In view of some unbearable tax requirements, it is virtually impossible for a national company not to use bribery. The taxman has tremendous discretion in applying the law and if a company refuses to bribe him, 'the company will be sorry', as an executive put it. For international companies, however, public authorities have to be more careful. Not only is there the danger of a scandal on the international scene, but in addition foreign companies can always refuse to bribe, divest themselves, and leave the country. Furthermore, it is more difficult to communicate with foreigners on such delicate issues and, in the words of an executive, 'there is a certain modesty *vis-à-vis* foreigners'. As a consequence, government officials feel international companies have too much freedom and are too little dependent on them. The same is true for national companies that engage in an international consolidation. Such companies escape, at least in part, from the need to engage in corruption. Governmental officials see that international link-ups entail a loss of potential bribery income for them, and they thus tend to oppose international concentration.

These personal reasons should not be dismissed lightly. In the eyes of the business community, they are important motivators for government opposition to international concentration. In fact, to many they are the cause of the greatest concern since they reflect the basic ill-will of politicians. Whereas the other reasons are either the result of misconceptions or emotional behaviour, the personal reasons are intrinsic characteristics of politicians. The former can probably be cured (be it only through time), but for the latter the only solution may well be, in the words of an executive, 'a complete regeneration of our political classes'.

It should be clear that it is not within the scope of this study to deal with this type of recommendation. Moreover, even recommendations for the 'economic' and 'emotional' reasons tend to be in the realm of political science discussions. However, it is possible to outline a few suggestions to governmental agencies. These are the synthesis of ideas managers presented primarily during the first set of interviews, which then were elaborated and confirmed during the second set. These ideas all have one objective in common: change politicians' perspective of the EEC from that of an addition of parts which remain distinct to that of a blending and interpenetration of these parts into an indivisible whole—in other words, replace the national horizons of politicians with European horizons.

The first suggestion is to give more power to the EEC Commission. Today, the Commission has principally an advisory role.[25] It is the Council of Ministers that makes the crucial decisions. This Counsel is composed of the Foreign Affairs ministers of the member states, which means it is composed of individuals who are representatives of nations and thus have a national outlook. In addition, individual states still have all power at the national level, and the important decisions are at that level, not at the Community level. If the Commission were granted more power, it could, as a supranational organ, make decisions for a truly European policy. Specifically, if the Commission had enough power, it could take action against governments which hinder transnational concentrations.

Second, an attempt should be made to Europeanize the scope of national governments themselves. Today, each country has a Minister of Foreign Affairs whose role is to represent his country abroad and to carry out its foreign policy. His bias, therefore, is *to defend* his country, to adopt a bargaining position in favour of his own country and *against* the others. Yet it is this same individual and his foreign counterparts who have the responsibility for the construction of Europe. Such an individual appears unfit for this task precisely because he has a national outlook. To correct this, it is proposed that a new Ministry for European Affairs be created in each member state. The new ministry would not replace the Foreign Affairs ministry; rather, they would coexist. The Ministry for European Affairs would make sure its country followed a policy compatible with—or headed towards—European integration, that it did not attempt to manipulate the Common Market for its own selfish benefit, but was laying the foundation for a gradual harmonization and integration. Among other things, the ministry would make sure that the country's industrial policy was not nationalistic, it would attempt to prevent such things as governmental opposition to international concentration.

If each country elected its own European Affairs minister, the scope of such a minister would probably still be somewhat national. To avoid this, a French interviewee proposed that each country elect a Minister for European Affairs, not for itself but for another member state. Such a minister, who might well be a foreign national, would introduce a truly European outlook in each member state; hopefully, he would avoid biased national loyalties. 'This would be a first step towards an integration of European governmental agencies', said the executive. While the idea certainly has theoretical appeal, its practicability in today's environment is questionable. Indeed, second set interviewees who were asked to appraise this proposal considered it premature though interesting. Generally, they felt an intermediary step was warranted: i.e., a minister in charge of European policy who would be a national of the country. He would have particular responsibilities for a Europeanization of the country's industrial policy. In addition, an advisory post for each government could be created, staffed by an 'observer' from another EEC country. His role would be a consultative one, directed towards a common EEC industrial policy.

Third, member states should agree to pool their resources in a definitive way in their industrial endeavours where this is economically desirable.[26] 'Definitive' means not on an *ad hoc* joint venture basis but on a permanent basis. For example, in government-sponsored high-technology projects for the development of military equipment, each country tries to be autonomous. Not only does this create wasteful duplication, but it is also ineffective because of the relatively small size of European countries. Often, the result of each country trying to be independent 'for national strategic reasons, is that nobody is independent because nobody can make it alone', as a British executive said. First, a pooling of resources in these fields would be economically efficient. Second, it would foster the Community spirit of governments. By their own industrial collaboration, governments would become more receptive to the private sector's business collaboration.

A fourth suggestion is general in character: to Europeanize the values of politicians. This calls for the creation of European schools for public administrators. In several European countries there are academic institutions designed to educate public servants; the finest are in France (e.g., Institut de Sciences Politiques or Ecole Nationale d'Administration). The non-European attitude of politicians is believed to stem from the strong national orientation they receive in their education. This could be counteracted by a European institute for the education of public servants.

On a broader level, national symbols should be Europeanized; specifically, expressions of nationalism should gradually be suppressed. Exaltation of national 'grandeur' reinforces the 'regionalism' of public representatives. The glorification of symbols like the national flag enhances nationalism. Ideally speaking, if a European army, for instance, were organized, it would certainly serve as a catalyst for bringing politicians closer together. In particular, symbols with economic overtones should be 'denationalized' as soon as possible. In this connection, monetary union would certainly bring about greater cohesiveness in the industrial policies of member states.

While recommendations in the area of governmental attitudes are naturally addressed to governmental agencies themselves, there is one important exception to this. In discussing advantages and disadvantages of the various hybrid models presented in chapter 2, it was found during the second set of interviews that hybrid solution II—creation of a common operating subsidiary jointly owned by the companies participating in the venture—offered considerable promise for bypassing governmental opposition to a consolidation. Such a solution is not a concentration until all the endeavours of the group are carried out through the subsidiary, thus leaving the founding corporations with just a holding company role. While such a process may take a long time, it is compatible with the desirability of implementing a consolidation in a gradual fashion (chapter 7 will discuss the desirability of carrying out such a gradual integration process from an organizational standpoint). It is possible for companies which face governmental opposition to their union to found a joint subsidiary which at the beginning is given only a limited share of the partners' activities. Government opposition to such ventures is typically far less articulate than it is against outright consolidations. The share can then be increased over time. In fact, rather than actually transplanting activities from the parent companies to the joint subsidiary, it should be possible to increase the subsidiary's range of activities by carrying out the new endeavours of the group at its level rather than at the parents' level. For example, in the aeronautics field, the parents could continue to develop those projects on which they are already working, while new projects could be undertaken at the subsidiary's level. If this policy is carried out consistently, the parent companies will reduce their range of operations as old projects are terminated until they finally have no direct activities at all.

The advantage of such a strategy is primarily its psychological impact on governmental agencies. Executives interviewed on the subject feel that a link-up can get by much more easily under such a legal set-up than under a set-up requiring the interplay of the financial or legal structures of the relevant companies themselves. In other words, the amount of resources two companies can actually pool together is greater than under any arrangement involving the financial or legal format of the companies themselves (e.g., exchange of shares of the companies). 'Governments perceive the parent company is not impaired, namely, they do not see any injury is done to the company itself', said one of these executives.

The real goal of such a strategy, however, is not to deceive governments. Rather, its proponents speculate that Europeanization of governmental industrial policy will increase, and with it, political opposition to consolidations should decrease. The objective is to prepare for such times. As will be seen in chapter 7, the integration of two industrial units is a cumbersome process which requires many years to be completed. The strategy just outlined calls for initiating such an integration process now and, as an Italian executive put it, 'Do as much as possible in the way of consolidating activities now and, above all, set up a structure which will enable you to go further in the integration process each time that governmental policy will make a step further in the direction of Europeanization'.

Other non-explicit institutional obstacles

This section examines four sets of obstacles. First, Europe's slow progress towards fuller integration, as a consequence of which the business community sees little incentive to pool resources on a European scale. Second, bureaucratic difficulties, namely, having to deal with cumbersome red tape. Third, the peculiar informal relationships between public and private administrators of some countries, which may constitute a psychological barrier for foreign executives. Fourth, environmental uncertainty, specifically the problems created by the perceived instability of some countries.

United Europe is perceived by management as making little tangible progress. At the Community level, up to a few years ago there had been concrete signs of progress towards European integration, but more recently, tangible results have become rarer. The explanation is that up until recently the prime industrial objective was customs union. Now this has been completed and harmonization is the key theme of the Commissions' work. This is not only a more complex endeavour but also requires more preparatory work and leads to fewer tangible results. While the Commission may be justified for what is perceived as lack of progress, the business community—probably again due to a lack of adequate information—understandably complains that little is done towards the further construction of the EEC.

At the national government's level, politicians in the past have not given sufficient emphasis to their European policy. Interviewees stated that political programmes often made little mention of European integration and that politicians did not seem particularly concerned with the problem. As a result there has not been an awakening of the consciousness of Europeanization. Europeanization has remained a theoretical concept deprived of much operational meaning, because the political sphere did not provide sufficient motivation towards it. (It should be pointed out, however, that this has been changing in recent times; more and more the European question is at the centre of the politicians' preoccupations.)

The fact that Europe is perceived as not making much tangible progress is a hindrance to international business concentration because it reduces the incentive for businessmen to join forces on a European scale.[27] The problem has two aspects. The first is psychological. It is generally felt that, if the European notion were concretized, it would serve as a stimulus to businessmen to get together simply in a 'me too' reaction. Moreover, this would serve as a catalyst for transnational consolidations in that it would reduce the psychological barriers of international unions. Today Europeans have the feeling of being 'different' from each other because they are foreign to each other. This creates human barriers to collaborative endeavours which true European integration would reduce.

The second aspect is that European business integration is more necessary if there is a macroeconomic union. If the EEC were really one economic entity, there would be one large market which, in turn, would increase the need for large European companies. From a superficial analysis, it may seem that the EEC is already such a market, as a result of the customs union. This, however, is far from being true. For example, while the customs union is theoretically completed, it is still necessary to clear customs when crossing the border between two EEC countries. Moreover, there are non-tariff quotas such as the technical regulations on products surveyed in chapter 3. Nationalistic government procurement is another example of a hindrance to a real economic integration of the EEC. As a consequence, managers encounter a certain protectionism surrounding each country, which reduces the urge to rationalize economic units on a community level.

The second obstacle is the bureaucratic difficulty involved in international consolidations. As was seen in chapters 2 and 3, a concentration often has to rely on special agreements with public authorities. *Ad hoc* arrangements may be necessary for fiscal and exchange control purposes. These arrangements are typically negotiated by top management itself with high-level public authorities. Managers report that, if the government has no objection to the concentration, these arrangements usually do not pose major problems. Similar arrangements are often made for the barriers arising at the operating level. These are usually made at the highest level of both the private and public administrations, and here, too, the bureaucracy involved is not overly cumbersome.

The real problems occur when these latter arrangements are implemented. At the operating level, representatives of the public administration are normally minor officials. Management has often complained about the difficulties of dealing with people who are accustomed to applying regulations in a routine fashion and are totally unprepared to cope with unexpected events. 'They hopelessly lack initiative', said an interviewee. In an international concentration there are bound to be unexpected events because of the uniqueness of the operation. No special arrangement can foresee all the eventualities. As soon as an unexpected event occurs, the public administrator appeals to his superior, who calls upon his own superior, and so on, until the highest echelons are reached. Here the matter is decided upon and passed down until the lower level is reached again. While in northern countries this process can be a relatively swift one, it becomes painfully slow in southern Europe.[28] The more the Mediterranean influence makes itself felt, the greater the number of echelons between lower and higher levels and the more time required for a file to go from one echelon to the other. While a file is in the process of being ruled upon, progress on the issue under consideration is paralysed. In addition, there may be bureaucratic difficulties for non-financial matters. This is particularly common for technical standards on products, as illustrated by the following hypothetical example reported by an executive. For automatic industrial scales, some European countries have requirements for precision expressed in kilograms, while others express them in pounds. Imports of scales from a country which expresses its requirements in pounds into a country which expresses its requirements in kilograms may be a cumbersome procedure. Officials of the latter in charge of checking the precision of the scales may not know whether they should accept the guarantee of the exporting country—which, if converted into kilograms, is satisfactory—or go through the checking of the scales themselves. Even worse, they may not be able to resolve the question themselves and may apply to higher authorities. It may take several months for an answer to come back, saying that the importing country is satisfied with the exporting country's control.

These bureaucratic difficulties hamper the day-to-day operations of an internationally consolidated group. It is a handicap for an internationally consolidated group to see its internal administration running into problems which typically hamper only the international operations of the company. As an executive of such a group said: 'We have internalized all the bureaucracy we were used to encountering only in our export-import business.' The financial hindrances are particularly inconvenient for cash management because it is often difficult to forecast when certain problems will occur and how long it will take to resolve them. In fact, any planning becomes difficult because it is hard to foresee bureaucratic bottlenecks, precisely because they are caused by unexpected events. Moreover, management may use its influence to expedite the ruling on a file, but this is a time-consuming process. Higher-level executives may appeal to higher-level public servants to obtain a faster decision, but this really requires that management have informal or social contacts with public administrators. For a foreign executive, development of such contacts may take a long time. It should be pointed out that bureaucratic difficulties were found to be an obstacle of far greater concern to those executives with international collaborative experience and were generally underestimated by firms prior to a consolidation.

The third obstacle is the peculiar informal relationship between public and private administration which is sometimes necessary to conduct business in a smooth fashion. Management reported that bureaucratic requirements may be so numerous and so time-consuming that one must have contacts in the public administration to simplify and speed things up. Moreover, it is necessary to be familiar with the right procedures in dealing with public authorities. There are two countries which pose particular difficulties on this account—France and especially Italy.

In France, governmental economic planning is particularly extensive.[29] The government tends to supervise the private sector, not in terms of a state-owned economy, but by encouraging private business to invest in certain areas, in certain fields, at certain times, etc. This planning can be detailed, and controls thereof quite elaborate. As a consequence, the public administration has extensive influence in various domains and, generally speaking, interaction with it is far more common for French businessmen than for others. Further, public and private administrations have very close social ties, and the success of the collaboration between the two is heavily dependent upon these ties. Within the French society, these ties are fostered by the fact that public and private administrators are typically of similar social extraction. Moreover, the fact that there is an exchange of administrators between public and private sector creates an osmosis of the two. Interaction is thus quite effective because it relies heavily on informal links which greatly expedite the process.

Obviously it is difficult for a foreigner to establish similar relationships with public authorities. Not only is the time involved too great, but the informal protocol of relations with the public sector is too complex for a foreigner to grasp readily. As a French executive described it: 'It is the product of a long established tradition and is composed of futilities; but these are very important for the kind of implicit and tacit understanding we need.' Finally, there is an element of nationalism among public administrators. In the words of another executive: 'They are jealous of their sovereignty and they unconsciously resist the penetration of foreigners in their invisible network of social powers.'

The situation is quite different in Italy. While the problem in France is a complex, overly refined social structure, in Italy the problem is one of values. As already stated, Italy today is going through a dramatic crisis which has social overtones. 'Corruption is deeply rooted in every part of the economy and it is virtually unavoidable for a businessman to live with it.' This statement was proposed to managers during the second set of interviews. Every manager who worked in Italy endorsed it unhesitatingly. The problem for a foreign businessman is twofold. First, he must learn how to bribe. It is not easy to avoid mistakes, particularly to avoid scandals. Large foreign firms are often favourite targets of public calumny, especially if this calumny is of leftist origin. A misplaced bribe can have catastrophic consequences for a manager personally, as well as for his company. Second, there is a moral decision the manager must make for himself: will he do like the Romans when in Rome and indulge in corruption, or will he stick to his own ethical standards? The typical answer to this question is—according to management—that foreign executives do not themselves bribe but allow their local collaborators to do so. Thus, they agree in fact to the bribery but apparently rationalize it by attempting to convince themselves that they are not actually doing it but are merely putting up with it. Indeed, a consultant observed that this dissonance could extend to the foreign executive convincing himself that he is not aware of the bribery.

This problem of peculiar relationships with public authorities is not in itself an obstacle to transnational concentration. A foreign firm consolidating with a French or an Italian partner can let the French or Italian executives handle the bureaucracy.[30] During the second set of interviews it was ascertained that the true obstacle here is psychological. Foreign managers feel uncomfortable when, in a 50–50 concentration, half of the organization becomes incomprehensible to them. It is a very different situation from that of a foreign branch of a multinational company operating in a country where the relationships with public authorities are elusive for a headquarters manager. Here, not only is the foreign branch a small part of the business but headquarters feel they have full control over the operation. Although the foreign branch manager's relationship with local authorities may be incomprehensible to headquarters, the manager is still a subordinate; he does not threaten headquarters with his ability to deal with public authorities. In the case of an international concentration, however, the situation is quite different. First, half of the organization is elusive for the foreign executive. This is far more disturbing than a foreign branch being unmanageable for him. In this situation, he may feel he is unable to manage the total enterprise because a large proportion of it is 'taboo' for him. Moreover, he feels at a comparative disadvantage relative to the French or the Italian executive: he is impotent *vis-à-vis* French or Italian public authorities, while his own public authorities are receptive to the French or Italian partner. As a consequence, the foreign executive feels inhibited by the relationships with the public authorities which he does not really understand. These relationships may indirectly hamper the mutual confidence of the two partners. The foreign partner may fear that the French or Italian partner is taking undue advantage of his familiarity with his own public authorities. On the other hand, Italian and French executives may believe that the foreign partner has an advantage since he does not have the obligation of complying with a complex bureaucracy. Executives with international concentration experience emphasize the necessity of making a deliberate effort to clarify such misunderstandings. One of these executives said: 'A major difficulty we had was to gain mutual confidence on issues deriving from the environment. Each partner tends to think that the other uses the excuse of environmental obligations to get an advantage over him. The only cure is to talk for hours in order to explain the dynamics of each national environment.'

The fourth obstacle has to do with international institutional uncertainty. Foreign businessmen feel that some EEC countries are too risky to become heavily involved in because of their uncertain environment. In an international consolidation requiring the commitment of half of a company's assets in a foreign country, the guarantees for environmental stability have to be much higher than for a foreign investment of a multinational firm, which constitutes only a small part of the company's total assets. This problem has two facets to it: a 'real' problem and a psychological problem.

First, some countries represent an economic and political risk; their internal macroeconomic situation is perceived to be unstable. Among these, Italy is by far the cause of the most serious concern to management. Traditionally, the country has been looked upon as having a risky business environment because its communist party is the strongest in the EEC. Moreover, the somewhat questionable morality of Italian bureaucracy has always generated a certain circumspection among foreign investors. However, the situation has deteriorated dramatically in the last few years. The economic crisis has its roots in the social and political situation. Leftist civil disturbances have become quite widespread. Companies are not only suffering from increased labour costs (which have risen 75 per cent since 1969[31]) and decreasing productivity, but also from disruptions which result in sabotage on the part of labour. For example, the Pirelli factories of La Bicocca near Milan have suffered incendiary fires which have destroyed considerable plant and equipment. In addition to strikes which have reached unbearable limits, absenteeism is plaguing manufacturers. For example, 'Mr. Agnelli, President of Fiat, blamed absenteeism which he said was running at a 14 per cent rate, for the loss of some 150,000 vehicles that might have been produced this year.'[32] On many occasions a limited number of workers in key positions on an assembly line have stopped working, thus paralysing a whole factory. The other workers stated that they were willing to continue to work and thus claimed they were entitled to be paid normally. As the few workers on strike were obviously in collusion with the other workers, it is clear that the objective was for workers to go on a *de facto* strike while continuing to be paid the normal salary.[33]

Understandably such a situation can be a considerable barrier to concentration with a foreign partner. A great many of Italy's industries are facing very serious profit problems. A potential foreign partner cannot share the burden of an Italian firm. As an Italian executive put it: 'Our bargaining disadvantage is completely isolating us from our Common Market partners. Why should a healthy foreign firm join forces with a sick Italian partner?' In fact, the situation is worsened by the difficulty of predicting its outcome. Management believes that in the next few years it is as possible for a communist government as for a rightist dictatorship to come into power. The best illustration of such collaborative difficulties is provided by the Dunlop–Pirelli union. 'As soon as the wedding took place', said Leopoldo Pirelli, Chairman of the Italian tyremaker, 'the bride [Pirelli] took to her sick bed with an attack of typhoid fever.'[34] The typhoid fever in question is 'the catastrophic situation of our country', as an Italian interviewee put it. 'Dunlop–Pirelli's central executive has launched a "special study" that has a short eight weeks to figure out ways of isolating Dunlop from new agonies in Italy.'[35] Indeed, the situation is so grave that rumours of a possible corporate divorce have circulated.[36]

While Italy's present situation is a very special one, other countries are sometimes looked upon with a certain cautiousness. In the past,

France was among these. Some executives—particularly Dutch and German ones—still express some reservations about France's 'revolutionary whims', but on the whole the country today is perceived as having one of the most promising economic growth trends in the EEC. Surprisingly enough, increasing concern is developing about Germany's sociopolitical situation. The first culprit is the leftist propensity of the present administration.[37] Further, some believe that the economy is overheated. The recent strikes are taken as an indication of the economic saturation. Finally, there appears to be a potential for radical changes in social values. Intellectual circles are still militant against the establishment and the younger strata of the population are often committed to a socialistic ideal. Many workers also tend to follow such leftist movements.

It should be clear that such environmental uncertainty can be a hindrance to international concentration. Management hesitates to engage in a permanent or long-term collaborative endeavour with a partner whose country it views as having a risky macroeconomic situation, particularly if management feels it does not have a sufficient understanding of this situation to be able to assess the risk involved.

The second facet of the problem is psychological and goes beyond the uncertainty attached to a macroeconomic situation. It pertains to the shakiness of institutional environments of certain countries perceived by foreign executives. Again, particularly for Italy, the implementation of laws and public policies is flexible. It was found that a foreign manager does not understand what factors influence one particular interpretation rather than another. Especially in today's troubled times, implementation of laws is heavily influenced not only by bribery but also by political and social factors. Several interviewees stated that certain court decisions are taken to temper public opinion on a given issue, while in other instances no legal suit is made against crimes in order not to arouse public opinion. For example, it has often happened that no action was taken against labour forces that had damaged company equipment during some violent strikes, for reasons that had little to do with business (e.g., sociopolitical reasons). A foreign manager cannot grasp those factors influencing the interpretation of the law, because they are deeply rooted in the social dynamics of the country. If what is judicially permissible depends not only on the laws but on intangible factors, a foreign manager cannot really have an adequate understanding of what he may and may not do. Management believes that this, in turn, has two effects.

First, firms hesitate to consolidate with a partner whose institutional environment they cannot fully grasp. They feel inhibited by the idea that half of their operations (in a 50–50 concentration) are in an environment of which they have little understanding. This, added to the peculiar relationships with public administrators, makes a foreign executive feel insecure. As a German executive put it: 'You have to play a game without knowing its rules, which means that you often don't know where you are going.'

The second effect is that of hindering the integration of the human organization of a consolidated group. A foreign manager always has the impression he is not 'at home' in an environment he does not understand. He knows he is dependent on local managers. This fosters the feeling that there is a 'difference' between the two partners. In other words, the fact that they operate in two totally different institutional environments increases the perceived differences between the two parties. This makes the integration of the 'human side of the enterprise' all the more difficult because it contributes to widening the gap between the parties involved.

For the four sets of obstacles discussed in this section, it is difficult to make specific recommendations. It should be clear that many of the problems will be resolved if further progress towards Europe is made at the macro-level. The uncertainty element of international concentration would be reduced. The bureaucracy involved in transnational operations would also be diminished and harmonization would have to come about in the informal organization of the public administration. In chapter 1 of this study it was stated that industrial integration should be a driving force for sociopolitical integration. The business community recognizes and generally accepts its responsibilities towards this endeavour. However, many interviewees point out the necessity for governmental authorities to keep up with the Europeanization movement. As a Belgian executive put it: 'We need tangible signs that the political sphere is following the European movement to be encouraged to continue to lead it.'

NOTES

1. See: 'Will Europe Face "the American Challenge"?' *Business Week*, 14 October 1972, pp. 60–63.

2. Nicholas Stacey, *Mergers in Modern Business*, Hutchinson, London, 1970, p. 121.

3. 'Will Europe Face "the American Challenge"?' p. 61.

4. See: Christopher Layton, *European Advanced Technology—A Programme for Integration*, Allen & Unwin, London, 1969, pp. 50–88 (particularly pp. 64–73).

5. See: Paul M. Goldberg, 'The Evolution of Transnational Companies in Europe', Ph.D. Dissertation, Massachusetts Institute of Technology, Sloan School of Management; and Michael B. Stewart, 'Transnational Enterprise: The European Challenge', *Columbia Journal of World Business*, July–August, 1972, pp. 5–13 at pp. 9–10.

6. See: Christopher Layton, *Cross Frontier Mergers in Europe*, Bath University Press, Bath, 1971, pp. 30–31; and Werner Feld, *Transnational Business Collaboration among Common Market Countries*, Praeger, New York, 1970, pp. 37–38 and 62–63.

7. Normally, these are cases where the company gave up pursuing the possibility

of consolidating quite early, as it found out very quickly that there would be strong governmental opposition (typically, a company finds this out through informal contacts with governmental authorities).

8. Robert N. Mattson, 'Mergers: European Style', *Mergers and Acquisitions*, Spring 1971, p. 30.

9. For a further description of this case, see:

(a) Werner Feld, *Transnational Business Collaboration among Common Market Countries*, pp. 63–64.

(b) *Le Monde de l'économie*, February 11, 1969, pp. 1–2.

(c) *Die Welt*, 'Bonn sagt nein zur Forderung de Gaulles nach Verkauf des Gelsenberg-Pakets', No. 6, 8 January 1969.

10. See: Walter P. Blass, 'Economic Planning, European Style', *Harvard Business Review*, September–October 1963, p. 112.

11. For a detailed discussion on the influence of the French economic planning on corporate strategies, see John H. McArthur and Bruce R. Scott, *Industrial Planning in France*, Division of Research, Graduate School of Business Administration, Harvard University, Boston, 1969.

12. This discussion should not give the false impression that this exchange between private and public administration is bad. Quite to the contrary, management feels the relationship is usually smooth and effective in fostering an ordered economic development of the country.

13. For further detail on this point, see:

(a) Luigi Einaudi, *Lo scrittoio del Presidente*, Giulio Einaudi, Torino, 1956, pp. 248–49 and 282–84.

(b) Luigi Einaudi, *Prediche inutili*, Giulio Einaudi, Torino, 1969, pp. 91–95, 101, 126, and 129–30.

(c) Luigi Einaudi, *Saggi sul risparmio e l'imposta*, Giulio Einaudi, Torino, 1965, pp. 115–17.

(Professor Einaudi has served as Finance Minister and as President of the Italian Republic.)

14. For a comprehensive discussion of this topic, see: Sergio Barzanti, *The Underdeveloped Areas within the Common Market*, Princeton University Press, Princeton, New Jersey, 1965.

15. A comparable discussion is to be found in Christopher Layton's *European Advanced Technology—A Programme for Integration*, p. 242.

16. This is consistent with Werner Feld's findings in *Transnational Business Collaboration among Common Market Countries*, p. 64.

17. See: Christopher Layton, *European Advanced Technology—A Programme for Integration*, pp. 64–73 (in particular, p. 72).

18. On this point, see the comments of Jean-Jacques Servan-Schreiber in 'Servan-Schreiber updates his "challenge"', *Business Week*, 14 October 1972, p. 66.

19. As an illustration of this, see: Gregory H. Wierzynski, 'G. E.'s $200 Million Ticket to France', *Fortune Magazine*, 1 June 1967, pp. 92–96 and 159–62.

20. It is interesting to note that the following comments on France, as well as the subsequent ones on Great Britain and Italy, have been made essentially by interviewees who were from a country other than the one to which the comments applied.

21. Recent developments seem to indicate that this was a sound policy from the national point of view (especially in view of a possible German recession—as the French are quick to point out).

22. See: Renato Mazzolini, 'Generating an Unconventional Hypothesis: Stockholders' Personal Objectives as Motivating Forces for International Concentration—The Italian Case', unpublished paper, Stanford University, 1971.

23. It is noteworthy that these arguments as well as the following were presented virtually only by private sector executives.

24. See: Luigi Einaudi, *Prediche inutili*, pp. 95 ff.

25. For a description of the EEC institutions, see:

(a) F. B. Jensen and I. Walter, *The Common Market: Economic Integration in Europe*, Lippincott, Philadelphia, 1965, Chapter II.

(b) M. Shanks and J. Lambert, *The Common Market Today and Tomorrow*, Praeger, New York, 1962, pp. 46–54.

26. For further discussion of this argument, see: Christopher Layton, 'European Advanced Technology—A Programme for Integration', in *European Business*, July 1969, pp. 33–36.

27. This corresponds to the analysis of Michel Drancourt and Henri Lepage in 'Obstacles psychologiques (et politiques) aux concentrations et aux fusions intra-communautaires', *Revue du Marché Commun*, No. 109, January–February 1968, pp. 139–41.

28. As evidence, managers in southern European countries raised the question more often and were more articulate about it, and managers with international experience who had had the opportunity to compare the various bureaucracies unanimously confirmed this situation.

29. For further details on the French economic planning system, see:

(a) Pierre Bauchet, *La planification française*, Editions du Seuil, Paris, 1962.

(b) Pierre Massé, 'National Planning and Business Enterprise in France' in George A. Steiner and Warren M. Cannon, *Multinational Corporate Planning*, Macmillan, New York, 1966.

(c) John Hackett and Anne-Marie Hackett, *Economic Planning in France*, Harvard University Press, Cambridge, 1963.

30. US multinational firms with direct investments in these countries have learned this well. When they have no local partner, they commonly hire the services of notables with extensive local relationships to take care of 'public relations with public authorities'.

31. 'Multinationals: The Unhappy Union of Dunlop–Pirelli', *Business Week*, 4 November 1972, p. 38.

32. 'Italy's Economic Woes Mount as Strikes, Layoffs, Profit Problems Plague Industry', *The Wall Street Journal*, 1 November 1972, p. 10.

33. See: Nino Nutrizio, 'Il male nuovo', *La Notte*, 28 October 1970, p. 1.

34. 'Multinationals: The Unhappy Union of Dunlop–Pirelli', p. 38.

35. 'Multinationals: The Unhappy Union of Dunlop–Pirelli', p. 38.

36. See: Enzo Passanisi, 'Per salvare l'unione Pirelli–Dunlop è necessario tagliare i "rami secchi" ', *Corriere della Sera*, 23 November 1972, p. 7.

37. The proposed enlargement of worker participation on companies' supervisory boards from one-third to one-half is an illustration of this leftist policy.

5.

SOCIOECONOMIC OBSTACLES

This chapter deals with obstacles which have their roots outside the business organization but are still somewhat related to its environment. The focus is on barriers originating in the social and economic scene in which the company operates. The first section analyses accounting practices and the financial framework. The second section deals with problems deriving from markets. The third section examines problems deriving from labour. The fourth section takes up two other obstacles: the opposition of stockholders and the opposition of the general public.

Accounting and finance

This section deals with problems whose roots are in the general area of finance. The first centre of attention is the difficulty deriving from conflicting business practices in Europe, mainly accounting. The second is the financing problems encountered by international concentrations.

Business practices are taken to mean non-codified rules of conduct a manager must follow. They are requirements which are beyond juridical regulations. These rules, self-imposed by the business community, may vary from country to country and can create difficulties for transnational collaboration. The greatest difficulties arise in the area of financial accounting.

Chapter 3 surveyed the differences in the legal requirements for corporate accounting. Here the discussion turns to differences in accounting methods which derive not from the legal regulations but from conflicting business practices.[1] It is noteworthy that the differences in business practices usually create greater problems than those originating in the legal requirements. This is because legal requirements are not as a rule very stringent and the business community is more demanding than the law. While there are strong dissimilarities within the EEC, it is with the United Kingdom that the differences are greatest.

The United Kingdom has Europe's most elaborate accounting requirements.[2] Its sophistication is traditional. Moreover, the London Stock Exchange has heavy requirements for the disclosure of the accounts of the companies it lists.[3] London is the most important stock exchange in Europe and virtually all large British firms are quoted on it. To satisfy the stock exchange, British companies are accustomed to complying with stringent accounting regulations. At the other extreme, Italy has very limited accounting stringency. The accounting profession there is flexible and accustomed to manipulating corporate accounts primarily for fiscal purposes.[4]

This disparity creates difficulties similar to those deriving from the legal differences surveyed in chapter 3. At the moment the concentration takes place, the task of evaluating and comparing two companies is very difficult.[5] Their financial data often have little in common. Not only do financial statements follow very different standards, but the underlying bookkeeping is also quite different. As a consequence, it is very cumbersome to render the financial pictures of two companies comparable. Despite the help of outside auditors, it often appears impossible to go beyond approximation. Management, however, considers that this particular problem should not be overemphasized. As will be seen in chapter 6, the evaluation of potential concentrators encounters more difficult problems than those posed by accounting.

The more serious stumbling blocks in management's experience are at the operating level, when an internationally concentrated group has to produce consolidated financial statements. Between two companies of countries which both have stringent regulations, it can be expected that the regulations will be in conflict. It thus becomes necessary to produce financial statements for each country. Where one of the countries (or both) has permissive regulations, it is also quite difficult to produce consolidated statements. Referring back to the Anglo-Italian concentration example, it is normally inconceivable for an Italian company to produce the type of information required by the British Stock Exchange. 'It would have catastrophic results', said an Italian executive. The principal problem, again, is fiscal: if the company complied with British standards, it would have to give a true and complete picture of its financial status. Not only might the necessary information be unavailable within the company but, even if it were available, nobody would think of publishing it; in the words of one executive, 'the company would go bankrupt under the fiscal burden.'

These differences in accounting practices find their solution in the hybrid forms of concentration. In the models discussed in chapter 2, it is possible to comply with the national requirements of each country because the legal person of each partner is maintained. In each partner's country the accounting is done according to national practices. Clearly, while this solves the problem from a technical point of view, the administrative hindrance persists. The impossibility of having a unified accounting for the whole group generates duplication of efforts.[6] Interviewees of internationally concentrated companies typically report that they keep two sets of books: one for national disclosure requirements; the other for the internal use of the company. The latter is based on common standards throughout the company and serves as a basis for internal managerial accounting. This duplication also adds to the administrative costs of hybrid solutions. However, executives of internationally concentrated companies say that there is a learning process which takes place, and that the inconveniences of such duplication gradually disappear. These executives also add that this learning could be expedited if a consulting organization were available to help set up an integrated accounting system. The greatest impact of such consulting would be in the 'debugging' of the accounting system resulting from the co-ordination of the systems of the companies participating in an international consolidation.

Another area of concern represented by differences in business practices has to do with the banking sector. Banks in the various European countries engage in different practices.[7] This hinders an international concentration in the banking sector itself because the policies of a bank in one country are not always applicable in another country. For example, German banks not only commonly engage in long-term loans but also hold sizable equity participations in commercial corporations. Moreover, the relationship between a German bank and its client company goes beyond a mere financial service and can be extended to the administration of the company. In other countries, banks limit their activity to short-term financing. As a consequence, some bankers tend to believe that they cannot pool their resources with their foreign counterparts because their expertise is not compatible with foreign business practices.

It should be pointed out, however, that bankers with extensive international experience believe this is an exaggerated view of the problem. More and more, bankers are realizing that 'good banking is good banking anywhere', as one of the interviewed bankers put it. Effective financial analysis is a skill that tends to exist in and of itself, and environmental constraints can be built into this analysis. International banking has proven that there can in fact be a valuable cross-fertilization in the collaboration of bankers of different countries with dissimilar business practices. Indeed, experience shows that the 'different ways of doing business' are less a technical barrier than a psychological hindrance. As one banker said: 'People think we do business differently and, thus, they do not even try to collaborate. This is the real obstacle, not the difference itself.'

FINANCING PITFALLS

The second centre of attention of this section is the inadequacy of the sources for financing available to European firms. The two sources discussed here are capital markets and banks (as well as other institutions specialized in corporate financing).

Capital markets in Europe are not yet as developed as in the US.[8] Indeed, 'most European capital markets cannot supply capital in the quantities and varieties demanded by local industrialists'.[9] Probably this is originally due to the fact that European companies are traditionally held by families or by closed groups of stockholders, often via banks. Moreover, with the exception of Great Britain, private individuals in Europe do not invest in securities as much as in the US, so that the volume of capital markets is further reduced. Besides, for debentures, the private sector has to face the competition of public issues.[10] The debt market is flooded by bonds either of public institutions such as cities or governments or by state-owned companies and financial institutions. This reduces the availability of funds for privately owned corporations. Finally, European capital markets are in fairly watertight compartments. With the exception of very large or well-known multinationals, it is difficult for a company to issue securities in a given European country if it does not have sizable operations in that country. Investors are dubious of the credit worthiness of a company which does not have substantial business in their country. As a result, a firm may not be able to issue securities on the most attractive capital market: if it does not have sizable operations in that market's country, its securities may not be received favourably.

Traditionally, European business has relied much more on banks and other institutions for its financial needs than on capital markets.[11] However, in recent years the availability of funds provided by banks has been the object of increasing concern to the business community.[12] Financial executives generally think that existing institutions are unfit to service multinational corporations. First, they do not have a sufficient network throughout Europe. One interviewee complained: 'We cannot use the same bank in all countries. An important advantage is thus lost: that of having a personal relationship with the banker.' Another even more significant advantage is thus lost: a company's credit worthiness is not adequately recognized throughout Europe. This means that if a company investing in a given country uses a local bank, it cannot easily transfer its credit worthiness from abroad in order to use it with the local bank. Second, multinational companies need multinational financial services beyond money. They need, in particular, assistance in the negotiations and launching of their new ventures: underwriters, brokers, etc. Here again, international executives complain about the inadequacy of such services across national boundaries. Third, multinational companies have increasing demands for larger sums of money. This is particularly true for the long and medium term. Larger companies require more debt to compensate their larger equity base. They also have higher working capital requirements. 'Multinational companies often have a difficult time in obtaining the necessary amounts of money', said a member of a professional association. Businessmen express concern about banks being too small, particularly for the future needs of transnational companies.

This situation has essentially four negative consequences for transnational concentrations. First, the fact that capital markets are in relatively watertight compartments may hinder the expansion of a transnationally concentrated group. As was mentioned already, two companies may consolidate in order to broaden their scope to EEC dimensions, i.e., join forces in order to operate on a truly European scale. In this endeavour it would be desirable that a concentrated group be able to issue securities on any European market, but the compartmentalization of the markets hinders this. Second, the difficulty of issuing debentures tends to force companies to revert to banks to satisfy their needs for long-term debt. This leads to problems which are now to be examined.

Third, traditional sources of financing are too limited to satisfy the needs of internationally concentrated groups. National banks have difficulties in serving the largest national companies, and are often unequal to the task when the client is the product of the amalgamation of several large national companies. This is of particular concern to high-technology industries. Executives point out that already in today's international joint ventures or co-operative agreements it is practically impossible to find a bank willing to finance an entire project. Several banks have to get together and share the responsibility of servicing the venture. However, executives complain that they themselves often have to solicit the formation of international banking consortia: without really promoting such consortia, they at least must actively support bankers to pool their own resources. Managers fear that when firms go a step further and actually consolidate with a foreign partner, banks will be unprepared to service them. Fourth, beyond the mere providing of money, banks do not have a sufficiently extended international network for financial services. Underwriting of new issues is thus more difficult. When an internationally concentrated group issues bonds, for example, it usually employs the services of a bank in each country in which it wishes to sell the bonds. Moreover, bankers are often not sufficiently equipped to advise companies on financial matters on an international scale. Executives complain that banks do not have the proper knowledge of foreign environments, and cannot counsel companies in their international financial policies. 'This is the area of major concern in the entire finance area', according to one international executive.

The most effective way to secure integration of capital markets would be monetary union throughout the EEC.[13] This would enable the free flow of investments from one country to the other. Monetary union would help banks to pool their own resources across frontiers. Short-run solutions would be for banks and other financial institutions to establish international networks.[14] These imply co-operative agreements designed for the long term (as opposed to one-shot joint ventures). While banks encounter practically insurmountable barriers to concentration, these agreements are temporary surrogates. In recent times banks have engaged in several such co-operative agreements and their number is rapidly increasing.[15] Beyond the often cited agreement between Crédit Lyonnais, Commerzbank, and Banco di Roma, one can point to Orion (formed by National Westminster, Westdeutsche Landesbank Girozentrale, Chase Manhattan, Royal Bank of Canada, and Credito Italiano) or the EBIC (formed by Amsterdam–Rotterdam Bank, Deutsche Bank, Midland Bank, and Société Générale de Banque).

It is not enough for banks to improve their ability to assist transnational companies. As we have seen, banks have difficulty satisfying the growing demand for funds by multinational business, and improvements are also needed in capital markets. Companies should be better able to satisfy their needs for external financing through capital markets. Firms might issue preferred shares and convertible debentures more frequently: these securities have the important advantage of not overly increasing the perceived risk for investors, while at the same time they do not dilute the ownership of closely held companies such as family-owned companies (i.e., the family retains control of the firm). In addition, a promotional effort should be made to get wider acceptance of private debentures and international shares by investors.

Markets

This section analyses the problems deriving from markets. There are four distinct areas of concern here. First, there is the nationalism of some consumers regarding certain products and services—a preference for those produced by national companies rather than foreign or multinational ones. Second, there are dissimilarities in market demand—differences in national tastes for certain products. Third, management often has misconceptions about markets—misleading preconceptions about certain characteristics of the market. Fourth, there is a lack of market data—insufficient information about certain aspects of the market.

In certain markets nationalism is expressed by a preference for national products, and one example often cited by interviewees is that of governments, which favour national over foreign products. Among foreign products, a trend is slowly emerging in favour of EEC products as against third-country products, but executives complain that this attitude is not yet sufficiently distinct. Moreover, other things being equal, a government tends to give preference to the product of a purely national company over the product of a transnational company composed of an amalgamation of firms of different nationalities, even though there is a firm of its own nationality participating in the group.

This nationalistic government procurement policy is, in management's experience, a hindrance to international consolidations on two accounts. First, inasmuch as governments favour national companies, there is an incentive for a national company not to concentrate transnationally as it might then lose the benefits of nationalistic governmental procurement. If the firm is the only national producer, this is not a major hindrance as its government will continue to buy from it because its product will still be the most 'national' one available. If there is a national competitor, this can be a problem because the government may give its preference to the other purely national firm. Consequently, the problem is greater in large countries, where there is a greater likelihood of their being more than one national producer of a given product. The problem reportedly is also greater in larger countries because smaller countries know that they cannot sustain a viable industry alone in sectors requiring high investments and their governments are thus more inclined to allow their national suppliers to link up with foreign partners. Large countries, on the other hand, tend to insist more on national suppliers because they see less need for a national company to consolidate with a foreign partner.

There is a second aspect of the problem of nationalistic governmental procurement which was discussed by management. As noted above, the choice by governments of foreign EEC products over foreign non-EEC products is still a limited one. Governments do not have a 'buy European' attitude. As a consequence, the loss of 'consumer preference' a firm incurs *vis-à-vis* its government when it concentrates internationally is not compensated by an increase in 'consumer preference' on the part of other governments. In other words, if two companies concentrate internationally, not only may they lose marketing goodwill with regard to their own governments, but they cannot count on the favours of other EEC governments—the hope that other EEC governments will prefer purchasing their products because they are European.

This problem of nationalistic governmental procurement is of particular importance because governments are the major customers in many sectors where there is the greatest need for transnational concentration. This is true for high-technology products such as aircraft, computers, or military equipment. Here the high investment requirements are such that it is economically desirable to have a pooling of resources cross-nationally. The fact that governments are often the prime customers for these products hinders this pooling of resources.[16]

It should be clear that this problem is distinct from the negative attitude of governments towards international consolidations discussed in chapter 4. There, the motivation was to maintain the national identity of companies. Here, it is a phenomenon of consumer preference. It is the product which preoccupies the government: the government wants a national product for its own perceived benefit. Nationalistic governmental procurement is an end in itself.

Governments do, in fact, sponsor international joint ventures in high-technology sectors, as a last-resort solution when there is no way of developing a project within national boundaries. Executives of companies involved in such joint ventures usually believe that, in their particular case, the joint venture route is insufficient and that an international consolidation is warranted. 'Governments are always a step behind; when they are brought to accept an international joint venture, it is really an international marriage which would be more in order', said one French executive.[17]

In addition to the nationalism of the government, marketing managers reported that there are other nationalistic consumers.[18] This is true where products are associated in some way with the prestige of the country. For example, some sports car manufacturers said that national customers buy their cars because they have been successful in international races. As a marketing executive put it: 'There is an element of the buying decision which is similar to that of buying a badge of the favourite team. When people buy one of our cars, they sometimes have the impression they are part of the factory team which they favour in the races.' This nationalism is also to be found in service companies, the best example being airlines. Market surveys have shown that people tend to fly on the airline of their nationality. While there is an undeniable convenience element here (e.g., the cabin crew speaks the mother tongue), there are also emotional reasons: the national airline is an expression of national power and prestige, in which the passenger takes pride.

The country in which the 'buy national' feature reportedly exerts the strongest influence is Britain. During the second set of interviews, the question was asked if the relative internationalism of the EEC consumers was a result of the Common Market, namely, if the EEC was believed to have encouraged a Europeanization of consumers' tastes. Managers responded that this was quite unlikely inasmuch as EEC consumers show no preference for EEC foreign products as opposed to non-EEC foreign products. Rather, managers thought the explanation should be sought in the traditionalism of British consumers, who have historically been insular in their tastes.[19]

The discussion up to now has dealt with ethnocentric consumer behaviour due to national pride. In addition, there is a certain category of products which gain from being associated with a country regardless of the consumers' nationality.[20] Several managers stated that some products benefit if a given national identity is associated with them. These are, again, prestige products. For example, one need only turn to perfumes, wines, or *haute couture* for products that benefit from the French image.

This nationalism is a hindrance to transnational concentration because a company of a given nationality may lose marketing goodwill if it amalgamates with a foreign counterpart. For example, if two European airlines concentrated, they might lose part of their consumers' loyalty. These consumers would not be as attracted by the transnational airline as they were by their national airline, and thus they may become indifferent to flying on the planes of the consolidated company or on foreign third companies. In the case of perfumes, if a French company concentrated with a foreign company, its products would lose some of their national image and thus consumers would end up purchasing perfumes of other companies which had remained 100 per cent French.

There are two solutions to the nationalistic market demand problem. The first is applicable to those sectors where there is a single producer in each country. Again, the best example here is the airlines.[21] If all European companies decided to pool their resources, this would bypass a substantial part of the nationalistic demand; there would be no choice other than buying from that company. The risk of turning to non-EEC companies is limited. Clearly the question arises, what would become of free competition? Here, there are two possibilities. The European company would represent all the industries of the EEC under the aegis of the governments. This would apply to airlines which are public or quasi-public companies. Here then, the free competition question would be dismissed because the group would be *de facto* a public monopoly. This possibility is attractive in high-technology sectors where the major customer is the government. The second possibility is that all EEC companies pool their resources not into one but into a few transnational companies. In other words, the concentration would lead to the formation of a few European giants competing against each other.

The second solution is that companies which concentrate internationally make a deliberate effort to retain their national image. This is particularly applicable to consumer products companies. In an international consolidation the participating parties can keep their national goodwill by a number of tactics. For example, the maintenance of the name of each company in its country is a convenient method of not calling the market's attention to the transnationalization of the company. As a French marketing manager remarked: 'The important thing is to integrate the inside of the concentrated group, namely, its finances and its administration, but to keep the outside well separated, namely, the markets.'

The second area of concern of this section is dissimilarities in market demand.[22] This refers to differences in consumers' tastes. Management reports that consumers desire different products in the various European countries, regardless of the products' nationality. Probably the most typical area here is the food industry, where tastes differ most from country to country and also are slowest to change. In fact, it is in the lower-priced products (e.g., bread) that this phenomenon is the strongest. This is clearly a stumbling block for international consolidations because of the requirement of tailoring the products to national markets. Demand differs most from country to country in the low-priced, mass-produced products; it is here that economies of scale deriving from a concentration are most notably jeopardized.

There are other sectors where management believes the demand for a given type of product differs across national boundaries. Many illustrations were given in the course of the interviewing. In the automotive industry, for example, certain markets like Germany have a distinct preference for two-door economy cars, while others such as the French favour four-door economy cars. Also, in countries like Italy where the cost of gasoline is the highest in Europe and where there is a high annual tax on vehicles with larger engines, consumers prefer cars with limited displacement. Another example is provided by the demand for technical surgical equipment, which depends upon the type of equipment surgeons have used in their training. As this varies from country to country, it is necessary to supply different types of products on the various national markets.

Reportedly, there are also differences in the marketing function itself, resulting from different purchasing habits of consumers. Hence the selling must be tailored to the local conditions of the market. For example, in the north of Europe department stores are now very popular and have been widely adopted by consumers. In the south, however, they still encounter some resistance and buyers tend to prefer small, individually owned shops. Differences in purchasing habits impede the full integration of the marketing function of a transnational company, which in turn goes counter to the reduction of the administrative expenses.

There are two sets of recommendations made by marketing managers with international experience to overcome the problem. First, it is possible to develop a basic model of a product which can be used in all countries with minor adaptations. This reduces costs in that it maximizes the part of a product which is produced in common for all countries and reduces the amount of tailoring to local taste. Careful investigation of market demand is required to identify what is unique about a particular national demand. Thus market analysis is required and the problem is to do this analysis successfully. Unfortunatley, as chapter 6 will show, the necessary skills for such analysis are often not available in Europe.

The second recommendation is that of trying to educate the consumer towards unified tastes. This is possible in such products as technical surgical equipment through a harmonization of the training programmes and through continuing education programmes designed to acquaint surgeons with the latest developments in medicine. It is, however, more in the purchasing habits that it is possible to educate buyers towards common practices. For example, the resistance to department stores might be countered with advertising that focuses on the merits of these stores (e.g., sanitation). Multinational companies involved in mass marketing emphasize that buyer behaviour can be manipulated far more easily than is commonly believed.

The third area of concern of this section is misconceptions about markets. There is a distinct tendency for managers to believe differences in market demand to be greater than they are in reality. This type of statement was typically made by marketing managers about general managers. Marketing managers are of the opinion that 'corporate strategists' believe that it is necessary to tailor products and marketing policies to individual markets far more than is really necessary. As a Dutch marketing manager said: 'People believe that the market for trivial products is influenced by profound cultural variables with deep historical roots. This is wrong for most mass production goods.' Further, marketing managers with extensive international experience tended to judge marketing managers of non-multinational businesses as entertaining a similar set of misbeliefs. As one of these international executives said: 'The typical marketer is convinced that in each nation consumers have a distinctive buyer behaviour. In western Europe this is wrong and the average marketer is myopic in this respect.'

Indeed, marketing requirements seem less differentiated than is commonly believed. US international firms have proven that it is generally possible to view Europe as one market. Even if there have been some failures in attempting to sell in certain countries products which are quite successful elsewhere, the American experience in Europe shows that the differences in markets have been exaggerated. Not only is it possible to sell a similar product throughout Europe but it is also possible to use the same marketing approaches. Standard Oil created a breakthrough with its 'put a tiger in your tank' message, which it used successfully in a multitude of countries. This advertising campaign surprised many European marketing managers because it contradicted their opinion that it is necessary to use special marketing messages for each country.

Thanks to the marketing policy of US international firms in Europe, some EEC companies are beginning to develop marketing policies with a European scope. These are usually far more successful than the expectations of the managers who launch them. Even in the food industry it is becoming obvious that many fears are unwarranted. A recent market study of one of the desserts of a food company has shown that even in this particularly traditional type of segment, it is possible to sell the same product throughout Europe. As an international executive put it: 'We were adapting our products to geographical areas not only for each country but also for each region. Then we tried to switch products from one area to the other, namely, put the type of product designed for area (X) into area (Y), and area (Y)'s product into area (X): the result was that sales increased in both areas!' Even if the explanation here may be that the sales increase was due to the innovation itself, there are strong reasons to believe that the tailoring of the product to the local market was, in the executive's words, 'the product of dreams'.

The erroneous conception that it is impossible to sell the same products in the same way throughout Europe is probably the major hindrance to transnational concentrations created by the marketing question. At the moment the decision to concentrate is made executives are often inhibited by the belief that no rationalization will be possible either in production or in marketing because of the perceived differences in demand. Furthermore, at the operating level, not all the benefits of integration are reaped because marketing managers do not question the alleged uniqueness of each national market. The solution is to do market analysis and pilot studies in order for managers to become convinced that markets are not as different as is often believed.

The fourth area of concern is lack of information on markets. This results principally from insufficient statistical data about demand. There are relatively few organizations in Europe which publish reliable data on markets. Executives complain particularly about the scarcity of information on the evolution of market demand and the lack of market segmentation analysis in sufficient detail. Furthermore, there are few published reports on buyer behaviour. Marketing managers complain that they have to enter a foreign market 'cold', without adequate information on tastes and consumer attitudes. It was found that companies tend to operate intuitively in their own national markets, which they know well because of their relatively small size and homogeneity. Large multinational companies make their own market surveys, which are not made available to third parties.

The lack of information on markets can be a problem during the preparatory stages of an international consolidation. A company seeking a concentration partner may find the search process difficult. The lack of information hampers the identification of the most appropriate country in which to look for a partner. But in fact, this is not a major hindrance in today's international concentrations among large companies. Companies rarely decide they want to concentrate before having identified a partner. Rather, they tend to analyse the desirability of concentrating with a particular partner in mind. Consequently, they learn about this market during the feasibility study itself. However, if international concentrations become more common, it is conceivable that the need for concentration will receive separate analysis and will precede the search for a partner. Companies would decide that an international link-up is desirable and would then establish criteria for the selection of a partner. Among these criteria the characteristics of the partner's market would be of major importance. It is here that the lack of data would become painful. In other words, under present conditions the lack of information has limited consequences. However, if international concentration should become less sporadic, then the need for better market information would become more dramatic.

Two basic types of proposals have been made by interviewees to overcome this lack of information. The first is to set up an organization designed to assist international link-ups, beyond purely legal, fiscal, or financial matters. This would be a data bank which would gather information on international management problems with particular attention to marketing data. The second is for existing professional associations such as the German BDI or the Confederation of British Industry to gather the data from large multinational companies that have generated the information for their own use. These companies could sell this information or receive royalties on its use by other companies. This task could, in fact, be a joint effort between various professional associations of different countries. In view of the as yet limited number of transnational consolidations, the second proposal appears more realistic.

Labour

In this section, the problems deriving from labour are analysed. It is important to reiterate that there are two types of issues raised by this question. The first is the legal problem of codetermination. This technical problem, which was surveyed in chapter 2, is relevant for the development of a statute for a European company or for the harmonization of corporate law throughout the EEC. The question is which model to choose for a European legal code: the German model which requires codetermination or the model of most other EEC countries which does not provide for codetermination?[23] The second issue—which will be discussed here—pertains to the actual difficulties that labour itself may create in an international consolidation. They can be divided into two groups: labour opposition to transnational consolidations and managerial problems deriving from labour.

Labour opposition to transnational concentration can take a variety of forms. The first is precisely through codetermination. In Germany workers may use the power which codetermination confers on them to oppose a concentration. They have at present a one-third representation in the *Aufsichtsrat*, which theoretically is not enough to block a consolidation. However, their influence is already sizable. German interviewees stated that if the rest of the decision-makers are not unconditionally committed to the concentration, the influence of workers can be decisive. Moreover, in coal, iron and steel companies, worker participation is 50 per cent. As was pointed out in chapter 2, there is a proposal to generalize the 50 per cent worker participation to all companies, thereby giving labour enough power to veto a concentration.

It was found that German codetermination can be a means to hinder a transnational consolidation even outside of Germany. It is enough that one partner be German for the codetermination to operate—indirectly—in the foreign partner as well. The foreign partner's workers can oppose the transnational concentration by asking their German counterparts to block the concentration. This was the major stumbling block of the Hoesch–Hoogovens concentration. The Dutch workers agreed that the German workers should oppose the consolidation through their *Mitbestimmung*. (In this particular instance, it is noteworthy that the firms involved were coal and iron and steel companies which gave Hoesch 50 per cent codetermination.)

In countries where there is no formal worker participation in management, labour can still influence management against a consolidation. According to several executives interviewed, there can be a constructive dialogue between management and labour in which labour explains its reasons for opposing a concentration. Management may give in to these reasons simply because workers' arguments are convincing. Alternatively, management may feel it had better give in to avoid unrest. Management, sensing that workers are determined not to accept a concentration, may feel that the dialogue will degenerate into worker militancy against the proposed consolidation.

If workers want to affirm their will in a militant fashion, they can strike or even commit acts of sabotage. If the discussion between workers and management does not lead to an acceptable compromise, workers may go on strike to carry their point. Alternatively, workers may go on strike even before discussing the matter with management. This is more likely in countries where the communist influence is greater, notably Italy. Italian workers are in ideological conflict with management and often refuse to enter any discussion. As an Italian executive stated: 'Here the strike is an end in itself; it is not necessary to have a reason to strike, a pretext is quite sufficient.'[24]

What are the motives of workers in opposing a transnational concentration? There are basically two sets of reasons: first, those which are directly connected with the link-up under consideration; and second, those which have little to do with the consolidation and for which the consolidation is merely an excuse.

The first have to do with issues pertaining to the concentration itself. The most important is the conflict over codetermination whenever a link-up is considered between a German firm and a firm from another member state. The German system calls for collaboration between management and labour. The system of the other countries is, at best, a situation of perennial bargaining and, at worst, what an Italian executive called ‘perpetual revolution’. As was seen in chapter 2, each system rests on philosophical foundations as different as they are deeply rooted. German managers, who often expressed considerable concern about this issue, reported that German labour is normally quite reluctant to engage in a consolidation in which there will be no codetermination. On the other hand, non-German management is strongly opposed to accepting codetermination in the amalgamated group. Further, non-German labour itself frequently does not welcome codetermination, preferring to remain in opposition to management.[25] Consequently, beyond the unwillingness of non-German managements to accept a codetermination system for the consolidated group, workers do not agree among themselves on an integrated policy and thus oppose transnational concentration because they fear they will be in conflict with each other. Moreover, they reportedly believe they will become relatively weaker because they are divided among themselves, while the patronate becomes stronger and more unified. If management joins forces while labour is divided into factions, workers fear they may lose some of their bargaining power.

The second reason associated with a concentration itself is the fear of rationalization. This is a problem in any consolidation—national or international.[26] Workers fear redundancy, principally due to economies of scale. In a transnational situation, the problem is aggravated by the relative ignorance of workers about foreign labour conditions. Management reports that the perceived risk of rationalization is increased by misconceptions about foreign labour. For example, Italian workers fear that a consolidation with a German firm might induce management to increase job opportunities for the more skilled German labour. Dutch or German workers, on the other hand, who have a higher per capita income, fear that management may favour cheaper Italian labour. Thus, not only is there a concern about fewer jobs but also a perceived threat to workers that their foreign counterparts have a competitive advantage and that they themselves will suffer more in the expected rationalization.

The second group of reasons for worker opposition to international consolidation is indirect; it involves motives which are not connected with their conditions as affected by the consolidation. Executives point out that workers often take advantage of an impending concentration to make demands that have little to do with the concentration itself. They request an improvement of their working conditions, threatening opposition to the concentration if they do not get what they want. For example, they allege that the concentration will bring about an improvement in the economic performance of the firm and that they are entitled to share in this improvement through increased salaries or reduced working hours. This is usually unreasonable, either because the improvement in the firm's performance is impossible to quantify or because the concentration is a defensive move designed to hedge against changing conditions of the environment such as increased competition. Moreover, there is little justification for the workers to be paid more because the firm earns more; a worker's pay is a function of his own performance, not a function of how well management utilizes his work. Executives believe that workers are aware of the unreasonableness of their demands and are simply using the excuse of the concentration to exert pressure on management for a betterment of their conditions.

Management has indicated that indirect motives can take another form. Workers do not always oppose the concentration *per se*. Rather, they are against anything which strengthens private enterprise. As was seen in previous chapters, there are in Europe leftist tendencies which have as their objective the abolition of capitalism. Communist working forces in particular oppose transnational concentrations because they strengthen private enterprise. Moreover, these communist working forces believe that this strengthening is accompanied by a reduction of control by public authorities over business: since governments as yet have no supranational authority, communists fear that governments will lose their influence over any firm which becomes transnational. This is of particular concern in those countries where leftist parties are powerful because their unions have strong political ties.[27]

The first recommendation pertains to the problem of worker participation in a consolidation involving a German firm. During the second set of interviews this problem received considerable attention. Two main alternatives emerged. First, it is possible in some instances to avoid codetermination altogether at the level of the decision-making organ of the consolidated group through the use of some loophole. For example, it may be possible to create a holding company outside Germany which centralizes the power for the total amalgamated group (hybrid Model V or VII). It is then not legally necessary to have worker participation for the holding company. Alternatively, it may be possible to create the holding company in Germany but organize it as a limited company (called GmbH); German law does not require worker participation for such companies provided they employ fewer than 500 people. This solution was adopted by VFW–Fokker, where the *Zentralgesellschaft* is not a stock corporation but a limited company located in Duesseldorf. While this type of solution bypasses the legal requirement, it is feasible only when the workers in the German company are not particularly eager to preserve codetermination rights.

The second alternative provides precisely for the case where co-determination must be preserved at the level of the consolidated group's higher decision-making unit. This calls for some sort of compromise. For example, Agfa–Gevaert agreed to have unity of command. Formally, however, the German working company has an *Aufsichtsrat* with worker representation, while the Belgian working company does not have this representation on its board. In practice, the consolidation is managed by one group of directors in which German worker representation is truly active in those decisions in which German labour is affected. Another example is the more cumbersome solution developed by Hoesch and Hoogovens. As seen in chapter 2, Hoesch and Hoogovens decided to adopt a type VII model. Their agreement calls for a one-third worker representation for a Dutch *Zentralgesellschaft* instead of the one-half which would be required by German law for coal and iron and steel companies.

Obviously there is no one clear-cut answer for the codetermination question. Rather, each consolidation requires a special solution. However, management tends to believe that a viable solution can always be found. The main problem is the time involved in negotiations with workers, which can sometimes take very long indeed (as for Hoesch and Hoogovens). Executives with transnational concentration experience emphasized the desirability of explaining the advantages of the consolidation to workers. 'The codetermination problem can be solved if you can count on the co-operation of the workers themselves. If you can, the legal problem of conflicting laws about codetermination becomes trivial. What you need is to convince workers to go along with the concentration.'

The second recommendation of this section pertains not only to the German situation but to others as well. It has been management's experience that most labour problems can be solved if enough time is spent in explaining why a transnational consolidation is done and in reassuring workers that they will not suffer from it. Assuming labour has a genuine concern (i.e., that it does not use the excuse of a concentration for some other purpose), it is possible to convince workers of the economic merits of an international link-up.[28] As a manager with transnational consolidation experience pointed out: 'Management generally does not take enough care in explaining these things to labour. People are too busy and they believe it is a waste of their time. As a consequence labour often objects because it does not know what is really going on.'

The second set of difficulties involves managerial or administrative problems deriving from labour—the problems management itself encounters with the administration of labour in a transnational company.[29] Two types of problems exist.

First, interviewees pointed out that salary levels are different throughout Europe, as are social benefits. Some workers prefer higher salaries and lower social benefits, and vice versa. For example, workers in Holland reportedly prefer high social benefits and high job security, while workers in Germany prefer high monetary rewards. Further, the skill of workers varies across national boundaries. In Germany labour has better training; in Italy unskilled labour is in greater supply.

These differences have three types of negative consequences for transnational concentrations. First, they add to the regulatory barriers on the free flow of workers across national boundaries which have been surveyed in chapter 3. 'Just as there are different technical standards for products, there are non-tariff quotas on the flow of human resources', said a French executive. A transnational company cannot benefit from mobile working forces, using them where they are most needed at a given time. This particular problem, however, should not be overemphasized. Except for skilled labour with special technical capabilities, human resources are not shuffled around in an international concentration. The second consequence is that it is difficult to integrate labour policies in a transnational company. Workers receive different treatment and have different rights. This means that they must be kept separate, from the administrative point of view. Consequently, it is difficult to rationalize the labour management, reducing the administrative cost savings that would otherwise be possible. The third consequence is that there is a risk of 'reciprocal contamination'. Executives point to the danger of workers of different countries adding up their demands, each one asking what the other one has already obtained. For example, in a concentration between a Dutch and a German company, the German workers will ask for as many social benefits as the Dutch, while the Dutch will ask for a salary increase to the German level. Neither one will, however, accept a reduction either in salary or in benefits. As one executive put it: 'If you bring them together, they start talking and they give each other all the bad ideas.'

The second type of problem reported by management is lack of information about labour in foreign countries. It is a particular problem at the moment when the decision whether to concentrate is being made. When evaluating the desirability of an international concentration, it is often necessary to take into account the labour variable. For example, for a German company it may be attractive to concentrate with a company in a country with much available labour. To evaluate this variable it is not enough to have quantitative figures such as salaries or social benefit requirements. As was seen in the previous chapter, certain European countries (Italy in particular) are witnessing an economic recession which has its roots in the sociopolitical dynamics of the nation. Here it is necessary to have information on the behaviour and performance standards of labour. This information often has to be very detailed with many nuances. To reflect the type of situation discussed in chapter 4, it is necessary to provide a descriptive report of the facts and to give an analysis of them which may have to be quite subtle to be both useful and understandable for foreigners. Such data are more often than not unavailable. While it may seem that this type of information can be obtained by firms through their own investigation, such a process is in fact rendered cumbersome by the complexity of the issues involved. To obtain such data it is necessary to take into account sociopolitical variables, often not fully understandable—let alone foreseeable—by local managers themselves.

With regard to recommendations for the managerial problems, the only cure for the differences in worker expectations and skills is an integration of the socioeconomic characteristics of the various EEC countries. Particularly for salary levels, a harmonization of European economies should bring about a levelling of the income expectations of labour. Also macroeconomic integration should foster an integration of labour's skills. As to lack of information, management generally feels that data on labour in foreign countries can be provided by professional associations. Executives complain that these associations are too national in scope. This is true for this type of information as well as for data such as market information. To correct this provincialism, it has often been suggested by interviewees that professional associations themselves pool their resources and develop a European effort. As one executive put it: 'Companies need assistance in their Europeanization policy; the most promising avenue for this is a Europeanization of those organizations whose task is to service management in its corporate mission.'

Two other environmental obstacles

Opposition to transnational consolidations comes from two other groups: from stockholders and from the general public.

Beyond the problems discussed in the accounting and finance section, there may be an explicit opposition of stockholders to transnational concentration. There are, in management's view, three possible reasons for this opposition.

First, financial executives report that stockholders often prefer to hold shares of a national company out of habit.[30] The more unsophisticated stockholders prefer to hold the shares of an old, well-established national company rather than the stock of a transnational group, largely unknown to them because it is abroad. Managers believe the certificates of national companies provide a sense of security, stemming from the company's long history of positive economic activity. These stockholders resist the transnationalization of the company because they do not know the partner. They are not familiar with its name or historical development. Moreover, they are used to *seeing* the national company, not only to seeing its stock quoted regularly on the national stock exchange but its physical assets as well. Executives emphasize the psychological impact of shareholders being able to visit the plant of 'their' company. One of these executives said: 'Even if they never really go and see the factory, they know it's there, they hear about it in daily conversations and they read about it in the press, and this gives them the feeling they have invested in something solid.' These shareholders cannot have quite the same feeling of a tangible holding in a transnational concentration. The fact that the partner is abroad unconsciously arouses some doubts about its identity. As an executive remarked: 'The geographical distance subconsciously increases the discount factor for risk applied to a security.' Finally, investors reportedly do not understand the hybrid forms of concentration, particularly because the Press emphasizes the complexity of the legal structure. Consequently they may be unclear about the venture, and thus uncertain. The result is excessive conservatism.

This problem applied above all to large, well-established firms whose shares would correspond to 'blue chip' stocks in the US. The shareholders of these companies are often unsophisticated investors with the motivations described above. Executives emphasize the need to explain the concentration to stockholders. Instead of going into great detail about the whys and hows of the concentration, these executives feel it is important to mention repeatedly a few key points, emphasizing a few clear benefits of a consolidation. Public relations managers emphasize the need to publicize the consolidation as early as possible in order to give stockholders time to assimilate the notion of an international link-up. As a public relations executive said: 'You have to give people time to buy the idea and you have to do your selling slowly so as not to build up a strong defensive attitude at the beginning.'

The second reason alleged by management is a nationalistic attitude of stockholders. They may prefer to invest in national companies because they feel they are behaving patriotically. They have the impression they are helping their own country and they take pride in owning part of a national firm. They oppose transnational consolidations because they wish to preserve the national identity of the company. Reportedly, they may sometimes be willing to forfeit a potential increase in their earnings rather than permit the transnationalization of the company. As an interviewee said: 'A stockholder of ours may feel guilty if he agreed to exchange one of his present shares for that of a transnational group.' This attitude is clearly most pronounced in Britain, as indicated by the interviewees.

The third reason is that stockholders may have dissimilar expectations in various countries. Several executives felt that stockholders might oppose a transnational consolidation because they feared that those of a foreign country might have different preferences. For example, Italian stockholders are perceived by foreigners as having a greater propensity towards risky investments, while British executives are said to seek so-called 'heavy shares', i.e., those of companies which are known for the stability of their economic performance. Management believes that stockholders exaggerate these differences. Here again, a promotional action is often desirable to show stockholders that these fears are unwarranted.

We now turn to the problem of the opposition of the public in general. Nationalism as a hindrance to transnational concentration has already been analysed in connection with the opposition of governments to international concentrations and with the discussion of markets. Here, the issue is the nationalism of public opinion. A number of interviewees expressed the belief that the general public might be aroused against a transnational consolidation because a company was viewed as part of the national patrimony. A company is often felt to be public property; it represents the prestige of a nation. Its transnationalization is viewed as a loss of national identity and a renunciation of national hegemony. Beyond purely nationalistic reasons, interviewees felt that public opinion may fear that an international consolidation will result in a reduction in potential domestic investments, and thus retard national economic development.

In fact, it was determined in the second set of interviews that normally public opinion does not by itself react negatively towards operations such as international consolidations. It is, typically, the Press which is responsible for focusing attention on such ventures. Management believes the motives of the Press are nationalistic or, more frequently, political. The Press can be a political instrument to hinder a concentration. Playing an aggressive role, it arouses public opinion to prevent a concentration. Alternatively, the Press can support political action; when a government takes action against a concentration, the Press can justify such action to the public. Here, it has a defensive role in that it plays up the official reasons for governmental action in order to discourage public protest.

A negative reaction of public opinion may affect the overall goodwill of the firm. This in turn may have three principal negative consequences. First, the market position of the company may suffer. In particular, marketing managers believe consumers may stay away from the products of the firm on the grounds that they do not want to contribute to the prosperity of a socially irresponsible organization. This attitude is more likely to occur in countries where there is a strong feeling of cohesiveness among citizens, where people are less individualistic and have a greater sense of their collective civil responsibilities. Great Britain is the best example here. British interviewees point out that sales are distinctly affected by the public's perception of the firm's socially responsible behaviour. An important element of the public image is the patriotic element as is best illustrated by the slogan of a large commercial bank—the Midland Bank—which is 'a great British Bank'.

The second consequence is financial. Several financial executives were quite articulate about the fact that a firm's loss of goodwill may decrease its capacity to raise money. Among possible effects, interviewees mentioned a reaction by the financial community not to finance a company it feels is behaving unpatriotically. Another possibility is that investors may anticipate that the firm's performance will be adversely affected by its diminishing goodwill: the result is a loss of confidence in the future performance of that firm, which diverts investors from it.

The third consequence is that a company may lose some of its ability to attract the most competent personnel. The weight given by interviewees to this point depended on the weight they gave to 'nationalism'.[31] In the countries where national awareness is highest—such as Great Britain—managers felt people may choose not to work for what they consider a socially irresponsible firm.

The best way to hedge against the negative public opinion is through a public relations campaign. As was seen, public opinion is influenced by the Press. A company can make an effort to explain and publicize its reasons for consolidation. Public relations managers emphasize that the difficulty is to predict the focus of the attacks in the Press in order to retaliate promptly. As an interviewee put it: 'The name of the game is to give tit for tat; but, as tit requires some time to be delivered, you win when you properly anticipate tat.'

NOTES

1. For a treatment of the types of problems dealt with in the forthcoming discussion, see: William P. Barsanti, 'Accounting Pitfalls in Foreign Acquisitions', Speech by a member of the staff of Arthur Andersen & Co., New York, 23 May 1968.

2. See: Leonard W. Hein, 'The Auditor and the British Companies Acts', *The Accounting Review*, July 1963, p. 508.

3. See: G. Maitland Smith, 'Obtaining a Stock Exchange Quotation', *Accountancy*, January 1964, pp. 23–28.

4. See: Michael B. Stewart, 'Transnational Enterprise: The European Challenge', *Columbia Journal of World Business*, July–August 1972, pp. 5–13, at pp. 12–13.

5. See: Kenneth S. Most, 'How Bad are European Accountants', in: K. B. Berg, G. G. Mueller, and L. M. Walker, *Readings in International Accounting*, Houghton Mifflin, Boston, 1969, pp. 208–22.

6. It is noteworthy that managers do not regard the difficulty of consolidating accounts *per se* as a problem: 'Many European companies with their propensity toward greater decentralization of foreign operations and the avoidance of consolidation of foreign country operations, do not face the problem at all.' From: 'Solving International Accounting Problems', Business International Corporation, New York, 1969, p. 25.

7. See: Otto Von Fieandt, 'Trends in European Commercial Banking', Euroeconomics, Paris, 1972.

8. For further detail on European capital markets, see:

(a) *The Development of a European Capital Market*, European Economic Community Commission, Brussels, 1966.

(b) Hermann J. Abs, 'The European Security and New Issues Market with a view to International Financing', a Report presented to the Institut International d'Etudes Bancaires at its 28th Session on 6 November 1964 (Knokke, Belgium).

(c) 'Capital Markets in Europe', a Report published by the Economic Research Group of Amsterdam-Rotterdam Bank, Deutsche Bank, Midland Bank and Société Générale de Banque, March 1966.

9. Paul Morton Goldberg, 'The Evolution of Transnational Companies in Europe', Ph.D. Dissertation, Massachusetts Institute of Technology, Sloan School of Management, 1971, p. 73.

10. See: *La politique industrielle de la Communauté—Memorandum de la Commission au Conseil*, Commission des Communautés Européennes, Brussels, 1970, p. 189.

11. The other financial institutions are typically public or semi-public institutions such as the Italian IMI (Istituto Mobiliare Italiano). In addition to the problems raised by banks, these institutions run into the bureaucratic inefficiencies discussed in the previous chapter.

12. See: James B. Warden, 'International Banking in the Seventies', *Columbia Journal of World Business*, July–August 1972, pp. 67–72.

13. See: Norman N. Mintz, 'Toward a Common European Currency', *Columbia Journal of World Business*, January–February 1971, p. 20.

14. See: Ugo Piccione, 'Cross-Border Banking', *European Community*, May 1971, pp. 14–15.

15. See: Michael von Clemm, 'The Rise of Consortium Banking', *Harvard Business Review*, May–June 1971, p. 125.

16. Christopher Layton makes a similar observation in *Cross-Frontier Mergers in Europe*, Bath University Press, Bath, 1971, pp. 99–100.

17. Examples of such exceptional joint ventures are Concorde and the Franco–German SYMPHONIE telecommunications satellite. For details, see Milton S. Hochmut, *The Effect of Structure on Strategy: The Government sponsored Multinational Joint Ventures*, DBA Dissertation, Graduate School of Business Administration, Harvard University, 1972.

18. See: G. D. McConnell, 'Behavioral Factors in World Consumer Markets', Long Range Planning Service, Stanford Research Institute, Menlo Park, California, July 1970, p. 10.

19. It should be pointed out, however, that no research data was found to support these assertions.

20. See: Ernst Dichter, 'The World Customer', *Readings in International Business* by John J. Coyle and Edward J. Mock, International Textbook Company, Scranton, Pennsylvania, 1965, pp. 225–37.

21. European airlines seriously considered a concentration known as Air Union.

22. Published material is available in this area. For example, see:

(a) Henry Deschampsneufs, *Selling in Europe*, Business Publications, London, 1963.

(b) Robert L. Brown, 'The Common Market: What Its New Consumer is Like', *Printers' Ink*, 31 May 1963, pp. 23–25.

(c) Ernest Zahn, 'The European Market-place: Social Change and Consumer Choice', in Philip R. Cateora and John M. Hess, *International Marketing*, Richard D. Irwin, Inc., Homewood, Ill., 1971, pp. 136–41.

23. For a discussion of the codetermination issue, see:

(a) 'Codetermination Rights of the Workers in Germany', published by the DGB, June 1967.

(b) Ernst-Gerhard Erdmann, 'The Myth of Codetermination', published by Bundesvereinigung der deutschen Arbeitgeberverbaende, Koeln, 1970.

24. For a discussion of unions' attitude towards concentration, see: Nicola de

Pamphilis, 'Azione sindacale e concentrazioni industriali', *Conquiste del lavoro*, 18–24 November, 1968, p. 7.

25. P. P. Fano, 'The Italian Labor Movement and Collective Bargaining', in *Western European Labor*, Alfred Kamin (ed.), The Bureau of National Affairs, Washington, 1970, pp. 99–108.

26. See: Winifred Raphael and M. W. Zimmerman, 'After the Take-over—A Study of Reactions of Employees in a Group of Companies', National Institute of Psychology, London, 1963.

27. In this regard, it was interesting to note that this issue, which preoccupied Italian managers most, had become even more important to them between the first and the second set of interviews. In the several months between the two sets, the situation of the country had deteriorated enough and leftist socioeconomic disturbances had increased sufficiently to cause a noticeable growth in management's concern.

28. For discussions of what information to release to workers in the case of a concentration, see:

(a) Winifred Raphael and M. W. Zimmerman, 'After the Take-Over—A Study of Reactions of Employees in a Group of Companies'.

(b) Geneva Seybold, 'Communicating with Employees about Mergers', National Industrial Conference Board Inc., New York, 1968.

29. See: Clyde W. Summers, 'Labor Relations in the Common Market', *Harvard Business Review*, March–April 1965, pp. 148–60.

30. Paul M. Goldberg, 'The Evolution of Transnational Companies in Europe', p. 73.

31. See the discussion in the next chapter.

6.

THE HUMAN SIDE OF THE ENTERPRISE

This chapter focuses on problems deriving from the human assets of a company. They are serious barriers to transnational concentration which are within management itself. It should be emphasized at the outset that these problems are a most serious area of concern to transnational concentration. As these problems are for the most part interrelated, the material has not been divided into sections. Instead, nine problem areas will be discussed in the following sequence:

- the language problem: the obstacle of communication and its by-products (e.g., resistance to use the partner's language on nationalistic grounds).
- the problem of the lack of relationships among top executives of different countries.
- the difference in the way work is organized.
- the problem of sizing up a potential partner (i.e., appraisal gap): a particular area of concern is the difficulty of appraising the congruency of two organizations along intangible variables (e.g., are the informal organizations compatible?).
- the problem of the lack of professional skills: finance and marketing are discussed. Then the lack of 'international business skill' is described as the major issue in this area. It corresponds to the inability of managers to effectively relate to their foreign counterparts.
- resistance to change: this is an area of considerable importance. There are two types of difficulties: the resistance to change in working methods and to the environment in which management operates.

- perceived threat of concentration: managers feel personally threatened by a concentration. There are four aspects to this important area: the reluctance to lose one's independence; the fear of rationalizations; the fear of loss of personal opportunities within the company; the fear that one's country's macroeconomic weakness will give the foreign partner a competitive edge.
- nationalism: in this area lie very serious obstacles. There are two broad sets of issues: animosities towards particular foreigners and ethnocentric attitudes.
- misconceptions: managers erroneously believe there are differences in mental structures and values between people of different nationalities which impede international collaboration. This too is an area of considerable hindrance to consolidations.

The chapter ends with a discussion of recommendations on educational systems, which are felt to be the main cause of the 'human' problems.

It should be noted that the last four problem areas represent the major obstacles considered in this chapter. Indeed, for many interviewees, it is here that the most serious difficulties for transnational concentrations lie.

Professor Tabatoni has written: 'There has been no serious in-depth research on the topic'.[1] While it is true that there has been little investigation of these types of obstacles to international collaborative endeavours between European firms, this chapter touches upon provinces which have been analysed in connection with other types of research efforts. References are made to this literature, which should be considered as background material.

THE LANGUAGE PROBLEM

The first problem area is language. The worst linguists are reportedly the British and the French, while the best are the Dutch. The problem of comprehension may be an important difficulty in a concentration between British and French companies because both nationalities tend to insist on speaking their own language. Interviewees also mentioned that some difficulties may develop in a Franco–German or Franco–Dutch collaboration because Germans and Dutch usually speak English rather than French as a foreign language. Otherwise, management believes French or English is spoken sufficiently well for people to make themselves understood.

Beyond mere comprehension, however, there are three by-products of the language problem which have been raised by interviewees.[2] The first is that communication within the organization is more difficult because of the risk of misunderstandings. As an executive of a transnational group said: 'Sometimes it's better that a man has no knowledge at all of a foreign language rather than having some and the belief he has more knowledge than he has in fact.' International business executives with very few exceptions have anecdotes about misunderstandings due to nuances in different languages. Several interviewees reported that communication has to be formalized; written communication is used more extensively than oral communication. Often, even in transnational companies that have been in existence for many years, interpreters are needed. The result is a good deal of red tape and a slower flow of information within the organization.

The second by-product is that differences in language hinder the integration of the human assets of a transnational group. The fact that managers have a different mother tongue hampers their socialization. Executives point out that, apart from professional requirements, company personnel of a given nationality tend to cluster because it is easier for them to communicate with each other. This is obviously a hindrance to the blending of two organizations in a transnational concentration.

The third by-product is psychological in nature, and was mentioned by several managers from transnationally consolidated companies. Normally, one partner's language is adopted. For example, in a concentration with a British company, English is normally adopted as the working language. The partner who has to give up his language resents this, feeling subconsciously that the other partner is favoured—that he is in a position of dominance and has most of the decision-making power. Executives may feel they are at a disadvantage *vis-à-vis* their foreign counterparts because of their linguistic handicap. Also, people may resent having to use a foreign language for nationalistic reasons. For example, several interviewees from companies which have collaborative links with German partners reported that some managers resist the use of German on xenophobic grounds. As noted later on in this chapter, xenophobia still may play an important role, and the language of a disliked people stirs up these feelings.

There are two types of recommendations that can be made for this problem: first, at the level of public education, and second, for companies. The last part of this chapter will synthesize the views of management on the problem of education; it has been left for the end as many of the obstacles dealt with in this chapter are connected with education. As for the firms, the advisable policy is for their managers to develop foreign language skills. International executives agree that courses are not enough. Managers must have the opportunity of living in the foreign environment prior to the concentration. As recommended in chapter 7, in the preparatory stages of a concentration, companies should deliberately make massive exchanges of managers. Among other things, this will force a familiarity with the foreign language on collaborators, reducing linguistic inhibitions. However, it should be pointed out that managers with extensive international business experience emphasize that companies cannot entirely solve the problem. At best they can attenuate it. 'The real potential for effective therapy lies in education', said one of these executives.

LACK OF PERSONAL CONTACTS

The second problem area is the lack of personal relationships among top executives of different countries.[3] Managers point out that social ties strongly influence professional relationships. Generally speaking, European business is less impersonal than US business, and personal contacts are crucial. They are strong within national boundaries, but across national boundaries these ties are much weaker, mainly because people have different social origins and education and do not have opportunities for daily contact.

Interviewees reported two consequences of this lack of international contacts. First, businessmen feel uncomfortable in international partnerships because they are unable to conduct business in the accustomed way. Domestically, executives are used to doing business on the basis of a deep mutual confidence and *entente cordiale*. Internationally, this is not possible because people do not know each other sufficiently well. This is of particular concern to British executives. British interviewees proudly indicated their custom of doing business on one's word, with no need to formalize a deal with a written contract. 'A handshake is enough' or 'doing business on the basis of gentlemen's agreements' are expressions that have been used by many interviewees. The fact that there are no comparable social links with foreign managers requires a more formalized relationship. This hinders collaboration between people who are not used to such a relationship. Moreover, the habit of working with friends reduces the mental adaptability to working with strangers. 'We don't know how to evaluate a foreign partner', said one interviewee, 'nor do we know what precautions we should take; so we become overly suspicious, which obviously is a hindrance for collaboration.'

The second consequence is that people do not think of joining forces. The fact that top managers seldom have the opportunity to meet their foreign counterparts hampers the possibility of fruitful discussion towards a concentration. As shown in chapter 7, a concentration often emerges from 'golf-course conversations'. The problem is precisely that there are too few golf-course conversations and that 'international consolidations do not even cross people's minds', as one interviewee remarked.

It is noteworthy that most of the companies with transnational concentration experience are concerned with this fact. For example, the Dunlop–Pirelli union was allegedly greatly facilitated by the personal friendship between Sir Reay Geddes, the Dunlop chairman, and Ingegner Leopoldo Pirelli, the president of Pirelli. Indeed, had there not been an exception to the typical social gap between executives of different nationalities, the link-up might not have taken place at all.

It is generally felt among managers that the solution to this problem, again, lies in education. The need for Europeanization of education, both general and managerial, is increasingly recognized. Education is still almost exclusively national in scope. This reinforces the national social ties already in existence between managers. An internationalization of education would broaden the social relationships of future managers. It would develop the skill of potential executives in working with strangers. As a Dutch executive put it: 'It would give people the ability to deal with a potential partner even if his family had not attended the same school for a minimum of three generations.'

THE DIFFERENCE IN THE WAY WORK IS ORGANIZED

The third problem area has to do with the ways in which work is organized.[4] It should be pointed out immediately that this is an area where perceived obstacles are overemphasized. Executives with transnational concentration experience are virtually unanimous in saying that here expected problems prior to the concentration are greater than those which actually occur. Among the 'real' problems managers raised in this area are differences in structure. Chapter 2 has discussed the differences in structure deriving from differing national company law. There are also problems which derive from managerial habits which have developed over time. In particular, German managers report that, owing to relatively strong American business influence, the decentralized company organized along product lines with profit centres has become quite popular. In France and Italy it was found that managers are unfamiliar with the profit centre notion, which often is still considered a theoretical concept. Companies tend to have a strong centralized hierarchical structure in which patriarchal influence of the patronate is strongly felt. These types of contrasting structures may be difficult to integrate because there are no reciprocal matches for the various organs of each organization.

Another area of concern to managers is the dissimilarity in the informal organization. In certain countries the organization can be very autocratic and rigid while in others it can be quite flexible. Consider the example given by a major consulting organization (Fig. 6.1). An organization has two independent departments (X) and (Y) which both report to a co-ordinating unit (A). A given task requires that (X) and (Y) have to work together. In a country like Holland where the structure is relatively loose and flexible, (X) and (Y) could have a direct relationshid and communicate in an immediate and informal fashion. In a country

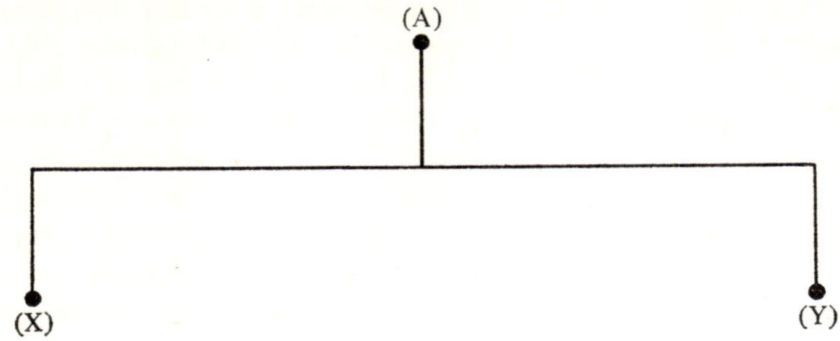

Fig. 6.1

like Germany, with a relatively rigid organizational structure, (X) and (Y) would probably go through (A) before being able to communicate with each other. They would tend to request (A)'s mediation in order not to disrupt the channels of the formal structure. These differences in the informal organization may pose more delicate problems for a concentration than the difference in organizational structures *per se*. They are intangible and therefore more difficult to handle. As an executive put it: 'First of all, you have to identify them; this already requires, normally, working together; then you have to modify them and this too can only be done by reciprocal influence in an actual collaborative situation.'

As mentioned at the beginning, this type of obstacle is not, in fact, a major hindrance. It is noteworthy that those executives with the least international business experience mention it the most. Executives of transnational companies emphasize that in a concentration the reorganization is complete, so that the original structures are blurred and the internal culture of the organization has to be built up *ex novo*. Moreover, as pointed out by one of these executives: 'The real problem is less the differences themselves than the misconceptions people have about these differences: people are convinced differences are quite important and consequently they don't even try to collaborate.' (The problem of such misconceptions will be discussed more fully later in this chapter.)

THE PROBLEM OF SIZING UP A POTENTIAL PARTNER

The fourth problem area is an appraisal gap. This refers to the difficulties management encounters in sizing up a potential partner. At the moment a concentration is considered, it is necessary to evaluate the partner's congruence with one's own organization. Beyond the difficulty of evaluating a partner due to a lack of 'factual' data (e.g., financial data), it is hard to appraise compatibility of the human organization. There are differences in the way people behave in an organization. These features are intangible and therefore difficult to assess. Managers express concern about identifying and evaluating the relevant variables. Questions such as the following illustrate this: 'What are the right questions to ask?' 'What are the parameters along which to evaluate the compatibility of people?' 'What makes a collaboration work?' While these problems exist in any concentration—national or international—there are two reasons why they are a particular hindrance in a consolidation across national boundaries: first, because dissimilarities between people are greater across national boundaries, and second, because within one country companies know each other better. They compete more directly, they are likely to have acquaintances in potential partners, and they are better able to 'spy' upon each other (e.g., through financial intermediaries). In a transnational concentration, companies may have had relatively little direct experience in competing against each other. This may be true in the most synergistic link-ups, when two companies have complementary product lines or complementary market coverage. (For example, in the Agfa–Gevaert concentration, the German company had a particular expertise in amateur photographic products, while the Belgian company had a distinct competitive advantage in the professional segment.) Not having competed directly, the two companies may have relatively little knowledge of each other.

This problem is compounded by the European business tradition of being particularly secretive. European companies are much less open than their US counterparts. As Krekel, Van der Woerd, and Wouterse write:

> Frankness in matters of finance, products, turnover and other vital business data, which in American enterprise is considered usual, not infrequently seems to the British to be a kind of obnoxious exhibitionism. There is an unwillingness to allow the outsider a glimpse of the details of a company and it is therefore extremely difficult to obtain data on companies with which one is not already in direct contact.[5]

In fact, it was found that this is a particular problem in southern European countries and most of all in Italy. The reason is that management's reflex is to disclose as little data as possible because of taxes. 'The less you say the better off you are. If you are doing well and you say it, you run the risk of higher taxes; if you don't say it, you run the risk of being in trouble because you lie', said an Italian executive. The consequence is that companies have become used to concealing as much as possible from anybody.

Beyond the clear desirability for companies to become less secretive (which is usually dependent on environmental factors), there are two distinct types of recommendations that can be formulated here. The first is directed to companies. Companies have too little knowledge of each other beyond national boundaries. Moreover, the need to concentrate takes companies by surprise and they have no background to appraise the organization with which they might consolidate. Instead, they should prepare for a transnational concentration by becoming acquainted with potential partners as early as possible.[6]

The second recommendation is directed to behavioural researchers. There is a clear need for better knowledge on how to appraise the congruence of two organizations. The development of a grid which highlights the crucial variables that have a bearing on organizational congruency would be most effective in reducing the appraisal gap. Specifically, work along the lines of Robert Blake and Jane Mouton (adapted to the European scene) holds considerable promise.[7]

THE PROBLEM OF THE LACK OF PROFESSIONAL SKILLS

The fifth problem area is the lack of professional skills.[8] European companies are still run in an intuitive, non-analytic fashion. There are three areas of particular concern to managers here. The first one is finance. Interviewees deplored the fact that there is little training available in financial analysis techniques. At the moment a concentration is evaluated, the effects of the pooling of resources from the financial point of view cannot be evaluated satisfactorily.[9] The potential synergies of a consolidation are not forecast appropriately. Moreover, at the operating level, European managers cannot be as effective on an international scale as their US counterparts. US executives are used to hedging against international monetary fluctuations, and indeed, to speculating on them. European financial managers are relatively uncomfortable in these operations. They feel that they compare particularly unfavourably in short-term money operations involving cash management.[10] For example, swap operations are still unknown to many finance managers.[11]

Another aspect of this relative lack of financial skill is the difficulty encountered in the control of an international group.[12] This refers to internal accounting aimed at monitoring the operations of a divisionalized group. In the view of the managers who were interviewed on the subject, the main problem is represented by the necessity of using different units of account. The absence of monetary union requires that figures be converted from one currency into another to allow any comparison between operations in different countries. The risk of fluctuations would warrant, for example, the use of probability theory to take the risk factor into account. Here again, European financial managers are typically ill-trained for this type of analysis.

Of course there are multinational companies in Europe which have solved the problem internally through an empirical learning process. The fact remains, however, that this not only leads to suboptimal results but also takes a long time. While firms with a tradition of international operations have developed in themselves the resources to adapt to the international monetary environment, the more national firms would benefit from formal training. Indeed, this problem was mentioned most by those firms which traditionally had a domestic outlook and for some reason suddenly found themselves operating in the international environment.

Owing to inadequate financial skill, European managers tend to be unable to make the most of a transnational concentration. They are relatively incompetent to supervise and to internally audit a transnational group. The inefficiencies involved may be particularly acute in large diversified organizations.

The second area of concern is marketing. Again, managers report that the lack of any analytical approach bars a full evaluation of the potential synergies of two companies. Beyond obvious features such as geographical coverage, there is little appreciation of areas of compatibility between two potential partners. As an executive of a US multinational company put it: 'Europeans just don't see the more promising areas for collaboration because they have but a superficial perception of the market.' Intuitive marketing, like any intuitive administrative practice, creates another problem. Intuitive practices are hard to harmonize because they are hard to grasp. Policies and procedures are not made explicit: managers learn by trial and error. Staff managers with US experience (either learning or working experience) recognize that Europeans acquire the knowledge of their job by intuitive methods and by random feedback from the market. This stimulus-response is essentially unsystematic and tacit. As a consequence, managers develop a 'feeling' for their task which remains unarticulated. When co-ordination of their job with the job of a concentration partner is to take place, the task is complicated by the absence of any realistic job description. As an executive of a transnational company described it: 'Integration is hard to bring about because there is nothing tangible to integrate.'

The third and most important area of concern is lack of 'international business skill'.[13] This aspect was brought up by a few international executives during the first set of interviews and was widely confirmed during the second set, when the researcher asked managers to comment on it. It refers to the inability of many European managers to adapt to foreign business environments. There is no particular body of knowledge involved here. It is the skill to size up and adjust to different working conditions, and is particularly important in relating to foreign people. As an executive described it: 'It is a sensitiveness which enables to feel the way foreigners think and react.' This skill enables a manager to overcome dissimilarities in human characteristics of foreigners, in their thought processes and values. It is important in any international collaboration endeavour, not only for working effectively in foreign environments but for reducing the inhibitions people have towards international environments. Differences with foreigners are not as great as people often believe they are and, in point of fact, they can be positive factors for the collaboration. Foreigners can bring new ideas and perspectives and can offer a stimulating challenge to one's business practices. However, as will be discussed in greater detail shortly, people feel inhibited by and uncomfortable with these differences. The international business skill makes it possible to reduce these inhibitions and to draw the best out of international collaboration.

This skill can be acquired by professional and social contact with foreigners: by living, working, or having educational experiences in international environments. 'One becomes cosmopolitan by actually living, working and having fun around the world; the last feature is important because the major hindrance to communication with foreigners is the lack of feeling for their sense of humor', said a top manager of an international firm. The problem is that many Europeans do not have this skill. They have been raised, educated, and employed in national environments. Even in the most cosmopolitan cities, foreigners are often avoided by natives because European societies tend to be closed and introverted. There are very few foreign executives working in European companies. Even in many international companies there is a reluctance to put local executives in key positions of foreign subsidiaries. Apart from Holland, European executives lack international business skill. Transnational concentrations suffer from this. European managers are unprepared to cope with the dynamics of international human relations. They often find themselves facing a situation in which they must suddenly, with no prior international experience, become dependent upon a collaboration with foreigners. This is a consequence of the attitude of European companies to put off internationalization as long as possible. Instead, it would be desirable to prepare for a transnational concentration by prior collaboration with foreign firms. This aspect falls in the realm of the strategic planning discussion which will be taken up in detail in the next chapter.

RESISTANCE TO CHANGE

The sixth problem area is what many executives called atavism: it refers to the difficulties of implementing change in many European companies. It is an area of major concern. The next chapter will discuss strategic inertia, the fact that European top management is often unable to make a strategic breakthrough. Here, the discussion focuses on the resistance to change at the organizational level, i.e., the barrier imposed by the bulk of management—excluding top management—to any radical modification of organizational patterns.[14] Specifically, interviewees have presented this problem in two ways.

The first is a lack of administrative flexibility. This was emphasized in particular by executives from mature industries such as mining or heavy metallurgic enterprises, and by executives of enterprises where the patriarchal influence is greatest, such as family-owned enterprises. The problem is that managers resist change. Any modification in work habits is unwelcome. Interviewees pointed out that people are used to doing the same task from early in their careers and that they have had relatively little exposure to change. As a mining executive put it: 'People enter their job in their twenties and get the cultural shock of their life in that they are exposed to a totally new environment. But that is it. There are rarely major changes in one's environment after that. At best there is an evolution as one (slowly) moves up in the hierarchy.' Indeed, job rotation has not really been introduced in Europe yet. A manager begins his career in a given department and progresses within it. He often has little opportunity to work with other departments. Moreover, mobility among companies is not typical; indeed, it is frequently frowned upon. This also reduces the individual's openness to new situations. In this way, managers are reinforced in their own work habits and have little mental preparedness for new ways of working. 'The adaptability of people is rusted', said a Belgian executive.

As a consequence, a manager has a strong tendency to stick to the working methods which he has been using since the beginning of his career. He has been accustomed to do a certain task in a certain way and has been reinforced in so doing by his past performance: if he has been at all successful, he will resist change, being convinced that his way is the best since it has been effective in the past. In a transnational concentration, this change can be quite dramatic. Integration of policies and procedures is likely to be arduous because each participating management will be reluctant to modify its own policies and procedures. Moreover, if an argument does occur between the participating managements over what method should be adopted for the new transnational organization, each partner will insist that his own way of doing things is the best, as demonstrated by his own success. There is always the risk, then, of reaching the conclusion that what is good for one is not for the other and that integration is not possible. Ethnocentrism is the end result, since both partners become more inclined to maintain their independence.

In a transnational concentration, this mental rigidity is a considerable hindrance. A consolidation entails massive reorganization and requires the full commitment of managers to implement change. Indeed, many companies which have engaged even in a national consolidation point out how long it takes to obtain the acceptance of new policies and procedures or of new organizational structures.

The second aspect of the resistance to change pertains less to the working methods themselves than to the working environment. In particular, older interviewees expressed the concern that a concentration is disruptive to the environment because it has a bearing on the prevailing atmosphere of the working group. People are anxious to preserve what a French executive called the 'genuine air of home'. They tend to resist any alienation of the national character of their environment. The perceived reason for this is that executives tend to have the same social origin, the same education, and the same acquaintances. This fosters the closeness of the social circle, which becomes particularly meaningful to the individual who feels 'cosy' in it. He is used to having a well-established position in, and recognition from, his milieu and feels threatened by any outside force which might modify his position.

The lack of flexibility and resistance to change of the professional environment is a hindrance to any consolidation—international or domestic. It is, however, a far greater hindrance to an international concentration, first of all because managers are unfamiliar with their foreign counterparts. Unfamiliarity with foreigners leads to a fear of them which, in turn, leads to resisting them. Unfamiliarity among EEC managers is a source of many troubles and will be analysed at further length later on in this chapter. Besides this problem, resistance to change is greater in an international concentration because the disruptive element represented by the introduction of strangers into a working group is far more pronounced where the stranger is a foreign national. In a domestic concentration the stranger probably has the same social background as his new co-worker. He is used to relating to the same environment and has similar values and thought processes, or at least he is likely to understand the partner's mental attitude. In a transnational concentration the alienation of the stranger is far greater. He comes from a totally different social environment, and is used to a different hierarchical system and to a different type of relationship with the outside world. A French executive put it this way:

> To collaborate with a compatriot is easier because you know he is not that different from yourself. The similarity of personalities facilitates the integration of jobs. With a foreigner it is far more difficult because you often have little in common: you have to start with a harmonization of the personalities. This resistance to any change coming from abroad is the first cause for ethnocentrism.

The cure for this resistance to change is for companies to make an explicit effort to train their human assets in the direction of greater flexibility. 'It is the challenge of the next decade to break as many social ties and professional habits as we possibly can; this is our major responsibility toward the younger of our people', said a French executive with US business experience. Firms should be committed to exposing their junior executives in particular to the perspectives of the organization of various departments. They should push them to work in their foreign subsidiaries and, where possible, in other companies with which they have a co-operative agreement. An executive of a transnationally consolidated group put it this way:

With hindsight, this resistance to change was among the major problems we had, particularly because we didn't really expect it. To any would-be concentrator I would recommend making a firm commitment to giving people ahead of time an improved ability to adapt to new situations involving foreigners. This can be done best by sending people to work and live abroad. This should be done as an investment, over and beyond the concern of putting the best man in the best place.

Another type of suggestion is made to alleviate the problem of management's resistance to change. It has been the experience of a number of interviewed executives that the creation of a new activity in common with another company is easier than the integration of existing activities. In other words, it is easier to set up a new common organization than to try to blend two organizations which already have a life of their own. This suggests that hybrid solution II may offer considerable promise where resistance to change created by a consolidation is particularly strong.[15] This solution calls for the founding of a jointly owned subsidiary to which the activities of the original companies are gradually transferred. An executive referred to this process as 'a reverse take-over', i.e., the common subsidiary gradually becomes more important than the founding parent companies. The transfer of activities ought to be gradual. In fact, interviewees suggest that transfer of activities *per se* be avoided as much as possible: the subsidiary should carry out the new projects of the group, while the existing projects should be kept at the parent companies' level until these projects are terminated (i.e., when they have reached the end of their life cycle). While this may appear to be a somewhat slow process, it is congruent with a progressive amalgamation process which is warranted in most transnational unions (see chapter 7).

Reportedly, management resists the creation of a common subsidiary much less than the amalgamation—even if gradual—of the existing organizations. In the jointly owned subsidiary model of consolidation it does not perceive an alienation of its present working environment. It is this notion of perception which is important: integration of existing organizations is perceived by management as impairing the *status quo*. While the creation of a joint subsidiary leads to a similar result (i.e., the emergence of a new organization with its own hierarchy and internal culture in lieu of the original organizations), management does not perceive it in this way. This is so because at the outset there is no need to talk about integration as such. Rather, there may simply be talk about the creation of a new activity, with no mention of further plans to fully integrate one's activities with the activities of the partner. As a top executive put it: 'What people are most concerned with is that their organization be preserved; they are much less concerned with the addition of new things, as long as they feel the old ones are there to stay.'

PERCEIVED THREAT OF A CONCENTRATION

The seventh problem area is the fear of managers that a concentration may be detrimental to their own position. This is, of course, a serious restraining force for any consolidation—domestic or international—and the literature on mergers gives considerable documentation on the problem.[16] It has, however, distinctive features in the framework of transnational consolidations in the EEC. Specifically, there are four aspects to the problem.

The first is the concern of top management to retain its freedom or, in more prosaic terms, 'to remain one's own boss'. In a concentration the problem is that neither management is willing to relinquish any of its decision-making power. There is what Robert Short has called the 'appeal of independence'.[17] Managers raised this issue many times during the first set of open-ended interviews. During the second set an effort was made to determine what characterized this problem in an international concentration, i.e., what—if any—were its distinctive features in an international as opposed to a national consolidation. To the question 'Is this problem greater in a transnational setting?' managers responded affirmatively. When, however, the researcher pressed respondents to explain why this was so, managers were unable to explicitly state their reasons. The discussion typically shifted from this issue, interviewees alleging other difficulties which in their view rendered the particular problem under consideration more complex. For example, some would refer to nationalism, that managers find it harder to relinquish their autonomy because the partner is a foreign one. Others would talk about mistrust among people of different countries due to lack of familiarity with each other, which makes the sharing of responsibility a more threatening prospect. In these examples the 'compounding factor' (i.e., the alleged reason which makes the problem of losing one's freedom greater in an international setting) is, in fact, the only variable which changes. In other words, the problem of having to relinquish one's freedom appears to remain constant between a national and an international link-up. What appears to interviewees a 'compounding factor' is simply one of the other obstacles analysed in this study. This means that a transnational consolidation would not be any more painful solely on account of the loss of autonomy than a national consolidation.

Clearly, this conclusion is tentative. Probably more behavioural research is needed in this area. However, it should be pointed out that it was possible in certain instances to carry the discussion quite far with interviewees. When at last the researcher brought up the fact that the importance of the variable of 'difficulty of acceptance of freedom's loss' did not really appear to change in an international setting, interviewees tended to agree with the analysis.

Obviously this does not discount the importance of the obstacle, both to national and to international concentration. Top managers took a pragmatic attitude when asked what solution they recommended, stating that the issue should be viewed in terms of a cost–benefit analysis. As a chief executive said: 'You have to decide for yourself if you value your own leadership position more than the long-run welfare of the company; if the latter comes first, you have to give up some of your pride, at your own personal cost.' In fact, if the desirability of a consolidation is clearly recognized, some sort of compromise solution should be found. The best example, in the framework of this discussion, is Dunlop–Pirelli, which has a top-level co-ordinating committee whose function is to harmonize the policy of the consolidated group. This committee is 'chaired alternatively by the two chairmen, Sir Reay Geddes and Signor Pirelli.'[18] Indeed, the chief executives interviewed about this believe that for a consolidation to take place successfully, personal relationships have to be so strong anyway that 'there is always a way to come to a friendly arrangement', as an Italian executive put it.

The second aspect of this problem is the fear of rationalizations. As is amply discussed in the literature, this is of particular concern to middle managers.[19] Any consolidation entails potential rationalizations. Integration of departments eliminates duplication of functions. For example, the control functions may be integrated and fewer people may be needed. The manager fears he may lose his job. While this threat exists in any concentration, an international concentration is felt to be far more threatening than a national one. The first reason for this is that there is a greater element of the unknown: less is known about the organization of a foreign partner than of a domestic partner. Particularly important is the lack of knowledge about the capabilities of foreign managers. Ignorance generates the fear that foreign managers are better: if a reduction in the number of managers takes place as a result of a consolidation, foreigners will be retained, while nationals will be terminated.

Beyond the problem of fear generated by ignorance about foreign managerial know-how, interviewees reported on the inferiority complexes managers have towards each other. The most important of these is a generalized inferiority complex with regard to German managers. The postwar economic success of Germany has generated admiration for German managers; this was encountered in virtually every country visited during this study. In fact, more than their superior managerial skill, Germans are viewed as having a remarkable working potential. Moreover, they are perceived as having the ability to discipline themselves to produce an outstanding collective effort. A special inferiority complex is that of French managers. France had a 'glorious past' when the French enjoyed intellectual and economic leadership. Their lack-lustre industrial development in the postwar period contrasts with this grandeur, and executives feel a certain responsibility for not having perpetuated the past. This sense of guilt generates the feeling that they are inferior administrators. Frenchmen tend to rationalize this by saying they are intellectually brilliant but lack an applications orientation. 'We conceptualize too much and are always up in the clouds. We should have some of the Anglo-Saxon down-to-earth behavior', said a French interviewee. Italy provides another example. It industrialized later than its Common Market partners and has traditionally been the needy country of the EEC. Its postwar industrial development has given it a competitive industry. Now, executives feel their success is due more to their entrepreneurial ability to improvise than to their administrative capability. They feel they are poor administrators because of their lack of rigorous training. This is a handicap in today's advanced stages of corporate development. As an Italian executive said: 'We were great at creating our industries but, now that we have them, we would need to be better administrators to manage them effectively.'

The result of these inferiority complexes is a fear among managers that, if the rationalization does indeed occur, they will be the victims, since their foreign counterparts are better administrators. The company will get rid of the less capable managers and will retain the better foreign ones.

Another motive leading managers to fear international consolidations more than national ones is the general mistrust of multinational corporations which has developed. Many interviewees pointed out that multinational companies are perceived as hiring and firing people more readily than national companies. The reason is allegedly the fact that multinational companies—primarily US-based firms—have affected public opinion by introducing a practice of higher turnover among their employees than was normal in the EEC. Working for a multinational group is perceived as more risky in terms of employment stability. As long as they work for a national company, managers feel secure, knowing that top management tends to be somewhat paternalistic. They consequently resist the internationalization of their organization through a consolidation with a foreign partner because to them such a consolidation connotes reduced job security.

Top management considers this fear of rationalization can be an important obstacle: if middle management is worried about its own future, its opposition will be very strong. As a chief executive said: 'One clumsy lay-off can raise enough hell to jeopardize the entire success of a consolidation.' It is not likely that middle management will become militant against a consolidation (i.e., that it will strike). Rather, morale will sink so low that the effectiveness of management will be severely impaired.[20] Top managers emphasize the need to explain at considerable length that rationalizations will not occur. Indeed, no rationalization should occur at all. This highlights the need to plan a concentration from the human assets point of view.[21] It is possible to reduce the economic inconveniences of avoiding lay-offs by carefully planning the development of human resources and by not hiring people who would have to be fired when the concentration occurs.

The third aspect of the threat represented by a concentration is managers' concern for their personal position in the organization.[22] The fear of rationalization is an extreme case. Managers can be relatively easily reassured that their job is not in danger. However, it is much more common in a consolidation for middle managers to worry about the opportunities which they may lose as a consequence of a transnational concentration. Because of the same type of inferiority complexes surveyed above, managers may fear that their career advancement will be hampered by their foreign counterparts. If foreign managers consistently perform better, they will progress more rapidly and will fill those higher hierarchical positions which the national managers would otherwise have reached.

The fear of losing career opportunities is a serious problem. It generates anxiety, which diminishes management's effectiveness. Interviewees with transnational concentration experience reported that prior to the collaboration and at its beginning, managers feel inhibited by their foreign partners. At this stage they may be inclined to hamper the collaboration. For example, one of these interviewees said that 'tacit political factions' developed to sabotage the consolidation: managers avoided any collaboration and pointed to administrative frictions to demonstrate the inadvisability of the collaboration.

There are two types of recommendations to solve this problem. The first is that of explaining the necessity of a concentration and of reassuring managers about their personal career development. If it is made clear that a concentration is desirable and that the future of the organization depends on it, management will be less inclined to resist it. If it is shown that not undertaking a concentration will make the company worse off, managers may be convinced that the consolidation is in their own interest.

The second recommendation is that the concentration be created by a gradual process. Chapter 7 will discuss how a concentration should be brought about progressively: co-operation should precede full amalgamation. Hopefully, this should solve the feeling of personal threat, caused by unfamiliarity with foreign managers. If managers are given the opportunity to work together before the consolidation, they will come to know each other and build up confidence in the collaboration. In a co-operative agreement, managers work with foreigners but they still remain part of a separate hierarchical structure. They do not run the risk of losing a personal opportunity because they are not in direct competition with foreign managers. This, then, gives managers a chance to work together and to become acquainted with foreign partners without having to risk their personal position. When the actual consolidation takes place, managers should be sufficiently well acquainted not to fear each other any more.

The fourth aspect of the problem of threat is of particular concern to top management. At present executives from several European countries feel an economic recession is hanging over them. Managers fear that such a recession will put them at a competitive disadvantage in relation to the foreign partners, who may take the upper hand over the consolidated group. In most of the countries visited in the course of this study, managers complained about the deterioration of national economic conditions. In Italy the crisis is now several years old and signs of recovery are still faint. Britain has a sluggish economy, and managers have complained about its lack of dynamism since the end of the Second World War. In France, despite a clear trend towards recovery from the crisis of 1968, managers adopt a prudent attitude. The country has too often witnessed set-backs due to sudden sociopolitical crises for managers to be unconditionally optimistic. In Germany there is a clear feeling that the economy may be overheated. Furthermore, the relatively leftist Brandt administration worries the business community.

A manager who perceives that his country has a weak economy relative to that of a potential concentration partner fears that his company will have a relative disadvantage in the concentration. This is a particular hindrance in the preparatory stages of a concentration and until the amalgamation is complete. The manager fears that the partner may avail himself of his favourable environmental conditions of the moment to take a decisive advantage in the consolidated group.

It is noteworthy that interviewees typically say their own economy is undergoing or may undergo a crisis in the near future, while most of the time they perceive other countries to be in economic expansion. A manager in a given country complains about national economic problems, while the neighbour indicates that this very country is doing well. When second set interviewees' attention was called to these contradictions, they invoked management's ignorance of foreign business conditions. International executives especially complained that businessmen in general are only familiar with national economic features. This provincialism is thought to be due principally to the domestic focus of the mass media and of the professional training of executives. Both these features will be discussed at the end of this chapter. From the firms' point of view, this is an additional reason to engage in a concentration in a progressive fashion. The inhibitions about the inferiority of the national economic environment are cleared away by actually working with foreigners and thus becoming familiar with their problems. As an executive of a transnational company said: 'When you actually work in a foreign environment, you quickly realize that, after all, they are just in the same type of mess you are in at home.'

NATIONALISM

The eighth problem area is nationalism. The behavioural literature emphasizes the importance of this problem for endeavours in general, calling for the interplay of people from different nationalities.[23] Indeed, a majority of interviewees have raised this issue, and to many of them the most important barrier to concentration lies in this area. Specifically, there are two sets of obstacles to be discussed here.

The first set can be called xenophobia.[24] There are in Europe certain animosities which have a national basis,[25] and impede harmonious relationships among people of different nationalities. In the context of the present study it was found that the people against whom the most xenophobic feelings are directed are the Germans. The reason is the Second World War. Those executives who have personally suffered under the Nazis 'can at best forgive but cannot forget', as one of them said. Thus, it is the older executives who tend to have these feelings. However, they are shared by younger ones when their family has been a victim of the Third Reich's atrocities. Among them, Jewish executives are the best examples.

In the course of this research, xenophobic feelings against Germans were expressed in two ways. First, interviewees reported that some managers—principally older middle managers—explicitly refused to work with Germans. Persons who were this explicit about their strong feelings were quite rare. Furthermore they are typically not key people and it is always possible to avoid their having a face-to-face relationship with the Germans in question. Second, these feelings have a subconscious negative influence on managers' minds. This is a far more important hindrance for transnational concentration; it is an unconscious bond affecting the decision of whether or not to collaborate. For example, a corporate planner of a Jewish family-owned company reported that talks for a co-operative agreement with a German partner failed because his company's top management could not be resolved to a close relationship with Germans. It was his observation that this reluctance was totally subconscious. At no moment did his top management express its animosity; rather, it showed 'no will to make it happen' and no confidence in the viability of the operation. These feelings are hidden, and people are unaware of harbouring them. The result is often apparently irrational behaviour by decision-makers, who refrain from undertaking an economically attractive venture for no ostensible reason.

Beyond xenophobic feelings towards Germans, interviewees reported other animosities between Europeans. There is a French–British animosity, particularly on the part of the French. This is seen to be due to the historical rivalry of the two countries. Several interviewees expressed the opinion that this rivalry is stimulated by the educational systems. French pupils are taught from the earliest age that the English are the all-time enemies and that there has been a traditional rivalry between the two countries. As a consequence, there is a conditioned reflex against the British. There is also the rivalry between the Belgians and the Dutch, which has an historical basis as well. For instance, an executive of a multinational company reported that his firm decided to centralize the decision-making unit for the entire Benelux area in Holland. Immediately the Belgian plant sent him a letter signed by the entire staff, complaining about this loss of autonomy, saying: 'We wish to remind you that in 1830 we fought a war against the Dutch to obtain our independence. This war is still not over.'

Such feelings are hindrances to a consolidation. A decision-maker may refrain from engaging in a consolidation because he himself is somewhat reluctant to enter into a permanent relationship with 'rivals'. Moreover, he may fear that his organization will react negatively to such a collaboration. He may expect that there will be frictions at middle-management level which will preclude any hope for constructive collaboration.

The second set of obstacles is what an interviewee called 'classical nationalism'. This refers to 'nationalism' for its own sake, i.e., ethnocentric attitudes. It is a bias in favour of maintaining the national identity of an organization on the grounds of economic or managerial 'patriotism'.[26] Managers are chauvinistic either because they take pride in being part of a purely national firm or because they personally have an ethnocentric attitude aimed at safeguarding the particularism of their organization.

There are here two types of problems. The first is one of personal values of top management itself. Interviewees who have had a chance to observe top managers while they were making crucial decisions involving close relationships with foreigners report that the chief executive often has a personal desire to continue working for a national company because this is a source of personal satisfaction to him. He then resists a transnationalization of the company. Although European top managers normally are not against internationalizing their company's scope, they often resist transnationalization. In other words, international business is desirable as long as the ties with the home base remain strong. European top managers are not quite ready yet to lose their national identity as is the case in a transnational concentration. They would feel alienated. Top managers usually are not explicit about such economic patriotism. Rather, as with xenophobic feelings, there is a subconscious bond which hampers a decision to consolidate internationally.

The second type of 'classical nationalism' is middle-management's resistance to the transnationalization of the company. Top management considers this an important hindrance to transnational concentration because it is middle management which is expected to work with foreigners on a day-to-day basis. Workers and lower-level managers normally do not resent the a transnationalization. The routine tasks they perform do not usually require any interchange with the new partners. Middle managers, however, do indeed collaborate on a permanent basis. It is they who actually bring about the integration of the companies involved. As a chief executive put it: 'If they are really nationalistically minded, you had better forget about any concentration altogether.'

There is another group which is nationalistically minded and thus hampers transnational concentration. This is technical and scientific personnel. Interviewees reported that engineers fear a loss of their freedom and autonomy. They are jealous of their know-how and do not want to share it with foreigners. This problem was mentioned in particular by high-technology firms and by those firms which had had experience in co-operative agreements or joint R & D projects. They stated that engineers have a certain intellectual snobbery towards managers. To them it is relatively unimportant if the administrative or the marketing side of an organization is transnational. However, they do resist a pooling of scientific knowledge resources. Executives are of the opinion that engineers identify their stock of knowledge less with the company than with the country. The fact that they have studied in national schools gives them the feeling that they have a national heritage which they are expected to build upon. As a French executive said: 'It is as if there were a national school of scientific thought; to share this school's knowledge with foreigners would mean betraying one's country.' It should be pointed out, however, that this particular problem is said to disappear very soon when engineers actually work on a joint project. The common purposive goal very quickly builds up cohesiveness and, in fact, it is among engineers that the feeling of belonging to the same group develops most quickly. The recommendation of executives who had to organize for collaboration among technical staffs of different nationalities is that considerable time should be spent at the moment the collaboration is planned in explaining the nature of the project in order to highlight the benefits of the collaboration in terms of technical synergies and to emphasize the fact that individual autonomy of the parties involved will be preserved. The last feature is, in fact, deceptive for engineers as the aim in a consolidation is to integrate the staffs completely. However, managers point out that this integration will come by itself and that technical people will be the first to endorse it. An Italian manager said: 'It is simply sugar you put in the medicine. What is important is the medicine's curative effect, but the sugar helps people to swallow the medicine.'

There are two countries where 'classical nationalism' was found to be most prevalent: England and France. On the other hand, Holland is the country where the phenomenon appears to be least prevalent. During the second set of interviews it was ascertained that the reason—in management's eyes—for the strong nationalism of British and French executives is, first, the educational system of the countries. This will be discussed in further detail at the end of this chapter. Moreover, Britain has always tended to remain in some isolation, primarily because of its insularity. British interviewees have often mentioned that people have a clear desire 'to retain some of their independence'. Indeed, beyond actual patriotism, Englishmen have a tendency towards particularism. One executive said: 'We want to remain distinct: we don't want to be like everybody else.' French executives, on the other hand, have a cultural superiority complex. They are not mentally prepared for the idea of needing to collaborate with foreigners. They are individualistic and they wish to remain economically and intellectually independent.[27] (A popular expression is 'Restons Français', which means: 'Let us remain French.') The Dutch are the least nationalistic. The reason for this is, first, that the country has traditionally been dependent on international trade. For centuries the Dutch have been great travellers, both as settlers in distant colonies and as merchants. Since the country is small, it has had to depend heavily on outside commerce. Its geographical location on the sea facilitated this international orientation. Moreover, the country has had a tradition of spiritual liberalism. Again, for centuries Holland has allowed considerable intellectual freedom. Interviewees believe this has had a double effect. First, it has attracted people from all over Europe who wished to enjoy this freedom: philosophers, scientists, or those seeking freedom for their religious beliefs. Dutch people have consequently acquired a habit of living in a cosmopolitan environment. Second, this freedom has enabled the Dutch to be open-minded *vis-à-vis* the outside world. They have been receptive to foreign ideas, values, and life styles. This open-mindedness has probably made the Dutch the best prepared people for the challenge of Europeanization.

Nationalistic attitudes lead to ethnocentric behaviour. As was mentioned several times already, people are motivated to remain within their national frontiers and refrain from Europeanizing their environment. This can take the explicit form of overt opposition to a transnationalization of a company or the form of a subconscious hindrance, hampering the decision to consolidate across national boundaries. Beyond this general resistance to transnationalization, interviewees reported specific hindrances deriving from nationalistic attitudes. For example, in a consolidation there may be a rationalization in which two departments are integrated. The result is that there is one boss. This in itself creates frictions. But nationalism compounds the problem. If the companies involved are a French and a German company and the boss of the integrated department is German, the French may not only resent this on chauvinistic grounds but may also experience a certain xenophobic feeling towards the German boss. This may be quite disruptive, to the point where it may be desirable to replace the boss or find an arrangement by which it is clear that there is some French representation in the leadership of the integrated department. Another example that was often mentioned is the problem of where to establish the headquarters of a consolidated group. Each participating company may insist on having headquarters on its own national territory. In fact, an argument the EEC Commission puts forth for the European company statute is that it will resolve this problem by giving a supranational image to the company. However, businessmen point out that the place of juridical incorporation of a company is of trivial importance. What counts is the geographical location of headquarters as well as the nationality of management.[28]

Practitioners advocate compromise solutions to these problems. For instance, the top management can be a group composed of an equal number of nationals of each participating company. The chief executive may be selected on a rotating basis between nationals of each country involved. Finally, many interviewees think that a trend may well develop towards locating the headquarters of internationally consolidated companies in a neutral country: in a transnational concentration between two companies the headquarters may have to be located in a third country.

MISCONCEPTIONS

The ninth problem area is a set of psychological obstacles and is labelled misconceptions. This refers to erroneous ideas managers have of foreigners' mental structures and values. Managers believe foreigners think and react differently and that this impedes transnational collaboration. These inhibitions, which can be considerable hindrances to concentrations, can be classified in four categories.[29]

The first is what is called in German *Denkkategorien* (meaning approximately 'thought processes'). Interviewees often stated that foreigners have a different approach to problems which hinders a joint effort on a given task. The French are perceived as dogmatic and the British as pragmatic. British executives who think of working with Frenchmen are disturbed by their tendency to 'philosophize and theorize'. The Germans are seen as analytical, but with little imagination. As a French executive said: 'They are great at perfecting the *status quo* but lack creativity.' The Italians are superior improvisors, but are incapable of organizing themselves. They tend to act intuitively and do little analytic thinking. The result of these alleged differences is that businessmen think they cannot collaborate across national boundaries. They think they cannot tackle a problem together with a foreigner and that it is preferable 'that one thinks about the problem by oneself and then compares results', as an interviewee said.

The second category of misconceptions is about people's values. The personal objectives of businessmen are seen as conflicting. For example, the Dutch place a high value on job security and social benefits. Even high-level executives are concerned with the stability of their professional position. Germans have a higher preference for liquidity and put a higher priority on financial remunerations. The Italians are perceived as having a doubtful morality. Foreigners know about the 'unconventional and folkloristic' relationship between Italian public and private administrations. They then tend to believe that the same code of ethics is in force within the private sector. In particular, the unreliable accounting gives rise to many questions about Italians' honesty. The reasoning is that, if Italians cheat with public administrators, they probably cheat with private administrators as well. As an interviewee put it: 'Italians' tendency toward "special arrangements" scares foreigners, who see no reason for Italians to have a stricter morality with private partners than with public agencies.'

The third category of misconceptions is about conflicting ways of doing business. Managers believe that their foreign counterparts have different ways of working which are in conflict with their own. A widely quoted example is the individualism of Latin people as opposed to the spirit of collectivism of the Anglo-Saxons. In particular, the French are perceived as incapable of working in committees, while the British have a superior ability for teamwork. Another example is the direct approach of the Dutch to a business problem in contrast to the somewhat involved approach of the French or the Belgians. The Dutch are more 'to the point' while the French and Belgians have a tendency to discuss general principles and get to the real issue only after some generic considerations. A final example is the hierarchical structure in the various countries. Here, two variables are of particular concern: formal versus informal relationships, and the amount of delegation. With regard to the former, the Dutch are perceived as having very 'democratic' and informal relationships between the various hierarchical levels. The Germans and the French are viewed as having more rigid relationships. With regard to the amount of delegation, Italian organizations are more centralized than, say, the Dutch or the German ones. This type of difference in the way work is organized generates the feeling that it is difficult for two management teams to work together.

The fourth category of misconceptions concerns the 'mentality' of people; the way people behave, over and beyond their professional attitudes. Managers fear they will not get along with foreigners on a social basis. The ways of living are different and tastes vary. The following are examples of preconceptions presented by interviewees. The Italian likes to drive fast sports cars recklessly, is short-tempered, and beats his wife at night. The Frenchman is romantic and is a heavy drinker. The German has a 'bull-dog' quality which takes away any glamour from whatever he does. The Englishman still lives with the illusion of ruling the world and thus is often condescending towards foreigners. People seem to believe that, in view of these differences, they cannot live together. 'Our philosophy of life is too different for us to get along with each other', said an interviewee.

A comprehensive discussion of these misconceptions is unwarranted. It would be possible to give many examples of such stereotypes about foreigners, but the preceding examples should suffice. Needless to say, these stereotypes are, for the most part, nonsense. While there are indeed differences in national traits, they are actually neither as great as people say, nor are they a hindrance to collaboration.[30] Executives with international business experience are unanimous in saying that transnational collaboration is not only possible but, in fact, can be a stimulating and rewarding professional experience. Foreigners impart new points of view which can lead to a constructive challenging of otherwise unquestioned methods. Moreover, international executives point out that, with a positive and open attitude, social contact with foreigners can be fulfilling and enriching from the personal point of view.[31]

Second set interviewees widely confirmed the hypothesis that the source of these misconceptions is the unfamiliarity with or ignorance about foreign environments. As will be discussed shortly, this in turn results from the fact that European cultures are in almost watertight compartments and from the scarcity of social contact between countries. The fact that people do not know each other generates lack of mutual trust and belief in popular stereotypes. Moreover, as was mentioned already, ignorance is inhibiting. It causes resistance to change. Managers shy away from transnational concentrations because of a more or less subconscious fear of the unknown, which they rationalize through stereotypes about foreigners.

RECOMMENDATIONS

Particularly in view of the psychological obstacles discussed in the last four problem areas, what recommendations can be formulated? This question can be answered in three ways: first, with reference to public agencies; second, to firms; finally, to areas where behavioural research is needed.[32]

There is a wide agreement among interviewees that European educational systems are unsatisfactory.[33] European managers advocate a Europeanization of educational systems. Today education takes a very ethnocentric approach to culture. First, the teaching of languages is inadequate. As an Italian executive said: 'They teach languages in an overly academic fashion, with no concern for practical usage. The student ends up having a few notions about the etymology and the literature but is incapable of asking for a cup of coffee.' Moreover, the emphasis of education is totally on national as opposed to European culture. For example, literature courses often make no mention of foreign authors, history programmes deal mainly with domestic history, and philosophy readings focus principally on national texts. Interviewees believe that Europeans are therefore relatively ignorant of foreign cultures. They tend to be myopic and to have little appreciation of foreign environments. An internationalization of European academic programmes would foster more open-mindedness to foreign ideas. In addition, gradual standardization of educational programmes would permit a greater exchange of students between academic institutions of different countries. This Europeanization of education would serve as a catalytic element to foster cohesiveness among EEC countries and would diminish the feeling of alienation among Europeans. People receiving a similar education would feel less remote from each other, which in turn would reduce inhibitions.

Beyond education, Europeanization of the Press is recommended. Many interviewees think that much of the provincialism of EEC managers and their consequent inhibitions has come about because the Press and other information media are national in outlook. 'In the EEC the only real international newspaper is American', said an international executive.[34] This provincialism develops a concern for purely local affairs by managers. Interviewees think it would be desirable, for example, to have a newspaper published throughout the EEC in several languages, but with the same content. In this connection, many interviewees argue that international concentrations should occur between newspapers.

These recommendations may appear somewhat far-fetched. It may seem that businessmen want to 'turn the whole world upside-down', just to make one segment of their own activity more effective. However, there are two types of justifications for such far-reaching policies. First, all these moves are congruent with European sociopolitical integration: what is good for business integration happens also to be good for EEC integration in general. Second, since business collaboration is to be a force for European integration, it is legitimate for business to expect a good deal of support from the environment. Executives generally believe that since European unity is first of all an economic need, it is logical that economic units (i.e., firms) should bring this integration about. However, as the environment has a strong bearing upon these units, and is also vitally dependent on them, it should logically facilitate their integration. For the long run there should be an effort towards the harmonization of the total environment. In the shorter run, the elements of the environment which are closest to business should receive most attention.

Specifically, a first step in the internationalization of the press might be to Europeanize the business press.

Moreover, beyond a Europeanization of education in general, it appears urgent that courses designed to prepare managers be harmonized. While graduate schools of business should generally be private institutions (an exception might be France), public institutions should focus on harmonizing those university programmes which are attended by future managers (e.g., the German *Betriebswirtschaft* studies or the Italian studies of *Economia e Commercio*).[35] In fact, most interviewees say that one should talk not about harmonization, but about 'the *creation* of European management courses at university level'. Today's university courses are typically so poor in terms of managerial training that there is indeed little to harmonize. Executives say that the necessity of starting adequate programmes from scratch provides an opportunity to initiate the same programmes throughout the EEC.

Turning now to recommendations addressed to businessmen, the overriding advice is to attempt to internationalize the scope of the firm's manpower. One way is by formal training. The company can insist that its managers take a crash programme designed to help them work in an international environment—most commonly language programmes. Furthermore, companies are increasingly advocating training programmes aimed at 'teaching people what we don't know', as an international executive put it. These are basically courses designed to call managers' attention to areas of potential friction encountered when working with foreigners. This has been referred to as 'developing skills in "learning how to learn" ',[36] namely, developing intercultural sensitivity or what was called earlier in this chapter 'the international business skill'. More than giving participants know-how in international business, these courses are designed to prepare people for the possible shocks of international relations.[37] The rationale is that, if people are warned and have thought about the potential problems beforehand, they will be less emotional about international collaboration and hopefully less prejudiced against it. Indeed, such courses should foster self-awareness and thus reduce the impact of such prejudices as nationalism. An interesting possibility would be to apply T-group techniques to international amalgamations. Among others, Ruth Streeter Hatch has proposed the use of sensitivity training in domestic concentrations.[38] It appears that these techniques offer some promise for international collaboration endeavours.[39]

The second step a firm can take is to encourage its personnel 'to learn by doing'. A company can gradually enlarge the scope of its managers by engaging in international co-operative endeavours prior to a concentration. If a concentration is planned sufficiently in advance, a company can induce its managers to gain experience in operating with foreign co-workers. Several interviewees stated that it may even be desirable to engage in transnational co-operation prior to the consolidation, if only for the sake of training human resources. Even if such co-operation is unwarranted on purely economic grounds, it should be done as an investment and regarded as a cost of doing a transnational concentration. Co-operation prior to the concentration gives managers an opportunity to become acquainted with foreigners without the pressure of quickly becoming an integrated group. Managers may become used to foreign working environments without the feeling that they have to renounce their national environments. They are introduced to an international professional and social life but spared the anxiety of being irrevocably committed to such a life.

These two steps can be combined. For example, two companies thinking of concentrating can begin to collaborate as early as possible. Once this collaboration is under way, sensitivity training sessions can be held, in which managers of the two companies are brought together. This requires two ingredients which are generally not available in Europe. First, T-group consultants are neither well established nor accepted by the business community. Indeed, there would be considerable potential for consultants in group dynamics such as Leadership Resources Inc. of Washington, DC, headed by Gordon Lippitt, or Scientific Methods Inc. of Austin, Texas, headed by Robert Blake.[40] However, even if they were available, such services would still face a credibility gap as businessmen are not persuaded of their usefulness.[41] The second missing ingredient is corporate planning. Co-operation prior to a concentration requires that the need for a concentration be forecast. The next chapter will show that this is often not the case in Europe.

The discussion of recommendations has, up to now, been addressed to the individual company. There is in addition an important recommendation which should be made to the business community as a whole. It pertains to the responsibility of businessmen to train future managers. There are as yet few graduate institutions for management training. Moreover, existing institutions are often national in scope. In fact, managers perceive those few schools that claim to have an international outlook as transplants of US business schools. They typically import US instructors and do limited research. It appears that the only schools which have a non-American scope end up having a national scope. 'There are either subsidiaries of US schools or national schools; there is nothing genuinely European', said a French executive. The result is that European managers have an inadequate training. Interviewees often expressed the opinion that professional schools for managers with a European scope could play a significant role in European business integration. This training would take Europe as its level of discourse (e.g., case material would draw on firms operating in the total European environment) and would have a European student body. Thus, students would work on European problems with European co-workers. Managers receiving this type of training would hopefully be more open-minded to the European concept: they would be aware of the risks and opportunities offered by the EEC and would feel comfortable collaborating with foreigners. Such institutions should be created under the initiative of private business firms. A pooling of efforts of European companies to organize and support such institutions is most desirable.[42]

With regard to areas where behavioural research is needed, it appears that there is a knowledge gap about the real differences among people and the effects of these differences. Social psychologists would make a considerable contribution if they could advance knowledge about people's thought processes and values. The main psychological problem is ignorance. Knowledge about the human traits of foreigners would allow an identification of areas of potential friction and thus make possible a smoother integration of two foreign management teams. It would also reduce the inhibitions deriving from ignorance about foreign managers. If managers could be 'taught' with some degree of confidence what to expect and how to behave, they would be less 'scared' of transnational concentrations. As an interviewee put it: 'The real problem of an international link-up is how to blend two proud and gallant management teams in which the main variable is the unknown (X) of human dynamics. The most urgent thing is for researchers to find out this (X).'

NOTES

1. Pierre Tabatoni, 'Remarques sur les obstacles psycho-sociologiques à la coopération internationale', *Revue du Marché Commun*, No. 109, January–February 1968, p. 104. (This quote was translated from the French.)

2. On this area of concern, see:

(a) F. C. S. Northrop and H. H. Livingstone, *Cross-Cultural Understanding: Epistemology in Anthropology*, Harper & Row, New York, 1964.

(b) Pierre Tabatoni, 'Remarques sur les obstacles psycho-sociologiques à la coopération internationale', p. 102.

3. A similar conclusion is reached by Nicholas Stacey when he writes: 'One of the reasons for their [international link-ups] slow progress in the EEC is the excessive individualism and often isolationism of manufacturers and traders.' Nicholas A. Stacey, *Mergers in Modern Business*, Hutchinson, London, 1970, p. 122.

4. On this topic, see: Werner J. Feld, *Transnational Business Collaboration among Common Market Countries*, Praeger, New York, 1970, p. 43.

5. N. R. A. Krekel, T. G. Van der Woerd and J. J. Wouterse, *Mergers—A European Approach to Technique*, Business Books, London, 1969, p. 64.

6. See: chapter 7.

7. See: Robert B. Blake, Jane S. Mouton, Larry E. Greiner and Louis B. Barnes, 'Breakthrough in Organization Development', *Harvard Business Review*, November–December 1964, pp. 133–55.

8. See: Roger Godino, 'The Importance of Advanced Management Education for Europe', *European Business*, No. 17, April 1968, pp. 54–59.

9. See: D. C. Damant, 'Investment Evaluation, Mergers and Take-Overs', *European Business*, May 1967, pp. 14–31.

10. See: David B. Zenoff and Jack Zwick, *International Financial Management*, Prentice-Hall, Englewood Cliffs, New Jersey, 1969 (particularly pp. 228–49).

11. See: Claude McMillan, 'The Swap as a Hedge in Foreign Exchange', *California Management Review*, Summer 1962, pp. 57–65.

12. See: David B. Zenoff and Jack Zwick, *International Financial Management*, pp. 453–508.

13. On this topic, see:

(a) H. C. de Bettignies and S. H. Rhinesmith, 'Developing the International Executive', *European Business*, January 1970, pp. 52–57.

(b) D. J. Hall and H. C. de Bettignies, 'Training Better Executives: Problems and Progress', *European Business*, January 1968, pp. 25–31.

14. See: Jacqueline Grapin, 'Il n'y a pas que des mariages heureux...', *Le Monde*, 5 September 1972, p. 17.

15. A comparable recommendation is made in chapter 4 when discussing ways to solve the problem of governments' resistance to transnational link-ups.

16. See, for example:

(a) Myles L. Mace and George G. Montgomery, *Management Problems in Corporate Acquisitions*, Graduate School of Business Administration, Harvard University, Cambridge, Massachusetts, 1962, Chapter 9.

(b) N. R. A. Krekel, T. G. Van der Woerd and J. J. Wouterse, *Mergers—A European Approach to Technique*, pp. 18–24.

(c) Rémi Sadoux and Rémy Arnaud, 'Les fusions jugées par ceux qui les font, par ceux qui les subissent', *Entreprise*, No. 851, December 1971, pp. 52–57.

17. Robert A. Short, *Business Mergers—How and When to Transact Them*, Prentice-Hall, Englewood Cliffs, New Jersey, 1967, p. 84.

18. Michael B. Stewart, 'Transnational Enterprise: The European Challenge', *Columbia Journal of World Business*, July–August 1972, pp. 5–13, at p. 13.

19. See, for example:

(a) Arthur R. Wyatt and Donald K. Kieso, *Business Combinations: Planning and Action*, International Textbook Company, Scranton, Pennsylvania, 1969, pp. 180–84.

(b) Rémi Sadoux and Rémy Arnaud, 'Les fusions jugées par ceux qui les font, par ceux qui les subissent'.

(c) Douglas V. Austin, 'We Contemplated no Changes in Personnel', *Mergers and Acquisitions*, September–October 1971, pp. 20–21.

20. A similar finding is reported by Wyatt and Kieso, *Business Combinations: Planning and Action*, p. 181.

21. See the discussion in the next chapter.

22. A similar analysis is to be found in R. W. Moon, *Business Mergers and Take-over Bids*, Gee, London, 1968, pp. 42–43.

23. See, for example:

(a) Amitai Etzioni, 'Social-Psychological Aspects of International Relations' in Gardner Lindzey and Elliot Aronson, *The Handbook of Social Psychology*, Addison-Wesley, Reading, Massachusetts, 1969, Vol. V, pp. 538–601.

(b) E. B. Haas and A. S. Whiting, *Dynamics of International Relations*, McGraw-Hill, New York, 1956.

(c) D. T. Campbell, 'Ethnocentric and Other Altruistic Motives', Nebraska Symposium on Motivation, 1965, pp. 283–311.

24. The literal meaning of the word 'xenophobia' (hatred of foreigners) is too strong for what is actually meant here. In this discussion the word is taken to mean an antipathy or a certain dislike of foreigners.

25. Werner Feld reaches a similar conclusion in *Transnational Business Collaboration among Common Market Countries*, p. 41.

26. See: Enid B. Lovell, 'Nationalism or Interdependence: The Alternatives',

International Survey of Business Opinion and Experience, New York, 1969, The National Industrial Conference Board.

27. See: Enid B. Lovell, 'Nationalism or Interdependence: The Alternatives', pp. 16–17.

28. Indeed, the question of location of headquarters cannot be dismissed lightly, as noted by Michael Stewart in 'Transnational Enterprise: The European Challenge', p. 13.

29. For a complementary analysis of these problems, see: W. G. Feld, *Transnational Business Collaboration among Common Market Countries*, pp. 40–48.

30. For a behavioural analysis of such differences, see: Mason Haire, Edwin E. Ghiselli and Lyman W. Porter, *Managerial Thinking: An International Study*, Wiley, New York, 1966.

31. Similar conclusions are presented in: Bernard Denoix, 'Une expérience de coopération internationale: l'IBM en Europe', *Revue du Marché Commun*, No. 109, January–February 1968, pp. 124–30. The author (who was interviewed during this study) is a top executive of IBM in France.

32. The following, basically, are conclusions developed after the first set of interviews, subsequently finalized during the second set.

33. For a complementary discussion, see: *La politique industrielle de la Communauté—Memorandum de la Commission au Conseil*, Commission des Communautés Européennes, Brussels, 1970, pp. 273–94 (particularly pp. 280–84 and 291–94).

34. He referred to the *International Herald Tribune*.

35. One should bear in mind that most universities in the EEC are state-operated.

36. H. C. de Bettignies and S. H. Rhinesmith, 'Developing the International Executive', p. 55.

37. For reports on experimental efforts aiming in the direction of developing such courses, see:

(a) S. H. Rhinesmith and D. Nylen, 'A Behavioral Approach to International Management Training', Pittsburgh, Graduate School of Public and International Affairs, University of Pittsburgh, 1969.

(b) A. Wight, *Handbook on Cross-Cultural Training*, Estes Park, Colorado, Center for Research and Education, 1969.

38. Ruth Streeter Hatch, 'Mergers and Men', *Mergers and Acquisitions*, Fall 1966, pp. 28–37.

39. In fact, T-group techniques have first to be adapted to the European environment. Several efforts have already been made in this direction. See, for example:

(a) C. Faucheux, 'Théorie et technique des groupes de diagnostic', *Bulletin de psychologie*, No. 158–61, 1959, pp. 397–420.

(b) J. Ardoino, 'Le groupe de diagnostic, instrument de formation', Institut d'Administration des Entreprises de l'Université de Bordeaux, 1962.

(c) Max Pagès, 'Le T-group ou groupe de diagnostic', *Hommes et techniques*, 1959, Vol. 15, No. 169, pp. 116–25.

40. See: Ruth Streeter Hatch, 'Mergers and Men', pp. 31–32.

41. Jacqueline Grapin, 'Il n'y a pas que des mariages heureux . . .', p. 17.

42. In fact, a few institutions have been created whose objective is to conform to this type of model. A good example is the European Institute of Business Administration (INSEAD) in Fontainebleau, France.

7.

CORPORATE STRATEGY

This chapter discusses issues which pertain to the strategic function of the firm. The first of the two sections examines problems resulting from inadequate analysis of the alternative of transnational consolidation in the strategic planning of European firms. While the set of problems dealt with in this section was not raised as frequently as others during the first set of interviews, these problems were emphasized most by the second set interviewees—once the researcher mentioned them. The second section does not present any new obstacle but spells out a normative model for implementing a concentration strategy which should reduce the impact of many of the obstacles described throughout this study. It calls for a gradual amalgamation process and is designed in particular to minimize the 'human' difficulties discussed in chapter 6.

Inadequate analysis of the concentration alternative

Strategic planning by European companies for cross-border concentration is inadequate. The alternative of a transnational link-up receives inappropriate analysis; hence the desirability of this alternative is not recognized early enough. There are two main groups of supporting arguments for this general statement. The first pertains to planning *per se* by European companies: inadequate strategic planning in general hinders effective planning of concentrations. The second pertains to the special difficulties of the specific planning for corporate link-ups.

The fact that European companies in general do not plan adequately is documented in the literature.[1] Moreover, in the course of the present research managers with professional experience in the US were unanimous in saying that European companies do not make sufficient deliberate efforts to generate and explore new strategic alternatives. One executive commented: 'In Europe there is neither creative search to generate strategic alternatives nor systematic thinking to analyse the corporate strategic posture.' One of the consulting firms visited during this study reported interesting data to corroborate this. Out of a sample of 28 European companies, 14 have no strategic planning at all; 9 have 'something which they believe is strategic planning but which, in fact, is useless, indeed misleading'; and 5 have an appropriate strategic planning system. The consulting firm added that the sample is probably biased in that the companies are clients of the consulting firm and thus are more disposed to sophisticated management techniques (i.e., firms which use consultants are more inclined to a professional management style and consequently more open to the planning concept). In addition, 2 out of the 5 companies which have an appropriate planning system have had it developed by the consulting firm itself. Thus a more representative sample of European companies should indicate an even smaller number of companies with appropriate strategic planning.

Indeed, the concept of long-range planning has not yet been introduced in many European firms. In all countries visited during this study it was found that the strategic function was inappropriately fulfilled.[2] It is noteworthy that the reasons which were given for this vary from country to country.

Italian managers believe national character is the main cause.[3] Italians allegedly have a natural inclination to improvise. Analytic thinking is deemed unnecessary and intuition is still considered the principal ingredient of business success. Younger executives tend to have an inferiority complex about analytic thinking. They are said to feel their training is inferior to that of other countries' executives. As a reaction, a cognitive dissonance phenomenon occurs and they tend to believe that analytical thinking is a 'Teutonic' characteristic less effective than their 'flair'. Since they perceive their analytic skills to be inferior to those of foreign managers, they tend to subconsciously denigrate the importance of analysis. Historical developments of the postwar period are said to have reinforced the national character. Italy's economic development is all the more remarkable because it was unplanned. As a consequence, Italians have been reinforced in their inclination to improvise. Moreover, Italian executives point out that it is hard to do any planning in today's troubled times of socioeconomic unrest.

Great Britain suffers from the businessmen's attitude of 'gifted amateurs'. This expression, which has been used by a large number of interviewees, refers to the unprofessional attitude of British executives regarding business. Interviewees reported that until recently executives have tended to be somewhat condescending about the management function.[4] Commercial activity has reportedly been viewed as low in prestige and thus the business environment has received little attention. This has alienated the planning function. As a British executive put it: 'We have suffered from a myopic view of the environment and an overemphasis on finances and accounting. We are not mentally ready for a global analysis of the organization and its environment.'

In France (and to a lesser extent in Belgium and Luxembourg) people are mentally open to the planning concept.[5] By his education the Frenchman tends to be analytic and is used to viewing a complex situation in a systematic fashion. As Roger Godino has noted: 'The Frenchman likes to look at planning as the main theme of the rational organization of the economy; and the cult of rationality he inherited from a long national tradition will lead him to support the principle of planning with conviction, even if in practice he will often deviate a great deal from it.'[6] In fact, managers observe that the Frenchman feels hampered in developing a corporate plan because of the uncertainty factor involved. His training is often scientific in emphasis and he allegedly encounters some difficulty in adapting his own rigourous mentality to the inexactitude of the business environment. In the words of a French executive with US business experience: 'The fact that a business plan is based on conjectural hypotheses and on inputs which are often rough approximations makes the rigorist Frenchman feel uncomfortable with the planning function.' Furthermore, it is in France that the influence of family ownership is strongest. Several interviewees believe that the resistance to change in top management is particularly strong, and planning is more or less unconsciously avoided as an undesirable questioning of the *status quo*.

It is probably in Germany (and Holland) that the planning function is most akin to national character.[7] Managers believe Germans have a propensity for organization and naturally tend to prepare any of their endeavours ahead of time. However, interviewees have pointed out two barriers that have impeded the full acceptance of the planning function among German firms. First, as in Italy, the postwar economic recovery has been dramatic but not programmed. As an older executive put it: 'We were too busy increasing our today's sales to plan for tomorrow's growth.' Second, Germans are scrupulous tactical planners. They forecast all the details of a programme with great care. But they tend to lack creativity with regard to the strategic decision. As a foreign executive put it: 'They lack imagination to develop a strategic breakthrough.'

Not only is there little strategic planning to start with, but it was found that the formal planning actually done is rendered ineffective by a credibility gap. Corporate planners as well as consultants have complained that their work remains an academic exercise and that it is not used when the strategic posture of the firm is actually determined. Top management does not take into account the analysis and recommendations made by planners. As a corporate planner said: 'I have the feeling of being an ornament. Top management feels it is more *à la page* with a planning department, so here I am. In fact, the only way to see my recommendations followed is when top management needs a report supporting an action against, say, a group of dissenting stockholders. Then, if I am willing to give them a report going in the right direction, it will be followed to the letter!'

The problem is that top management has little faith in a long-range plan. The absence of formal training for managers is believed to foster an over-reliance on intuition. 'People have been reinforced by their past successes which were based on hunch; they have a resistance to analytic methods which they often do not really understand', said a consultant. The planning literature emphasizes the need for top management involvement in the process.[8] European top management remains more often than not outside the process. This widens the gap between the plan and reality. As a planner said: 'How can one expect them to follow our conclusions which have a bearing on the total business when they have no idea of how we reach these conclusions?'

The insufficient amount of planning and the credibility gap are a hindrance to transnational concentration. It is the strategic planning function which should identify the need for a transnational concentration. Only through a deliberate effort aimed at the formulation of alternatives can the international link-up route receive proper evaluation.

SPECIAL DIFFICULTIES

Beyond the inadequacy of strategic planning surveyed above, five factors render strategic planning ineffective for transnational concentration.

The first reason given by interviewees is the production orientation of European management. As was discussed in chapter 1, production economies of scale do not normally constitute a major driving force in favour of transnational concentration. In most fields it is possible to reach the optimal size of plant within national boundaries. Marketing can, on the other hand, strongly benefit from an international link-up. In particular, marketing managers complain that European 'corporate strategists' typically think in terms of production costs; consequently, the advantages of a transnational concentration are often not apparent enough. This is aggravated by the fact that EEC companies do relatively little market forecasting. Reportedly, the consequence is that strategists do not see the trend which is often the most important stimulus for a transnational consolidation: tastes are becoming more similar throughout Europe, but segments for a given product are becoming more and more numerous. This means that it is increasingly possible to sell the same products throughout Europe, but that specialization is also increasing, i.e., the market is requiring an increasing number of models for a given product. This latter feature obliges producers to supply a greater variety of types of products, which increases costs. These costs can be hedged by an international concentration, which takes advantage of the gradual harmonization of demand while it permits the organization to reach a size sufficient for economic production of many models. Market analysis and projections would show these trends which, in turn, would highlight the desirability of international link-ups. As a Belgian executive put it: 'When thinking of a concentration, Europeans think only of production economies of scale because there is an intrinsic production orientation as opposed to a market orientation.'

The second reason is somewhat related to the first. Particularly interviewees with international business experience stated that planning in Europe still consists primarily of financial projections. According to one of these executives: 'Strategy is formulated by finance people who tend to focus on the forecasting of accounting data.' Recently an effort has been made to give greater importance to marketing data, but this is still an exception. American executives in Europe often express the opinion that Europeans have the feeling that qualitative strategic plans lack credibility and cannot be taken seriously. 'They believe only numbers have credibility and status', said one of these executives. As a consequence, the more intangible benefits of a transnational consolidation are not recognized. For example, the learning process resulting from a transnational amalgamation is difficult for a European manager to include in the 'pros' of such a strategy. This would refer to the development of human resources, namely, the benefit in a concentration of enlarging the organization's scope to international dimensions. The European executive feels this is not concrete enough to be included as an objective of a strategic plan. As an executive of an internationally concentrated group put it: 'The fact that European companies do not plan for the development of their human assets is a major obstacle to transnational concentration because this does not bring out the invaluable didactic benefit of these operations.'

The third reason is that, traditionally, European companies have had a national scope. Interviewees, and especially younger ones, believe European managers have been concerned with domestic affairs and have devoted little attention to international business. Allegedly, the result is that European management has not been open to international collaborative endeavours. Two major exceptions to this are Great Britain and Holland.[9] Historically, British firms have had an international scope but have tended to focus on the Commonwealth. Several British interviewees have noted that as a result British executives have developed a bias in that they expect to be the dominant party in any transnational collaborative endeavour. Thus, the scope of British executives does not extend to international business within the European framework. Holland, in fact, is the only real exception. This relatively small country has a remarkable history of international trade, and today it has the best examples of European-based multinational companies (e.g., Philips).

Apart from Holland, European management has tended to concentrate on its own national market. Companies have been busy with the postwar reconstruction and have had plenty of opportunities domestically. Management points out that it would have been ineffective to look to foreign markets when the potential was so great within national boundaries. As a consequence, companies have developed little transnational scope. Management has not been accustomed to looking abroad for new strategic alternatives. Now that there is a need for wider markets and a European corporate strategy, management recognizes the handicap of this national outlook. In particular, European managers' scope is not international enough to identify the desirability of a transnational concentration. As one executive said: 'We still have to internationalize our horizons in order to capitalize on the opportunities of international business; *a fortiori* we have a long way to go before we are able to identify the opportunities of transnational link-ups.'

The fourth reason given by managers is the entrepreneurial inertia of some European companies. These companies have a static strategic posture which is a slow evolution of past strategy; there is no attempt to challenge the fundamental direction of the business. Two reasons are alleged for this. First, a number of executives, particularly in Germany and Belgium, have stated that business is influenced by mature sectors such as mining or heavy industry. In other words, businessmen in general are affected by the mentality of mature industries. These industries have a long history of 'doing the same thing'. Basically, the administrator's task is to maintain the present state of affairs. As a German executive stated: 'There is a spillover effect from those sectors in which perpetuation of the past is a rewarding strategy, into those sectors where change should be the normal way of life.' Second, some companies have been started by a dynamic entrepreneur, whose way of doing business can still be felt. His family is still in control of the business and tends to perpetuate his work methods. This was found to be most common in France where the mark of the founder is preserved by his heirs. The result is that the company continues its line of business and no innovative policy is sought.

This entrepreneurial inertia leads companies to continue along traditional guidelines. Clearly, one of the strongest of these guidelines is the national framework. It should be emphasized that there is no aversion here to internationalization; there is no ethnocentrism as such. Rather, companies do not *see* the possibility of transnational consolidation, i.e., the way their strategy is developed does not allow adequate consideration of the concentration alternative. In this connection a Belgian executive made an interesting analysis which subsequently was submitted to other interviewees, many of whom agreed with it. In the past companies were usually conducted by the aristocracy of Europe. These men had received a cosmopolitan education and had a considerable international business tradition. They did not hesitate to invest in the farthest parts of the world and they created Europe's industrial units, thanks to their considerable entrepreneurial spirit. Then, a gradual socialization of management took place and lower-class people with a more regional *Weltanschauung* moved up into key positions. Their education was the product of local institutions and they had fewer opportunities to live in cosmopolitan environments. As a consequence, the scope of European firms shrank to provincial dimensions. The Belgian interviewee concluded: 'How can you expect a man of a rural background who may never really have had a chance to visit foreign countries, to be prone to make a deliberate search for business opportunities abroad?'

The fifth reason is the relative inexperience of European firms in the business of consolidations. As noted by Nicholas Stacey: 'Mergers and acquisitions may have been developed into a fine art by Anglo-American businessmen, but to the vast proportion of European businessmen this is a comparative novelty.'[10] Indeed, while US firms often have entire departments devoted to concentration activities, the majority of European managers reported they never even had to consider the possibility of a link-up. As an Italian interviewee put it: 'We in Europe are much too preoccupied with preserving our corporate identity and autonomy to be able to accept the idea of opening up our organizations to outsiders; we do it only in exceptional cases and not as a normal way of operating, as many American companies do.' The result of this unfamiliarity with corporate amalgamations is that the option of growing through a pooling of resources with external partners is not contemplated by European managers.

Those interviewees who had been exposed to US management practices were particularly articulate in saying that this state of affairs created an important handicap for transnational concentration because the alternative of a consolidation is simply not considered when a strategic plan is being developed. Further, even when such an alternative happens to be generated, it does not receive thorough and objective analysis. As a consultant said: 'In those instances where it does come up as a possibility, people analyse it with a negative bias; as they are unfamiliar with the process, they are scared of it and thus their analysis is really a search for reasons not to do it.'

The impact of this inadequate strategic planning for transnational concentration can be viewed in two distinct areas. First, cross-border consolidations are not generally considered, and their potential advantages are not recognized. Second, inadequate planning hampers an optimal development of those consolidations which actually do take place. These two areas will be discussed in turn.

UNAWARENESS OF CONCENTRATION POTENTIAL

The lack of appropriate consideration of the possible benefits of a link-up means there is no systematic search for potential synergies. Because they do not plan, companies neither realize the potential threat of isolationism in view of future business conditions nor the opportunities the international amalgamation route offers. Companies with international concentration experience often point out that they themselves were not previously aware of the true potential benefits of a concentration. 'People don't know what an international concentration can do for them', said an executive of one of these companies.

Inadequate analysis of the alternative of consolidating not only delays the potential benefits of a concentration, but also may expose companies to the risk of suddenly being surprised by the need to consolidate. This is less a need of today's business conditions than of the future competitive environment. Interviewees widely agreed that most sectors can at present accommodate large national companies on a viable economic basis. Should this not be enough, co-operative agreements across national boundaries are normally sufficient to allow companies to operate efficiently. It is only in rare instances that an international concentration is a necessity. Usually this was found to be the case either in high-technology, high-investment industries, or specialized sectors where competition from outside the EEC is particularly stiff and where there are no appropriate domestic partners. These are exceptional cases. In view of the *developing* environment, however, it is often desirable to form a transnational concentration. For example, while R & D costs can still be efficiently shared by two companies joining forces for a particular project, it is becoming clear that for many advanced industries the joint venture route soon will no longer suffice. For instance, in the computer business, basic research is reportedly reaching such dimensions that it is necessary for companies to join forces on a permanent basis. Only in this way can they develop the required basic knowledge on which specific individual projects rest. This situation in the computer business will become typical in other sectors. At that point European transnational companies will become a necessity.

The problem is that an international concentration cannot be improvised. As the second section of this chapter will discuss, it is desirable that a consolidation between two large companies of different nationalities be a gradual process. This is necessary to minimize disruption and clashes between the two organizations. A concentration must be prepared and sufficient time allowed before two companies can really operate as an integrated group. Consequently, it is necessary to begin the amalgamation process now if a concentration is desirable in the future. Depending on the sectors, the age of the company, and its ability to implement internal change, executives estimate the time required to complete the amalgamation process is between five and twenty years. This highlights the importance of strategic planning. It is vital to identify the need for a transnational link-up well ahead of time.

Management agrees that in the absence of appropriate planning the strategic posture of a company is determined by the current environment, not by a forecast of tomorrow's environment. In transnational collaborative endeavours an illustration of such sudden reactions is provided by the way international co-operative agreements have occurred. Reportedly, when companies realized they were unable to remain fully autonomous, they engaged in joint ventures in an abrupt fashion. Planning even in the high-technology, high-investment fields was fairly superficial. Moreover, most of the preliminary work was at the political rather than the managerial level. (Governments typically sponsor these ventures and public authorities spend considerable time to establish what each government has at stake.) In the words of an aircraft industry executive: 'International co-operative agreements took place on a rushed stimulus-response basis. Management reacted abruptly to the environment of the moment. It was a random, impulsive and disorderly process.'

While improvisation may be acceptable for co-operative agreements, it is not for concentrations. For co-operative agreements it may be bearable because the participating organizations remain essentially autonomous. The collaboration often involves direct contact of only a limited number of people and, in any event, the organizations remain basically unaltered; there is no radical blending and formation of a new organization. A consolidation, however, requires a very different sort of commitment. The original organizations must disappear and a new structure must emerge. This amalgamation requires several years to come about. While it was possible for companies to adapt rapidly to the need for co-operative agreements, they may well be caught short in an international concentration precisely because of the length of time needed to blend the organizations involved. Indeed, one may forecast that there will be a sudden wakening of companies to the necessity of transnational link-ups and that a number of such operations will take place. However, they may well run into serious trouble because there will be great pressure to integrate rapidly in order to meet the requirements of operating on a joint basis. Companies will have waited until environmental pressures make themselves felt. At that point it will be desirable to be able to *operate* as an integrated unit, but they will not be ready and will attempt to join forces too quickly. The above-mentioned computer sector may be the closest to such a point. In fact, as an executive of a US firm said: 'That point has already passed without people appearing to be aware of it. It seems to me that for Europeans to be able to efficiently compete against IBM would have required that they be really integrated since several years. This means they should have started to work together since at least the early 60s.'

In addition to the fact that they may not effectively capitalize on the opportunity of transnational concentration, companies may build up additional barriers to future concentration. In their attempt to remain autonomous, they adopt policies which render any future amalgamation with foreign companies difficult to realize. It was found that there are two principal areas where additional barriers are created when companies attempt to pursue a strategy of autonomy.

The first is that, by remaining autonomous, companies often engage in policy moves which reduce their complementarity with potential partners. Today managers report that companies in various countries tend to have distinctive expertise in a particular area, and are specialized in a given type of product or technique. This is reportedly because national demand has traditionally preferred a particular type of product or because the entrepreneurial initiative which has directed a company reflects the entrepreneur's particular ability or interest in producing that type of product. For example, pasta has been produced primarily by Italians, essentially because the demand was in Italy. However, with the gradual harmonization of demand, companies are marketing similar products throughout the EEC. To use the same example, pasta is now sold throughout Europe. If companies concentrate internationally, they have different products which they can sell in the various European countries. If an Italian company concentrates with a British company, it is conceivable that pasta would be sold in Britain through the distribution channels of the British partner, while gravy might be sold in Italy through the existing sales organization of the Italian partner. Here, then, companies are complementary and the synergistic potential quite high. If companies do not concentrate, however, they will have to expand their product line and start supplying products which they did not produce but which a foreign company might be producing. Since the national market will start demanding these products, national companies will have to begin producing them to hedge against imports. Pasta will have to be produced by non-Italian companies, and Italian companies may have to produce gravy.[11]

It should be clear that such policies are inefficient not only because there is a duplication of effort (as national companies have to commit resources to develop products which are already marketed by foreign companies), but also because this reduces the complementarity of the companies. As each company develops an increasingly similar product line, potential synergies disappear. This diminishes the attractiveness of international consolidations. Appropriate strategic planning should avoid these wasteful policies.

Not only are companies far from drawing the best possible advantage from concentration; they often build up additional barriers to any future link-up. Several executives reported that the lack of appropriate planning leads companies to commit themselves to co-operative agreements which end up obstructing possible concentrations. Quite often each new project involving a co-operative agreement also involves a new partner; in other words, each time a company engages in a co-operative agreement, it seeks out a different partner. The result is that every company has several co-operative agreements with as many (or nearly as many) partners. Executives report that when co-operative agreements are no longer sufficient and concentration is sought, companies find they cannot consolidate with a particular company because they have commitments to others; the multiple co-operative agreements stand in the way of a concentration with one definite partner. The best example was provided by interviewees of a large aircraft company.

About two decades ago it was still possible to be a viable aircraft producer within the national boundaries of European countries. Then with the increasing investment requirements for the development of new models, it became more and more difficult to produce new aircraft alone. (Probably the last big success of a purely national commercial air transport was the French Caravelle developed in the late 'fifties.) It became apparent that co-operative agreements across national boundaries were necessary. As a consequence, virtually all European companies signed such agreements. Indeed, each company signed several co-operative agreements with various partners. For each new project a new partner was selected. This was facilitated by the fact that the industry permits considerable isolation of groups of people working on different projects in the same company. A company can have a co-operative agreement with one partner for a given model and be in competition with him for another model.[12] A remarkable web of international co-operative agreements has developed, and these agreements impede concentration because each company is committed to every other company. Conflicting loyalties make concentration very difficult, in addition to which cooperative agreements in the aircraft industry usually cover several decades. Figure 7.1 presents charts provided by the company, indicating the co-operative agreements in existence today which are expected to still be in existence in 1983. This shows that concentration will stumble over conflicting co-operative agreements for several years.

It is expected that companies will have to concentrate despite these links. A few large transnational groups will emerge and there will be spin-offs of departments of certain companies engaged in a conflicting co-operative agreement. For example, if in group (A) there is a company

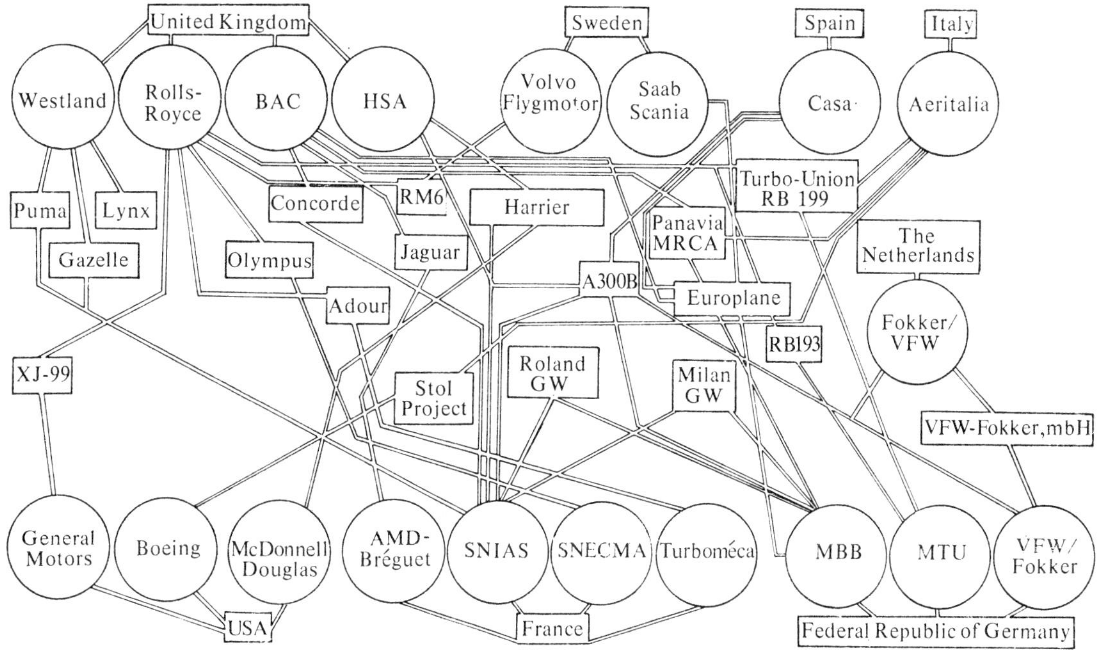

Fig. 7.1a. Existing collaborative links likely to be still functioning in 1983 among European aerospace manufacturers.

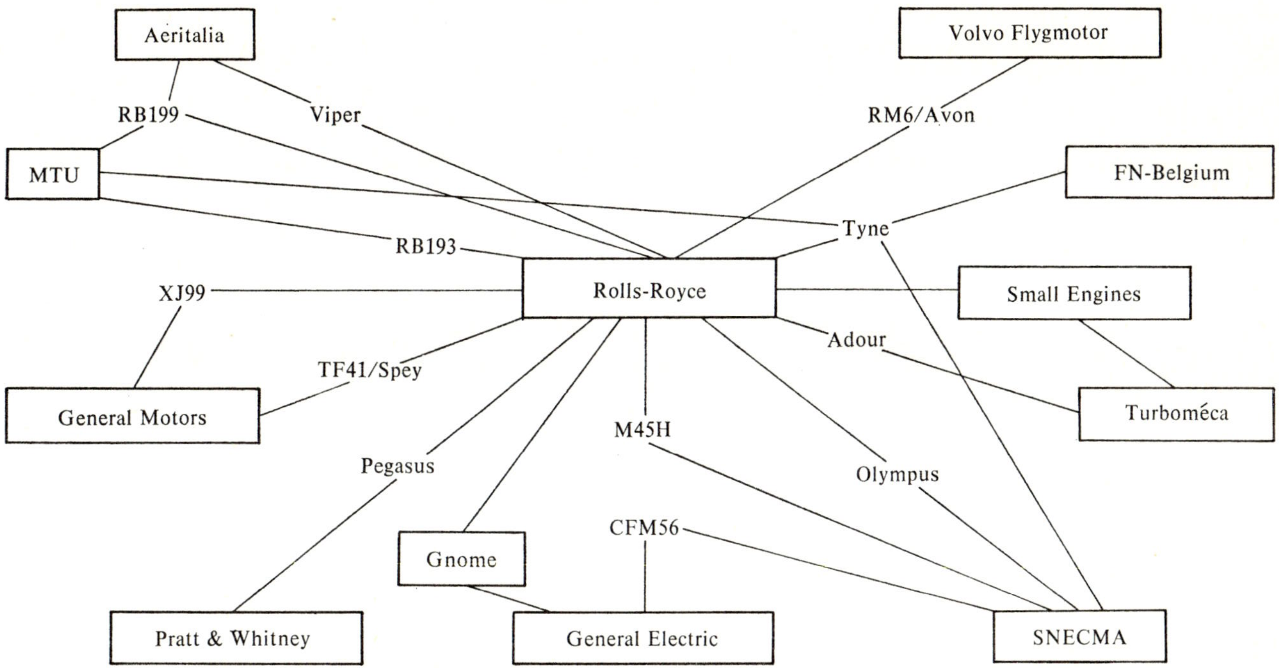

Fig. 7.1b. Existing international collaborative links likely to be still functioning in 1983 among air frame manufacturers.

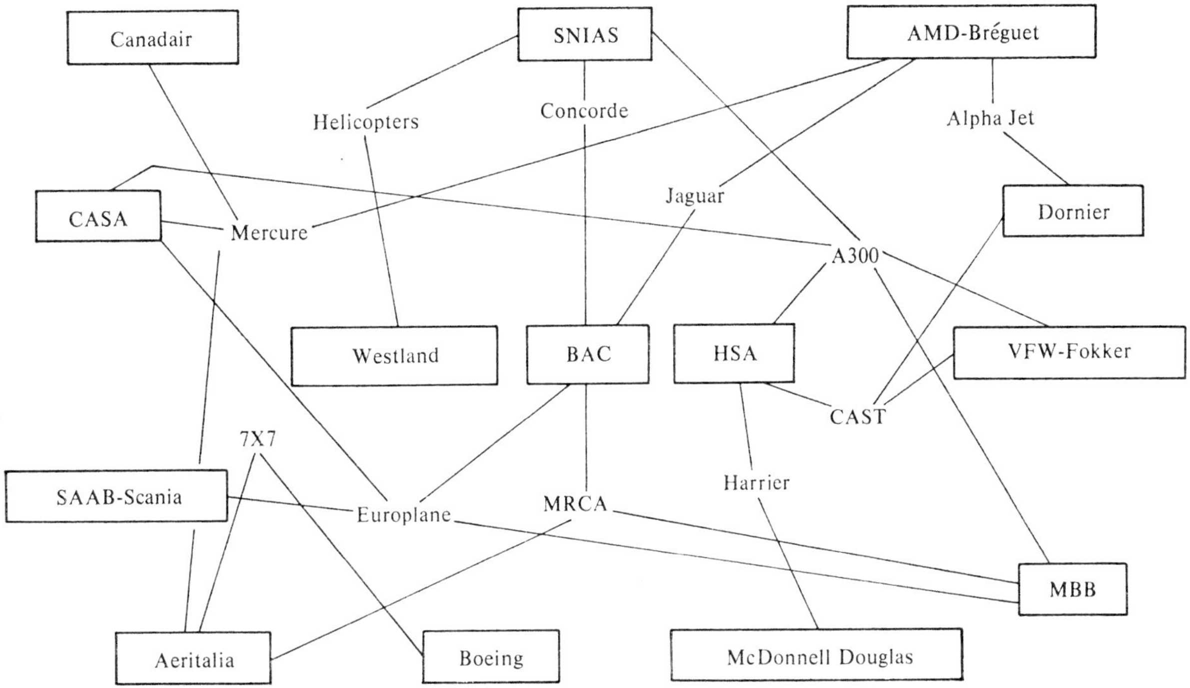

Fig. 7.1c. Existing international collaborative links likely to be still functioning in 1983 among aero-engine manufacturers.

which has a co-operative agreement for project (X) with a company of group (B), the department of one of the two companies working on project (X) might be sold to the other group. Clearly, this is not efficient. Executives are the first to deplore this state of affairs, which could have been avoided with appropriate planning.[13]

A comparable state of affairs can be found in several other fields, quite apart from high-technology sectors. For example, banking may be headed in a similar direction. Individual banks often engage in several co-operative agreements at a time, with various partners.[14] This is a realistic response to present difficulties in concentrating. However, several of the interviewed bankers think that the day may not be far distant when a concentration of banks will become viable. These bankers believe that if it is not planned for, banks may well be in a position similar to that of the aircraft industry where conflicting links will hinder a concentration. Some banks are in fact taking steps which will avoid such conflicts. While they too are adapting to the current necessity of co-operating, they are doing so in a way which will not hinder possible concentration in the future. Indeed, their co-operative agreements are so designed that they would prove to be a useful preparation if a consolidation were actually pursued. The best example is the agreement between Commerzbank, Crédit Lyonnais, and Banco di Roma. These three banks have chosen to respond to the pressure for co-operation in a way which may be comparable to what other banks are doing.[15] Their co-operation aims at achieving the same goals as other banks' co-operative agreements.[16] The difference is that they have made an explicit commitment to achieve these goals through a co-operation among themselves, as opposed to the policy of loose co-operation of other banks, which calls for 'selecting the best partner for each project', as one banker put it. Several interviewed bankers have criticized this agreement precisely because they feel it is possible today to achieve better results by preserving one's autonomy and engaging in *ad hoc* joint ventures with the most appropriate partner for each project. However, it may well be that in the long run the three banks will prove to have adopted the most rewarding strategy. If, indeed, further EEC integration occurs, those banks which engage in co-operative agreements in an orderly fashion should be better prepared to face the need for further integration. As one of these bankers observed: 'If you bet on Europe, you have to give up some flexibility today to be stronger tomorrow.'

SUBOPTIMAL EFFECTS

Turning to the second area of impact of inadequate strategic planning, let us consider those few consolidations which actually do take place. Even in the absence of effective planning, the possibility of a consolidation may still occur to a 'corporate strategist'. It was found that often some exogenous event may cause the strategist to pursue the possibility of a consolidation. In such instances, the lack of systematic strategic analysis hinders the optimal development of the concentration.[17]

During the data analysis of the first set of interviews there was evidence that today's unions may have been the product of a less than rational process. During the second set of interviews respondents widely confirmed these doubts. Specifically, the decisions which have led to corporate link-ups may have been close to the following model: (1) chance contact with partner → (2) fortuitous birth of a concentration idea → (3) emotional or quasi-emotional commitment to concentrate → (4) *ex post facto* rationalization of the decision. In this process the two future partners have a relationship caused by some outside event in which the idea of joining forces emerges casually, for instance, during 'a golf-course conversation'—as a British executive put it. In connection with this, several interviewees pointed out the importance of the 'me, too' type of motivation. A French executive said: 'Concentrations are now in style, so people talk about them at cocktail parties. Then they fall in love with the idea. Concentrations are often the epilogue of passionate love affairs.'

This discussion applies both for a national and a transnational concentration. The distinctive feature of a transnational concentration is that the 'chance contact with partner' is less likely to occur because managers have fewer opportunities to meet internationally or to be acquainted with one another across national boundaries.[18] In fact, much of the evidence to support this model comes at present from national consolidations. In this respect, Jacqueline Grapin writes about the fusion of the French companies Ugine and Kuhlman: 'It was said that their presidents liked to play golf together. At least, they often lunched at the same table.' She then goes on to imply that this friendship was the prime basis for the consolidation.[19] Further, executives of companies that are the product of consolidations agree that there was neither a search for an optimal partner nor an adequate investigation of the pros and cons of a concentration. 'We decided to concentrate, then we found out why', said an executive of a consolidated company. On the international scene there is also considerable evidence that consolidations are often due to chance events. An example, previously noted, is the preponderant role allegedly played by the personal friendship between Sir Reay Geddes and Ingegner Leopoldo Pirelli in the Dunlop–Pirelli union. Furthermore, it is noteworthy that when asked why a particular partner was selected, executives of transnationally concentrated groups frequently say that it was because the partner was the foreign company with which their own company was best acquainted.

There are two reasons why such a decision-making process leads to suboptimal concentration policies. Both derive from the inadequate planning described above. First, there is no search for the best possible partner. The decision to go ahead and concentrate is not taken on its own merits, but rather with a particular partner in mind. There is no analysis of the desirability of concentrating *per se*, and no assurance that the company is joining forces with the best possible partner. Hopefully an adequate planning system would avoid such a risk. Once the advisability of consolidating has been established in principle, separate analysis should be made of the possibility of joining forces with each potential partner in order to identify the best partner.

In fact, this problem is normally of limited importance in today's concentrations among very large firms. There are usually few potential partners for these companies and they are sufficiently well known to management. As a consequence, the search problem is greatly simplified. However, should smaller firms become involved in transnational amalgamations, the search problem would be of greater importance because of the greater number of available partners.

Second, there is a high emotional commitment involved in a decision to concentrate which strongly reduces the possibility of objectively evaluating its advisability. Interviewees widely believe that once the idea of a concentration is born, people become emotionally committed to it and that the decision to consolidate is made without a true analysis of the facts involved. As a member of a professional association put it: 'The whole decision to concentrate is emotional. It is only after the decision is made that people try to rationalize it for the outside world. When the President announces to his staff that he wants an investigation of the possibility of a concentration, he has already decided—more or less subconsciously—that such a concentration shall take place. He has made this decision based on intuition, without any systematic examination of the pros and cons involved.'

The result of such an emotional decision-making process is that there is little candid evaluation of the desirability of concentrating in the first place, or of the desirability of joining forces with the particular partner under consideration. Here again, a systematic planning process would normally take a more rigourous approach to the decision of concentrating. As stated by a corporate planner of a recently consolidated group of companies which was encountering considerable difficulty in its amalgamation process: 'If we [corporate planners] were really given a chance to have our say, there would be a substantial reduction of the inefficiencies which derive from going into a consolidation on such an impulsive basis. Choice of partner, timing, and overall modalities of the concentration would be optimized.'

The fundamental recommendation one can make for the problems discussed in this section is that of improving the strategic planning function. Generally speaking, European companies would often do well to establish corporate planning departments which would truly report directly to top management. It was found that many companies had planning departments, but that these departments had little or no direct contact with top management. What is important is that there be a *true* interaction between the staff of the planning department and the head of the line, represented by top management. In this regard, the necessity of top management's involvement in the planning process (namely, the involvement of whoever actually determines the strategic posture of the firm), as well as the involvement of the planner in the development of the corporate strategy itself, cannot be too strongly emphasized. In addition, in order to temper what an American executive termed 'Europeans' impulsiveness in management' it may be advisable for firms to refer more to outsiders when developing their corporate strategy. Professional consultants should add to the objectivity as well as the thoroughness of the analysis. As was discussed several times already, company link-ups are a very sensitive area for Europeans since, in the words of a French executive, 'the organization's freedom and thus its dignity are at stake'. In view of the emotional nature of the problem, the potential contribution of a consultant is particularly important in the concentration decision.

Finally, and more specifically with regard to the decision-making process for a consolidation, the following model should improve the effectiveness of the strategist's analysis of the desirability to join forces with a partner: (1) generation of the strategic alternative of an international link-up → (2) in principle resolution to concentrate with 'ideal' partner (specification of his characteristics) → (3) search for partner → (4) feasibility study → (5) decision to concentrate. In this process the corporate strategist analyses the firm's resources and its environment in a dynamic fashion. In so doing, he identifies the desirability of joining forces with another firm. He then establishes the features of the ideal partner, namely, that partner with whom the consolidation would be most synergistic. He then searches for the potential partner that best approximates the ideal partner. Negotiations take place which, if successful, lead to an in-depth analysis of the possibility of actually consolidating. If this analysis indicates that the concentration is attractive, the decision to join forces is made.[20]

Clearly, this is a theoretical and simplistic model of the decision process. However, it should highlight two major features of a rational way to tackle the concentration question: first, the felt need for a link-up precedes the analysis of a possibility of joining forces with a particular partner. In this way the corporate strategist may examine the advisability of a concentration without the bias of having a specific partner in mind. He is thus able to establish criteria of what an 'ideal' partner should be. Further, once this is done, he is able to search for the optimal partner; he is uncommitted and free to seek the partner that best fits his needs. Second and most important, there is a deliberate effort to generate the strategic alternative of a union. This alternative does not occur to the decision-maker by chance. He makes a conscious attempt to analyse the possibility of a concentration on its own merits.

Implementing a concentration in sequential policy moves

Throughout this study the desirability of creating a concentration in progressive stages has been mentioned. This section describes a model of a gradual amalgamation process. It should be viewed as a recommended action plan designed to circumvent many of the obstacles discussed previously.[21]

At the outset, one point should be re-emphasized. It is addressed particularly to the US reader. As noted by Krekel, Van der Woerd, and Wouterse, American literature makes little distinction between mergers and acquisitions, and concerns itself for the most part with the latter.[22] It is important to re-emphasize what was discussed in chapter 1: this study is concerned mainly with the fusion of two large economic entities of comparable size. The model which will be described shortly is designed to alleviate the problems deriving from the amalgamation of two similar organizations in which the hierarchy of one clashes with the hierarchy of the other. In an acquisition these problems are far simpler and a gradual amalgamation process far less necessary.

This is all the more important for American readers, as for many US companies 'mergers and acquisitions are a way of life and nearly an objective in and of themselves', as an executive of a US company put it. Several American companies pursue a growth strategy explicitly based on 'mergers and acquisitions'. The best instances are conglomerates, which are far more widespread in the US than in Europe. Here, not only is the combination of companies virtually always a take-over, but normally there is no true integration of the acquired company into the acquirer's structure. The union may amount to little more than an investment by the acquiring company in the acquired firm, which more often than not is left as an autonomous organization. The use of a gradual amalgamation process in such instances is limited. Indeed, the model is most effective where there is to be a full integration of the firms involved. It is in these cases that all the organizational problems discussed earlier in this study (particularly those discussed in chapter 6) appear fully, and it is these problems which this model is designed to solve, at least in part.

In fact, the model might often be totally out of place in the context of an 'acquisition strategy' as carried out by US conglomerates. The model requires several years for a consolidation to be implemented. In an 'acquisition strategy' this would normally be too long in view of the competitive environment: a slow concentration process may result in many opportunities being lost to competition. Generally speaking, this is not true in the type of consolidations discussed in this study. Here, it is possible to forecast the competitive environment and thus plan the concentration to adapt to it: if the need for concentration is forecast, then companies can initiate the amalgamation process sufficiently in advance to be ready when the environment makes it desirable for them to operate as concentrated units. The situation large European companies face is indeed quite different from that of the US-type conglomerate. Their problem is typically not to implement a strategy of capitalizing on a number of opportunities through a series of 'mergers and acquisitions'. Rather, their problem is to join forces with their foreign EEC counterparts in order to form European corporations with a sufficiently broad scope to be competitive on a global basis. The competitive pressures requiring such pooling of resources are much more amenable to advance forecasting than the environmental variables a conglomerate has to react to in its acquisition policies. As a consequence, it is possible to programme the implementation of a consolidation with a much broader time perspective than is generally possible in an 'acquisition strategy'.

The above discussion highlights the link between the need to plan adequately for a concentration and the gradual implementation of a concentration.[23] Implementing a concentration in progressive stages appears to carry with it considerable promise for reducing the impact of many of the difficulties dealt with in this study. It requires, however, many years for its completion. This re-emphasizes the need for strategic planning: the amalgamation process should be started several years before the companies involved face the actual need to operate as an integrated group.

A hasty implementation of a consolidation reduces the effectiveness of a joining of forces of two organizations. A number of the clashes discussed throughout this study could be avoided through a gradual amalgamation process. Specifically, it calls for four stages.

Stage I can be called 'sowing one's wild oats'. It calls for companies to become used to working with foreign partners. Specifically, it consists of companies engaging in international *ad hoc* joint ventures. These agreements are 'one shot': they do not tie the partners together beyond the one particular activity for which they desire to collaborate. As was seen in chapter 6, European companies are often overly national in scope and do not feel sufficiently at home in an international environment. It is desirable that they engage in international operations prior to a concentration. Joint ventures with foreign companies provide this experience while they familiarize management with collaborating with foreign counterparts. Activities such as import-export are not enough to provide the necessary experience. Managers of different countries actually have to work together with a common objective and become accustomed to being interdependent. This should generate a certain feeling of mutual trust. In this first stage, companies should also begin to learn to identify the type of partners they are best able to work with. A good example of such *ad hoc* joint ventures is provided by the banking sector. Banks often undertake joint financial operations (with one or several foreign partners), which do not involve any particular intent of further collaboration. Other examples are common procurement from a single source of supply for a given product, common distribution of certain products in certain foreign markets, and exchange of know-how on selective activities.[24] Indeed, it is important that these joint ventures *not* become binding over the long run. Companies would otherwise fall into conflicting co-operative links of the type surveyed in the first section of this chapter.

Stage II can be called 'engagement'. Companies select a particular partner with whom they feel especially compatible. Specifically, close co-operative agreements are warranted—typically with no financial participation. The agreement is no more an *ad hoc* joint venture. It is a commitment tying two companies together for the purpose of collaborating on a substantial portion of each other's overall activities. The companies actually work together and have a strategic commitment to each other, but they retain their juridical, financial, and organizational autonomy. They have a common goal, or at least very similar goals, and are dependent on each other for the attainment of this goal, but they retain their independence. This means they have separate managements (possibly, with co-ordinating units) and separate financial structures (possibly with an elaborate system of transfer prices for the sharing of costs). This gives a company the opportunity to work closely with the partner it may finally choose for concentration. The companies may size each other up while they take steps to increase their congruence. They may prepare for integration by making their respective product lines more complementary. They may make massive exchanges of managers in order to expose their people to the partner's organization and to his environment. They may even begin to integrate and rationalize parts of their organizations (e.g., R & D or marketing departments). Examples of such co-operative agreements are the MAN/Saviem agreement in the trucking industry[25] or the Commerzbank/Banco di Roma/Crédit Lyonnais agreement.[26] In fact, this stage might also apply to those agreements in which the parties collaborate on a particular large-scale project. An example here is the agreement between SNIAS of France and BAC of Britain for the development of the Concorde—a supersonic commercial airtransport.[27] Although the companies may not have an explicit commitment to any collaboration beyond the particular project, the scope of this project and its time frame are so broad that the agreement should be considered as Stage II (instead of Stage I).[28]

Stage III can be called 'concubinage'. Here companies actually consolidate. This corresponds to the amalgamations as defined in this study. If Stage II has been successful and if the companies have convinced themselves of their congruence, they may decide to fully integrate their operations. This is a *de facto* merger. Companies adopt an integrated strategy and operate as a single economic entity. There is a common organizational structure and a single top management. Rationalization is progressively brought about. It is, in fact, a mere continuation of the integration begun in the second stage. Managers are used to working with foreigners and thus have fewer psychological reservations. Examples of these forms of link-ups have been discussed throughout this study. Besides bypassing the impossibility of doing a *de jure* merger, the hybrid solutions described in chapter 2 allow enough flexibility to tailor the format of the collaboration to the particular needs of the companies, while calling for their full amalgamation.

Stage IV can be called 'marriage'. It is the *de jure* merger. It merely consists of a formalization of Stage III. The amalgamation of the companies is complete, and management wishes to give it its final juridical form. There are as yet no examples of such mergers. The first reason is, of course, the legal impossibility of merging discussed in chapter 2. In addition to the legal barrier, it is important to point out that there are very few companies which would be ready for this stage.[29] The vast majority of interviewed managers believe there are no companies which have yet reached a sufficient degree of internal integration to warrant an international merger, even if this were legally possible.

At this point, the question arises of how long it takes to complete the amalgamation process. No clear-cut answer can be given here.[30] The first stage really depends on the degree of 'provincialism' of the companies. Certain executives felt that their organizations were so traditionally national in outlook that it might take as long as eight years to develop a sufficiently international perspective for the smooth implementation of a link-up. Other firms are so international that Stage I could be skipped completely. Furthermore, Stage IV today encounters the problem that there is no legal instrument. In fact, how long it takes from Stage III to Stage IV really depends on what type of legal instrument is made available to the companies. If it is the statute for a European company proposed by the EEC Commission, it can be predicted that the time will be quite long. If it is a more flexible instrument such as the closed limited company proposed by CREDA, the time may be as short as two years.[31]

What is most relevant here, however, is the time needed between the beginning of Stage II and the end of Stage III. This covers the period from the beginning of the collaboration to full integration—the progress two companies make from the point where they actually 'choose' each other (to the exclusion of third companies) to the point where they form a single economic entity. The second set of interviews revealed that this period can vary between five and twelve years.[32] Executives believe three major factors have a bearing on the length of this period.

The first factor is the size and complexity of the companies involved. If the companies are large diversified organizations, the amalgamation will be slow. The second factor is the extent to which synergies are tangible. For example, if the synergies concern the product line the amalgamation will be faster. In the Agfa–Gevaert concentration the companies had clear areas of competence in their respective product lines (Agfa in the amateur segment and Gevaert in the professional segment). The fact that the product lines complement each other renders the integration easier 'because things complete each other in such an unlabored way that everything falls into its place in a natural fashion', as one executive said. If, on the other hand, synergies are of a more intangible nature, the integration will be slower. For example, the consolidation of the basic R & D activities can pose delicate human problems. Here it is necessary for the R & D departments to share their know-how, and the people involved may resist the disclosure of knowledge. This is rendered more complex by the tendency of engineers to undervalue the economic benefits of a pooling of interests. 'They don't really care about economic reasons and it is hard to sell them on the desirability of collaborating with foreigners', said an interviewee.

The third factor influencing the length of Stages II and III is represented by some of the 'human' difficulties surveyed in chapter 6. Specifically, the compatibility of organizational structures plays an important role. If two companies are organized in a similar fashion—say, on a product line/profit centre basis—the integration will be swifter than if the organizations have different patterns. A more important variable is the degree of management's resistance to change, namely, the internal ability (or willingness) of the organization to adapt to new working methods.

One factor which should not have a major influence on the length of this period is the degree of 'provincialism' of the managements involved. It is important that companies do not engage in international collaborative endeavours if their management does not have a sufficiently international scope. This internationalization should take place in Stage I: Stage II should not commence until Stage I is completed.

Such a gradual amalgamation process seems warranted in view of the organizational and human problems surveyed throughout this study and, in particular, in the last two chapters. The advantage of this process should be that it trains people for an international concentration prior to its occurrence. As will be discussed shortly, it is designed to maximize synergies and to minimize clashes. In enabling people to 'learn by doing' it overcomes 'provincialism' and the lack of effective formal training courses available to internationalize the scope of managers. They are gradually exposed to an increasing degree of transnational collaboration and given experience with foreigners before they have to make a union with them. Indeed, as stated in the *EEC Memorandum:* 'Co-operative agreements generally represent an indispensable stage prior to a more integrated type of co-operation between two or more enterprises. By preserving the personality and the autonomy of the partners they do not provoke the same psychological inhibitions as a fusion or an absorption. Benefits and difficulties of collaboration can be evaluated during this phase, which often represents an indispensable test for the implementation of any type of more advanced economic integration.'[33] Specifically, there are four principal areas in which this process offers advantages.

The first should be to reduce the appraisal gap. Stage I should provide management with sufficient exposure to foreign environments and foreign companies which might become collaboration partners. Furthermore, it should develop their skill in identifying areas of compatibility and areas of friction. Working relationships with foreign organizations should teach management to appraise their behaviour and the possibility of integrating their own organization with the foreign one. Also, it should bridge the information gap on foreign markets and general working conditions. Stage II should provide an opportunity to verify the compatibility of the partner, which might become the concentration partner. This is, in a way, an acceptance test to ascertain whether a permanent union is desirable and what form it should take.

Second, this process should develop skills required in a transnational collaboration as well as congruence of the organizations involved. Managers should learn international business methods (e.g., become familiar with international finance techniques, exchange control restrictions, customs, etc.). Even more important, they should acquire the 'international business skill' discussed in chapter 6, namely, the ability to collaborate closely with foreigners in an effective fashion. Moreover, it should prepare companies for the concentration by increasing their compatibility. An effort of each company to emphasize its distinctive competences should result in increased synergy. For example, the development of new products can be done in such a way as to avoid duplication: each company can make a deliberate choice to restrict itself to those products in which it has an advantage (instead of trying to cover the whole line of products on its own). At the same time, companies may gradually adapt their organizations and internal procedures to each other. For example, control systems may gradually be harmonized.

The third advantage is that this process reduces the impact of management's resistance to change. Interviewees with transnational collaboration experience strongly emphasized this point. The fact that the collaboration is progressively brought about generates far less reluctance to co-operate. As an interviewee of a company which might be considered in Stage II said: 'Foreigners are sources of change and of contestation of the *status quo*: if you bring too many of them in at once, people will resist them because it is simply more change than they can take. If you introduce only a few sources of change at a time, people will digest them much better. This will avoid the typical rejection phenomenon of concentrations.' Furthermore, this process will reduce the impact of the perceived threat of a consolidation. The fact that managers have a chance to begin to collaborate in relatively minor co-operative agreements will enable them to become familiar with this type of endeavour without feeling the pressure of a full-fledged concentration. In Stages I and II managers are exposed to their foreign counterparts but are not 'competing' against them because they are not part of the same hierarchy. Consequently, they have a chance to realize that no anxiety is warranted in collaborating with foreigners, that foreigners do not constitute a threat to their personal careers. Finally, Stage II should foster mutual trust. Cohesiveness should develop for both managers and technical staff, who work together towards a common goal. Indeed, gradual integration should avoid the psychological disruption of a sudden consolidation, while fostering the feeling of belonging to one group.

The fourth area is—in the eyes of managers—as important as the third one: the process reduces the effects of 'nationalism' and 'misconceptions' discussed in chapter 6. To repeat, these barriers are, for the most part, either the result of inhibitions due to 'provincialism' or of ignorance about foreigners' human traits. Stages I and II of the amalgamation process are aimed, among other things, at resolving these two types of problems. Managers are given the opportunity to broaden their scope to international dimensions at a pace which fits them best (i.e., a very nationally oriented organization will spend more time in Stage I). As a German interviewee put it: 'The nationalistic feelings of a man permit him to go only so far in a collaboration; he can work together with a foreigner but he does not want to be dependent on him. However, once he gets used to this relationship, he unconsciously encroaches on his nationalistic beliefs and slowly gets used to becoming quite deeply involved in international relations.' Moreover, the first stages of the amalgamation process reduce the *a priori* misconceptions about foreigners. The fact that people do not feel the immediate pressure to become totally involved in a collaboration enables them to be more open-minded about working with foreigners. The first stages are, in this respect, a surrogate for training opportunities which would provide knowledge about foreigners.

Despite the limited number of international consolidations which have actually taken place, there is some evidence that those link-ups that were the product of a gradual amalgamation process were smoother and more successful than the more hasty consolidations.[34] For example, VFW–Fokker was a happy union. The two companies were international in outlook and had extensive collaborative experience, as they had worked together for several years on a co-operative agreement basis (e.g., they jointly produced the Lockheed Starfighter).

A different example is provided by Akzo–Glanzstoff. Prior to the amalgamation the Dutch company AKU (which subsequently consolidated with another Dutch company KZO, thus forming AKZO) had a stock participation in the German company Glanzstoff. The top managements of the two companies had frequent opportunities to see each other and had worked together since 1929. Moreover, some departments of the firms had also collaborated for many years. However, for the rest AKU and Glanzstoff operated as two independent organizations and the majority of the companies' people had little exposure to each other. When the two companies decided to consolidate in 1969, top management took it for granted that the organizations were familiar with each other. Because of their own contacts, they failed to perceive the actual gap which existed among the two groups. As a result, the amalgamation was resisted by the organizations. While there were relatively few difficulties at top management level, there were serious clashes at other levels. However, integration in those departments which had been collaborating for several years created far less difficulties than integration in departments which were strangers to each other. Indeed, the AKZO–Glanzstoff case provides an interesting illustration of the benefits of collaborating prior to a concentration: within the same company, the blending of people who had been exposed to each other in advance was notably smoother than that of people who were strangers to each other.

In fact, a number of executives of internationally consolidated groups believe that their own consolidation was too rapid. They report that the integration had to be implemented more slowly than they had planned. In the first few years following their formal concentration, the degree of amalgamation was less than they expected. In terms of the model discussed in this section they were *de facto* in Stage II, while they had adopted the form of Stage III. In this connection, the more recent concentrations (e.g., Dunlop–Pirelli) might be regarded as in Stage II.

This model has two implications. The first is for companies. Besides being normative and thus prescriptive in its very essence (i.e., it is *per se* a recommendation), this model highlights the necessity for strategic planning. For two companies of different nationalities, many years are required to become fully integrated. Top management may be well advised to give serious thought to the desirability of transnational link-ups in the perspective of business conditions expected a few decades hence.

The second implication is for governmental agencies. As was mentioned in chapter 2, the EEC Commission's efforts are out of temporal focus. It attempts to make international mergers possible, while companies are not ready for this. Normally, they are ready for Stage II, or at best, Stage III. It is the legal operations of these stages which should be perfected. Specifically, the fiscal barriers encountered by the hybrid forms of concentration need the most urgent correction[35] (primarily the operating fiscal barriers).[36] Indeed, it appears that the availability of the merger route could even lead companies into error. As with certain concentrations, companies may rush the amalgamation process and engage in the ultimate stage of the process before being ready for it. This would unduly reduce their flexibility while causing painful organizational disruptions.

NOTES

1. See, for example:

(a) *La politique industrielle de la Communauté, Memorandum de la Commission au Conseil*, Commission des Communautés Européennes, Brussels, 1970 (hereinafter cited as *EEC Memorandum*), pp. 275–76.

(b) Philip A. Klein, 'The Development of Planning in European Business Firms', *European Business*, No. 4, February 1965, pp. 30–41.

2. This was determined essentially through the insights of interviewees who had been staff executives or consultants (particularly interesting were those who could make comparisons with US companies). These interviewees always felt that the relative lack of planning was one of the most serious handicaps of European industry. In the subsequent discussion about the reasons for this inadequate planning, especially valuable data were provided by the reported experiences of people who had worked with managers of another nationality.

3. In 1968, among the large Italian firms, only 17·9 per cent were said to have any long-range plan for strategy formulation. See 'Il consulente aziendale in Italia', *Successo*, No. 12, December 1968, pp. 133–45, at p. 140.

4. Younger interviewees with formal business education were more articulate about this point.

5. For a discussion of the planning function in France, see:

(a) Hans Schoellhammer, 'Corporate Planning in France', *European Business*, July 1969, pp. 22–31.

(b) John H. McArthur and Bruce R. Scott, *Industrial Planning in France*, Division of Research, Graduate School of Business Administration, Harvard University, Boston, 1969, Chapter V, pp. 153–81.

6. Roger M. Godino, 'A propos du Séminaire International sur le Long Range Planning', *European Business*, No. 4, February 1965, p. 20. (This quote was translated from the French text.)

7. For a discussion of planning in Germany, see: H. J. Worms, 'How Does German Industry Plan?' *European Business*, February 1967, pp. 20–30.

8. See: Paul E. Holden, Carlton A. Pederson, and Gayton E. Germane, *Top Management*, McGraw-Hill, New York, 1968, pp. 42–44.

9. The following discussion, which at first was the product of the researcher's speculations, was widely confirmed by second set interviewees.

10. Nicholas Stacey, *Mergers in Modern Business*, Hutchinson, London, 1970, p. 122.

11. The pasta example is, in fact, a real one. Particularly in France, national companies are producing pasta at an increasing rate.

12. Thus the British Aircraft Corporation has a co-operative agreement with the French Bréguet for the production of the Jaguar—a supersonic military aircraft. A few years after the agreement was signed, Bréguet was bought by another French company, Dassault, which was itself producing an aircraft—the Mirage, which is in competition with the Jaguar.

13. It should be pointed out that these executives allege that they had to engage in co-operative agreements and could not prepare for concentrations because of governments' opposition to the transnationalization of their companies.

14. See: Mary Campbell, 'The Top 300', *The Banker*, June 1971, pp. 628–97.

15. See: James B. Warden, 'International Banking in the Seventies', *Columbia Journal of World Business*, July–August 1972, pp. 67–72.

16. Ugo Piccione, 'Cross-Border Banking', *European Communities*, May 1971, pp. 14–15.

17. The following discussion is, in fact, conjectural. In a way, it amounts to formulating a hypothesis which might be usefully tested by behavioural researchers. Nevertheless, based on this study's data there is strong evidence for the plausibility of such a hypothesis.

18. See the discussion in chapter 6.

19. Jacqueline Grapin, 'Il n'y a pas que des mariages heureux...', *Le Monde*, 5 September, 1972, p. 17.

20. For a similar discussion, see: Fred W. Taylor, 'Anatomy of a Merger', *Mergers and Acquisitions*, November–December 1970, pp. 8–19.

21. This model was developed as the result of the analysis of the first set of interviews: in view of the problems managers described, it seemed an effective way of implementing a consolidation. The model was then amply discussed with second set interviewees who widely agreed to its potential usefulness.

22. N. R. A. Krekel, T. G. Van der Woerd, and J. J. Wouterse, *Mergers—A European Approach to Technique*, Business Books, London, 1969, pp. 6–7.

23. See: Michel A. Carré and Philippe M. Bouvard, 'The Courtship and Honeymoon of Successful Mergers', *European Business*, April 1970, pp. 36–43.

24. For examples of this type of agreement, see any of the issues of *A Weekly Report on the Economy of the Common Market*, Opera Mundi Europe, Paris.

25. For a description of this Franco–German agreement, see: Werner J. Feld, *Transnational Business Collaboration among Common Market Countries*, Praeger, New York, 1970, pp. 34–35.

26. For a description of this agreement, see: Paul M. Goldberg, 'The Evolution of Transnational Companies in Europe', Ph.D. Dissertation, Massachusetts Institute of Technology, Sloan School of Management, 1971, pp. 194–200.

27. For a description of this agreement, see: Christopher Layton, *European Advanced Technology: A Programme for Integration*, PEP, George Allen & Unwin, London, 1969, pp. 136–42.

28. For further illustration of such co-operative agreements, see: *Grenzueberschreitende Unternehmenskooperation in der EWG*, Comité Européen pour le Progrès Economique et Social (CEPES), Vorkel Verlag, Stuttgart, 1968; in particular pp. 75–143, which present thirty case studies.

29. In fact, among the companies which were interviewed in this study, only one stated that it was ready.

30. A similar analysis is made in: Michel A. Carré and Philippe M. Bouvard, 'The Courtship and Honeymoon of Successful Mergers', pp. 42–43.

31. See note 67 in chapter 2.

32. Comparable data can be found in N. R. A. Krekel, T. G. Van der Woerd, and J. J. Wouterse, *Mergers—A European Approach to Technique*, pp. 67–125, at p. 117.

33. *EEC Memorandum*, p. 142. This quote was translated from the French text.

34. It should be clear that the following examples do not attempt to *prove* the validity of the model. Rather, they are designed to illustrate it, as well as to provide some support for its realism.

35. See the discussion in the third section of chapter 2.

36. It may also be desirable to develop a legal instrument for Stages II or III, such as the *Groupement d'Intérêt Economique* (see note 67 in chapter 2). This would,

essentially, correspond to a tool which leaves considerable freedom to the parties involved. However, it should be pointed out that such an instrument would not basically alter the actual results of collaboration as companies are able to do it today; it would not make a substantial contribution to companies' economic or managerial integration. It would simply provide a formal framework. In this respect, its major contribution might well be that of reducing the inhibitions deriving from the hybrid forms of concentration discussed in chapter 2.

8.

SYNTHESIS

This chapter recapitulates the material presented throughout this study. The first of the three sections is a synthesis of the most important obstacles to transnational concentration from top management's perspective. A special attempt is made to convey the relative weight of the most important obstacles. The last two sections sum up the principal recommendations made to overcome these obstacles. Specifically, the second section takes a broad view of the courses of action business should pursue to render the policy of international consolidations a more effective one. The third section sums up recommendations to governmental agencies and to researchers.

The most important obstacles to transnational concentration

This summary was originally developed by the author after the first set of interviews. Although the analysis was cast in a systematic framework, some subjectivity was unavoidable.[1] The product of this analysis was thus presented to executives during the second set of interviews. Here the emphasis was to substantiate and complete the conclusions of the first set, with particular attention to defining the degree of emphasis as accurately as possible. The end result is a synthesis of the data of these second set interviews.

There are four obstacles which are of prime importance and which arise in most consolidations. In addition, there is one which is really a potential obstacle (i.e., it may become a serious difficulty in the future), and there are three which are important only in certain types of concentration.

The two most important obstacles to transnational concentration are the strategic inertia discussed in the first section of chapter 7 and some of the 'human' problems discussed in chapter 6. Strategic inertia essentially refers to the fact that the possibility of doing a transnational consolidation does not receive adequate attention by the corporate strategists of European firms. It was found that management widely agrees that transnational concentration is far less warranted in today's competitive environment than it will be in the competitive environment of the future. The relative lack of strategic planning hampers the identification of the forces leading to concentration. Further, on a more general level, the absence of adequate strategic planning results in what a second set interviewee termed 'a mental apathy *vis-à-vis* any strategic breakthrough'. Several interviewees pointed out that the strategic function is unfit to promote the type of dramatic change implied by a transnational link-up. As an executive with extensive US business experience put it: 'People are lethargic. They do not question the strategic posture enough to come to such radical conclusions as that of consolidating. Their minds are rusted and they don't even come to the idea that the present strategy might be questioned.'

This problem was not mentioned very frequently during the first set of interviews. Here it was mostly considered a major hindrance by interviewees with transnational business experience or with a distinctive competence in the strategic planning function (e.g., consultants). During the second set, however, when the researcher submitted that strategic inertia might be an obstacle, interviewees recognized the magnitude of the problem. In this connection an executive who was visited twice in the course of this research reported that as a result of the first conversation his company had given serious thought to the possibility of a concentration for the first time. During the first visit it was clear that this executive was not at all convinced of the potential benefits of an international link-up. Before talking about the obstacles to concentration, he asked the researcher to present reasons why a concentration should be considered in the first place. During the second visit, he stated that the first conversation had started him thinking about the possibility of a link-up. He reported he had since ordered an investigation of the possibility by his planning staff. 'Indeed, I did not expect there would be so many potential benefits', was the executive's conclusion.

Some of the 'human' problems discussed in particular in the latter part of chapter 6 constitute an equally serious area of concern. While strategic inertia results in strategists not 'seeing' the desirability of concentration, this problem is one of resistance to concentration. The former is an absence of driving force towards corporate link-ups; the latter is a restraining force.

This area of concern is represented by four interrelated issues. The first is management's reluctance to implement change *per se*. Management in Europe is less often exposed to organizational change than its US counterpart, and is strongly attached to its working methods and environment. The second issue is the perceived threat of a concentration. A consolidation with a foreign partner 'scares' managers because they are unfamiliar with their foreign counterparts: unfamiliarity generates dread. The third issue is nationalism. Managers have deep sentimental ties to their national environment and have a strong desire not to dilute the 'character' of this environment. The fourth area is misconceptions about foreigners. Managers mistakenly believe there are differences between two groups of people of different nationalities which hamper an amalgamation. These four issues combined result in management resistance to a link-up.

The third obstacle to be discussed in this section is governmental opposition to transnational consolidations, which was analysed in the first section of chapter 4. On the whole, its importance is second only to the two obstacles just discussed. Governments tend to favour the maintenance of the national identity of very big industrial units. They perceive these units to be part of the national patrimony. Further, governments resist the transnationalization of companies in the more prestigious sectors. It so happens that these are often the sectors that need concentration most, since they typically have high investment requirements. High-technology sectors such as the computer industry are examples of this. By their obstinate desire to retain these industries within national boundaries, governments often may jeopardize the development of a viable European industry in those very sectors in which they would value EEC autonomy most. With the exception of Italy (where politicians' personal motives are particularly strong), the most important motives for governmental opposition to concentrations are the 'emotional reasons' (e.g., the prestige of having a strong national industry).

The perceived importance of government resistance varies considerably according to the type of firm. For some it can be a very important, even the most important, obstacle (indeed, some interviewees stated it was insurmountable); while for others it may be a trivial issue. Generally, it is a major hindrance for very large firms and for high-technology firms. On the other hand, in relatively low prestige industries and industries that are neither traditional nor well established (i.e., they are not symbols of the national industrial power), the obstacle is of minor importance.

The obstacle that ranks fourth in importance is the by-products of the legal format question, discussed in the last section of chapter 2. Specifically, two misconceptions are serious hindrances. The first one is the belief that a concentration is impossible or, at least, extremely complex because of juridical difficulties. Executives are unfamiliar with the hybrid forms of concentration and are often convinced that consolidation is virtually unfeasible. The second misconception is that the hybrid models are not conducive to 'real amalgamation'. Management thinks the absence of juridical integration hampers the economic or organizational integration. Here the cause is lack of information or misleading information which results in managers assuming that transnational consolidations are very difficult to bring about because of juridical stumbling blocks. Interviewees with international concentration experience are the most articulate about management's impression that the legal and fiscal problems are more complex than they are in reality, and its consequent shying away from the idea of a concentration before giving it appropriate analysis.

There is one obstacle which is serious in view of its potential importance in the future. This is the operating tax issue surveyed in the second section of chapter 2. Hybrid solutions face potential fiscal burdens among which the risk of double taxation is the most serious. Today transnationally concentrated groups manage to attenuate the impact of the problem either through manipulating transfer prices, which reduces the cash flows as recorded in the corporate accounts, or by special *ad hoc* arrangements between the company and the fiscal authorities. These solutions only partially eliminate double taxation, and they carry with them an intrinsic element of contingency. There is always a possibility that the internal revenue will shorten the reins either by acting against the liberal transfer price system or by refusing to grant a special agreement. (The former is more of a risk for the very large corporations, while the latter is more likely to happen to smaller firms.) Should this happen, the fiscal barriers could become a major stumbling block.

Three obstacles can be serious hindrances in certain types of concentrations. These are the labour question, the uncertainty of a country's macroeconomic situation, and state ownership in industry.

As discussed in the third section of chapter 5, the labour question may be important when a German company is involved. The problem then is codetermination. German workers may insist on *Mitbestimmung* for the concentrated group, while the foreign partner—both management and labour—may refuse it. Indeed, German interviewees were very articulate about the problem.

The second section of chapter 4 described how Italy's macroeconomic conditions create considerable difficulties for a concentration. This obstacle is related to the labour question (although completely different from the German type of problem) in that it is the working classes who 'raise all the hell', as an Italian interviewee put it. The country's economic crisis has its roots in the sociopolitical situation. Certain interviewees believe it may be unacceptable for a foreign firm to join forces with some Italian companies today.

As discussed in the latter part of chapter 3, there are quite serious difficulties in transnational link-ups involving a nationalized company.

Such difficulties arise both at the level of a nationalized company itself and at the level of a potential private partner. State ownership in industry is an area of major concern because firms are often nationalized in those sectors where transnational concentration is most desirable (e.g., aircraft manufacturers).

The areas of difficulties discussed in this section should by no means be considered the only really important problems encountered by transnational consolidations. In some instances, they may even be unimportant, whereas other obstacles may be much more important. (For example, for smaller firms the finance question may become quite serious, while the opposition of governments may be a trivial issue.) Moreover, while on the whole the obstacles discussed in this section are the most important ones and those where corrective action is most urgently needed, the other obstacles combined can create 'a real barbed wire entanglement'.[2] Here managers with transnational business experience feel the underlying problem is often a lack of adequate information and guidance.

While the discussion up to now has been devoted to the most important obstacles to concentration, a word is in order about what are often perceived as being major obstacles but were found by this study to be relatively minor issues.

Chapter 1 indicated that commentators typically believe legal and fiscal issues are the main stumbling blocks for transnational concentration. Although a number of first set interviewees mentioned the impossibility of doing a *de jure* merger, the vast majority of them stated that this was not an important barrier. In fact, many interviewees acknowledged that they talked about the problem only because—in the words of a French executive—'so much has been written on the subject that you have been used to thinking immediately of the legal problem as soon as the word "international union" is pronounced; but this is far from meaning that the problem is a serious one.' Indeed, several interviewees specifically mentioned the problem only to say that commentators were wrong in believing it to be a major hindrance.

Similar (though less dramatic) findings were made for the set-up fiscal problem.[3] Although a hybrid form of concentration is far from being exempt from fiscal burdens, management typically believes that the cost of the operation is bearable. As a German interviewee put it: 'If you have decided to undergo such a radical change in your strategy and organization, the fiscal cost of building the juridical structure is not high enough to jeopardize the operation.'

Summary recommendations to business

This section synthesizes the principal actions the business community can take to alleviate the major obstacles to transnational concentration which were surveyed in the preceding section. It is organized in two parts. The first presents recommendations to the individual firm. The second presents recommendations to the business community as a whole.

There are two fundamental actions an individual top management should take: the first is to overcome its own strategic inertia, i.e., to improve its own ability to plan in the total European environment; the second is to overcome the resistance of its organization to international link-ups.

To overcome its own strategic inertia, top management should first of all improve the corporate strategic function in general. This calls primarily for an awareness of the need for explicit strategic analysis. Top management should recognize the desirability of allocating a substantial part of its own resources to strategy formulation. In this regard, it should make a conscious effort to become personally involved in the planning process. It is also necessary for top management to realize the potential contribution of professional consultants to help develop the strategy of the firm.

Furthermore, top management has to Europeanize its own scope. In order to take advantage of the attractive avenues offered by the EEC as a whole, it is important that the strategic function have a European outlook. This means that there must be an active search for new opportunities beyond national boundaries. This, in turn, requires an effort by top managers to overcome some of the 'human' problems discussed in chapter 6 and, in particular, their subconscious motivation to stay within national boundaries. In this connection, executives with extensive international experience have made two types of suggestions for top managers of national companies. First, national companies need to become involved in international operations, even if only to invest in the development of a 'think European' attitude. Operations on an international scale will broaden the outlook of top management, who should become open to seeking strategic opportunities on an international scale. A French international executive said: 'The philosopher Pascal wrote that he who wanted to believe in God should kneel down and pray; the faith would come by itself. International business is the same. You have to force yourself to do it; then you will start thinking in international dimensions.' Second, companies should make a deliberate effort to develop strategic plans in which the environmental variables are European as opposed to national. This is a commitment to analyse the total EEC environment and to generate strategic alternatives within this environment. It should be emphasized that this should be done over and beyond the need to have a European strategy in the short run. Rather, it should be considered as mental exercise for its own sake, to become used to thinking in European terms.

Finally, a special effort should be made to improve the analysis of the particular opportunities offered by transnational concentration. As surveyed in chapter 1, many of the competitive trends in Europe warrant concentration. It is essential to forecast these trends, particularly because of the time required to implement an amalgamation. In view of the analysis of these trends, companies should begin to generate the alternative of an international venture, or the alternative of a concentration—international or domestic. In other words, once the forecast of tomorrow's environment has indicated increased competitive pressures, consideration should be given to the alternative of responding to these pressures through a transnational consolidation. As an executive with transnational concentration experience put it: 'Companies are unconscious of the benefits, indeed in many cases, of the necessity of an international link-up. One of the most important tasks of European chief executives is to identify the problems of tomorrow's business and to search for solutions to these problems in the joining of forces with foreign companies.'

In addition to combating its own strategic inertia, top management has a responsibility to overcome the resistance of its organization to international amalgamations. This resistance is basically represented by the 'human' problems discussed in chapter 6. It appears that many of these problems would be alleviated by a more gradual concentration process. The model presented in the second section of chapter 7 should help in this direction. Top management should anticipate the need for an international link-up and prepare for it progressively. The organization should be given experience in co-operation with foreign partners, and special attention should be given to the broadening of the individual scope of those managers who actually will be responsible for bringing about the union with the foreign partner. In this connection, young managers in particular should be exposed to international collaboration. An effort should be made to make them responsible for operations involving direct contact with foreign environments and people. The internationalization of junior executives is important not only because they are the ones who have the potential to lead tomorrow's consolidated group, but also because they have fewer ethnocentric inhibitions. Indeed, younger people are more open to working and living in international environments.

Beyond this, recommendations to the individual top manager can be summarized by a general statement. It appears fundamental that the corporate strategist become aware both of the opportunities offered by international consolidations and the risks of isolationism and of the true obstacles to concentration. This study has pointed out a number of misconceptions which create an unwarranted impression of complexity in concentrations. Good examples are the misconceptions about the legal problems, such as the impossibility of doing a *de jure* merger, perceived as hindering the integration of the operations of two enterprises. These misconceptions unduly scare executives away from consolidations. It appears that, if top management gains an awareness of the true nature of the obstacles to transnational link-ups, a major hindrance to these operations would be overcome. It is hoped that this study has made a contribution in this direction.

The discussion of managers' misconceptions introduces the first recommendation to the business community as a whole. There is a need to secure better information about transnational concentrations. In particular, better information is necessary about the legal and fiscal issues and especially the hybrid solutions. Information is also warranted in areas such as markets or foreign businesses. This information gap could be bridged by professional associations either through the concerted action of the national associations or through international organizations. The idea has also been formulated 'that some kind of common European agency or marriage bureau be established as a catalyst'.[4]

In addition to information, professional consulting to assist firms in transnational concentration should be made available. First, there are needs in the legal and fiscal fields, with special emphasis on the development of hybrid models. Second, there are needs in the accounting and financial domains. Third, consulting would be warranted to help firms in the implementation of a transnational amalgamation; this refers to 'people-oriented' consultants such as group dynamics consultants. Fourth, consulting would be desirable in the top management function; this calls for assistance to companies for the development of their strategy. In particular, with regard to the latter two, there is in fact not only a lack of consulting availability, but also a necessity for businessmen to bridge the credibility gap faced by such activities.

Executives with international business experience believe that the major impact of more extensive information and consulting would be to help management confront the combination of obstacles to concentration. One of these executives put it this way: 'If you consider the help information and consulting can bring for each individual problem, this help is often trivial. However, they carry considerable promise for the manager who faces the entire range of the problems of an international union. If there is information and consulting available, he has the impression he has something to hold on to. In this respect, their major contribution would be psychological.'

Another area where there is urgent need for action by the business community is management education. While most of European education is state-run, the private sector should take its own share of responsibility for business training. Today, in view of the virtual absence of adequate management courses in public institutions, the business community should itself fill the training gap. Tomorrow, even if public institutions offer more appropriate business training availabilities, the business community would still have a major interest in complementing these public institutions with its own schools. Indeed, it appears that firms should make a considerable effort to sponsor the development of institutions designed to train professional European managers.

In addition, the business community should support actions by governmental agencies and researchers to facilitate transnational concentrations. Firms should join forces to lobby for institutional changes. They should also sponsor research aimed at advancing knowledge in areas critical to international collaboration. This is particularly important for behavioural research. While it is here that the knowledge gap is most dramatic, it is also here that management is most reluctant to finance research. Behavioural sciences still face a credibility problem among European managers who are unwilling to promote research whose result they perceive to be too intangible.

Summary recommendations to governmental agencies and researchers

The primary recommendation which can be offered to governments is that they adopt a more European attitude. Specifically, they should not oppose transnational consolidations. They should realize that their opposition to international link-ups goes counter to European economic integration, and is a threat to continued European independence. The true problem is that this opposition is an unofficial process, which hides the fact that the negative attitude of governments is a generalized phenomenon. This attitude and its consequences should, in fact, be publicized. (The EEC Commission, for example, could make known this behaviour of national governments.)

If European integration is to be pursued, governments should really encourage international collaborations. They should realize consolidations are driving forces for integration, and publicize their importance. Indeed, governments should make it clear that they want companies to join forces across national boundaries (e.g., that they favour transnational concerns for governmental procurement). They should simplify the bureaucracy which hinders transnational collaboration.

The EEC Commission should be given more power, particularly in connection with the Common Market's industrial policy. The Commission can be expected to have more of a European outlook than national governments, and should have less desire to preserve the national identity of companies. Alternatively, the proposal has been made that the Commission check the negative tendencies of national governments towards concentration. The Commission could be made responsible for monitoring the industrial policy of national governments, to make sure that their actual attitude is congruent with the official position which favours European industrial integration. Moreover, the Commission should make a further effort to clarify its position on antitrust issues, in order to dispel businessmen's fears that its policy is more stringent than it actually is.

From a strictly legal and fiscal point of view, the most urgent amendments needed are those concerning the fiscal problems encountered by the hybrid forms of concentration. The operating tax problems should be acted upon; in particular, double taxation should be eliminated. Also, an effort should be made to achieve a greater freedom in the flow of funds. Finally, harmonization should be implemented in those areas where a few relatively easy changes in the law could greatly facilitate the operations of internationally concentrated groups (e.g., elimination of disparities in technical standards).

Finally, public agencies have a major responsibility for education. The long-run objective should be to harmonize the whole educational system of the EEC countries. While this may appear far-fetched, it seems legitimate to expect such reforms since they are in the direction of European sociopolitical integration. In the shorter run, the focus should be on those university courses which are taken by future managers. An effort should be made to harmonize and give a European scope to these courses.

A promising avenue for research lies in the juridical sphere. There is a need for thorough but practical comparative analyses of the legal and fiscal environments in the various EEC countries in order to optimize the hybrid forms of concentration.

The most important area of ignorance in which research is needed is human behaviour. There is a great need for scientific knowledge about foreigners' traits and, in particular, knowledge which can distinguish true differences among people of different nationalities from stereotypes and misconceptions about foreigners. Moreover, normative work should be developed as to what actually can be done to bring foreigners closer together (e.g., sensitivity training). Finally, valuable research could be done to devise a method of evaluating the congruence of two organizations. It would be most useful to have a type of grid to evaluate the compatibility of two would-be 'concentrators'.

The principal objective of this study has been to define the obstacles encountered by top management in transnational consolidations. It has also proposed some recommendations for their solution. These recommendations, however, should not be considered definitive. Specialists' work is clearly warranted in many areas (e.g., fiscal matters). To repeat, here the main emphasis has been to describe the areas of concern to practitioners and to indicate what direction corrective action should take. It is believed that, if proper corrective action were taken, the number of transnational concentrations would increase. The movement towards transnational business integration should accelerate—first in high-technology sectors, then in sectors requiring a high marketing commitment, and finally in all the sectors requiring large investments. This should carry with it considerable promise for European industry. Indeed, it appears to be the best means for the old continent to develop a competitive position on world markets. This is true not only for those industries where transnational concentration is the only hope for achieving a sufficient size to become competitive, but also in great part for the rest of the economy: the industries just mentioned are typically motors for the whole economy. For example, the work of supersonic aircraft manufacturers is a stimulus for a multitude of industries which are subcontractors. A pooling of resources of aircraft manufacturers will make them competitive on a global basis, and improve the EEC economy as a whole. European transnational concentration should thus offer three main advantages: it should improve the economic performance of the firms involved in consolidations; it should have positive effects for the EEC economy as a whole; and it should serve European sociopolitical integration.

NOTES

1. See the discussion on data processing in Appendix 1.
2. This expression was used by the Dunlop chairman, Sir Reay Geddes. Quoted in: R. Marsh, 'The Dunlop–Pirelli Union', Speech given at the Institute of Chartered Accountants, Summer Conference, Oxford, July 1971, p. 8.
3. The importance of antitrust is also often exaggerated.
4. Christopher Layton, *Cross-Frontier Mergers in Europe*, Bath University Press, Bath, 1971, p. IX.

APPENDIX 1: A FURTHER WORD ON METHODOLOGY

The objective of this appendix is to supplement the third section of chapter 1 and to provide additional insights on how this study was conducted.

A letter similar to that shown in Fig. A.1.1 was sent to 280 organizations using one of the following languages: English, French, German, or Italian. The rate of favourable responses was expected to be about 60 per cent, which would have meant interviewing approximately 160 firms. The actual rate turned out to be 80 per cent, as 220 firms responded favourably. In view of the time constraints, the researcher deliberately chose not to interview all of the 220 companies. The 155 companies actually interviewed are listed on page xiiiff.

While it is difficult to make a thorough investigation of the reasons why 20 per cent of the companies did not respond or did not respond favourably, informal research revealed that companies had very good and specific reasons, thus excluding any negative conjecture on the representativeness of the sample actually interviewed. For example, one had just undergone a radical change in its internal organization from a family-owned to a publicly owned company, and the request for an interview had never even reached the new management. Another was close to bankruptcy and was in the process of being nationalized. Another one was under the scrutiny of the EEC Antitrust Commission and preferred to defer any discussion to a later date.

The question has arisen why so many interviews were conducted instead of using the more conventional approach of a few case studies of consolidations which had taken place. There are two main reasons for this. First, when analysing the obstacles to international concentrations,

Mr. Eric O. Faulkner, Chairman
Lloyds Bank Limited
71 Lombard Street
LONDON E.C.3

September 20, 1971

Dear Mr. Faulkner,

I am a Ph.D. candidate at the Stanford University Graduate School of Business and I am currently preparing my dissertation. My topic is "Transnational Concentration in the E.E.C." I am taking the liberty of enclosing a brief outline of this research.

My study depends heavily upon data gathered with the cooperation of over one hundred and fifty major European companies. I would greatly appreciate the benefit of your comments on this subject. Specifically, I would like to have your views on what obstacles prevent a greater degree of international concentration in the E.E.C. and Great Britain and any suggestion you may have as to the most appropriate means to overcome these obstacles.

If at all possible, I would be interested this coming fall, in interviewing you and/or other members of your top executive staff as well as members of your planning department. May I assure you that no confidential material will be requested and that complete anonymity will be preserved if interviewees so desire.

Thank you for your time and interest. Looking forward to hearing from you, I remain

Yours sincerely,

Renato Mazzolini
Graduate School of Business
Stanford University
Stanford, California 94305

enclosure

Fig. A.1.1

it is not enough to talk about the experiences of those who actually have consolidated. It is important to look at those who refrain from doing so precisely because their reasons for not concentrating are the main focus of this work. Moreover, those who concentrate tend to be subjective in dealing with the problems they encountered. Second, only a few concentrations have actually occurred, and it is not possible to draw any valid inference from this limited sample. The views of those managers who are potential 'concentrators' needed to be investigated. These opinions are strongly influenced by personal experience. Because they are bound to be quite varied, it is necessary to have a broad sample, if any valid generalizations are to be drawn.

Interviews were conducted in the four languages mentioned above. This means that all interviews were held in the mother tongue of executives except for the Dutch where German and English were used. There seems little reason to believe that this caused any loss of content, as the Dutch have a tradition of proficiency in these two languages. (Indeed, in some Dutch companies visited, the working language was English or German.)

The tape recorder was used in virtually all interviews. Here again, bias was minimal as respondents quickly forgot about the machine; control interviews done without the tape recorder revealed that there was no loss of content when the machine was used.

The reliability of the responses can be questioned in two ways: Are respondents being honest? Are their answers correct? The second question finds its answer in the very title of this study, 'Top Management's Perspective'. The objective is to define the problem as it appears to a strategic decision-maker. The underlying assumption is that a concentration occurs or fails to occur according to how top management sees the problem. Theoretically, then, the 'true' obstacles become irrelevant. However, the researcher's personal belief is that top management's view of the problem is accurate.

There are three reasons why the question of honesty should be dismissed. First, if the respondent takes his time to talk about the problem, it is probably because he believes it is an interesting one, and feels its solution will make him better off. If he is interested to see the problem solved, he will be motivated to contribute to this endeavour and will be honest. Second, no confidential company material is necessary to the study. The question of secrecy, which is the main threat to candidness, is thus irrelevant. Third, absolute anonymity is guaranteed to the respondent. He will not be identified with any of his statements, which will be absorbed in the bulk of a great many responses. He will thus not have to worry about withholding information for fear of being misquoted.

The main problem of the data processing has been to synthesize the data without introducing bias (i.e., data reduction without distortion). To do this a technique of data reduction in successive steps has been used, each time increasing the degree of global synthesis. Specifically, from the tape a report was made for each interview. Here, the obstacles were presented as the respondent talked about them. The same headings of obstacles presented were reported and the comments on each obstacle were given with strict fidelity because the tape permitted the preservation of the full content of the interview. From these reports a list was drawn of all the headings of obstacles that respondents presented. In the list no reduction of obstacles was made at first. Then, headings which were similar were merged. For example, if one heading read 'preconceptions about foreigners' and another '*a priori* opinions about foreigners', they were taken to mean the same thing and were put together. This simple exercise was particularly useful for language variations, in drawing up a list of headings in a common language. Using this list, a set of working files were constructed. This consisted of a file for each heading in which comments of interviewees on the obstacles corresponding to a particular heading were reported. Then, subsequent sets of working files were made in which files were merged along common characteristics: recurring themes in two or more files were identified and files embodying similar themes were put together. The result was a reduced number of files synthesizing the various views of respondetns on very similar issues which they labelled differently. For example, the concepts of ethnocentrism, chauvinism, nationalistic particularism, and patriotism are similar and might all be embodied in a broader concept such as nationalism. It is important to note that this can be done safely only if the meaning respondents give to a concept is controlled through their comments on that particular concept. It is not enough to merge headings alone any more; it is necessary to check the meaning attached to the headings through an analysis of respondents' comments on the particular headings under consideration. This explains why files were merged after the details on each obstacle had been transcribed. After several iterations, the end product is a report presenting the obstacles categorized, including for each obstacle the various perspectives different people have had on the particular issue under consideration.

A particularly important methodological problem which was encountered concerned the degree of emphasis interviewees attach to each obstacle. The objective here was to evaluate the relative importance of the obstacles without losing content in terms of the description of the barrier itself.

The first method that came to mind for determining the relative weight of the obstacles was to ask respondents to evaluate the importance of items proposed by the researcher, say, on a five-point scale. The drawback was, of course, that the researcher himself would have imposed the items on the respondent and thus would have introduced some bias. Moreover, the items would have had to be formulated in an *a priori* fashion; there would be no guarantee that all the relevant issues would be raised because not enough reliable material was available from which to build the items. Consequently, this method was rejected. The second method was that of asking the respondent to evaluate items he himself proposed. Specifically, during the interview the researcher could have kept track of the obstacles the respondent mentioned: then, at the end of the interview, he could have asked the respondent to rate the obstacles he had mentioned. While this route had much theoretical appeal, a pilot study revealed its limited practical use. It is very difficult to ask top managers to fall in with such an exercise after an open-ended type of conversation. The most fruitful interviews were often those during which the interviewee became quite involved in his arguments and even somewhat emotional about them. It is then that the best insights are provided on the more delicate issues such as politicians' attitudes *vis-à-vis* consolidations. It is virtually impossible to request that a high-level executive become 'a bookkeeper after having been a philosopher', to use the expression of an Italian manager.

The choice was consequently made to forego high precision on the relative importance of the obstacles, in order to maintain the richness of the qualitative description of the problem. It was decided that relative importance would then be approximated in two ways. First, a frequency count was to be made. How many times has each obstacle been mentioned? This was to be done on the data of the first set of interviews. The main limitation of the method is that some obstacles may be very obvious; the fact that everybody mentions them does not necessarily mean that they are important. Indeed, everybody can agree that they are trivial, but the frequency count would show a high weight for such items.

Second, a questionnaire was to be employed in conjunction with the second set of interviews, presenting a synthesized list of the most important obstacles as determined from the data of the first set of interviews. Respondents were to be asked to rate these obstacles on a five-point scale. Some difficulty was encountered here. Respondents were often unable to give a relative weight to the obstacles, in view of the variety of issues under consideration; it was often difficult to make comparisons between obstacles whose nature differed so dramatically. Further, the problem was encountered of asking a high-level executive to be quantitative for a given part of the interview, while for the rest of it judgemental issues were discussed. This is the problem alluded to before. Although the second set of interviews was less open-ended than the first, the problem was still encountered, though to a lesser degree. Because of these difficulties, results of this questionnaire should be taken with some caution.

Indeed, it is recognized that none of these methods alone gives a satisfactory answer on the weight of each obstacle. However, it is believed that, taken together, they do give a meaningful approximation of relative importance. This data is presented in Appendix 2.

In view of the imperfection of these methods, importance was, in addition, determined qualitatively. A particular effort was made to assess the degree of emphasis given to an obstacle during the interview. Here, the researcher's own judgement played a crucial part. The researcher determined the importance of the obstacle as he perceived the respondent's own evaluation of it. Because of the obvious danger of subjectivity, corroboration was sought by eliciting management's comments on the researcher's own evaluation. Specifically, after the first set of interviews, the researcher determined what he thought the most important obstacles were in management's eyes. During the second set of interviews, executives were asked to comment on this analysis. Because this was not in quantitative form, respondents were much more prepared to share their reactions. While harder to convey, this qualitative appreciation appears more realistic than any statistical analysis.

APPENDIX 2: STATISTICAL APPROXIMATIONS

This appendix presents statistical data. A frequency count of the obstacles is given, i.e., how many times an obstacle was mentioned by executives during the first set of open-ended interviews. Moreover, the relative weight of obstacles is given, i.e., what importance the second set interviewees attributed to obstacles which the researcher brought to their attention. As suggested by the title of this appendix, it is important to bear in mind what the limitations of these data are. The reader is referred to Appendix 1, where these limitations are discussed.[1]

Six tables are presented (one for each chapter discussing the obstacles to transnational concentration). Each table has six columns:

- column 1 indicates the pages in the text in which the obstacles are discussed;
- in column 2 obstacles are presented; there are here obstacles and sub-obstacles (e.g., within the obstacle 'operating fiscal problems', 'double taxation' is a sub-obstacle);
- column 3 indicates what percentage of respondents mentioned a given obstacle during the first set of interviews;
- column 4 indicates what percentage of respondents mentioned a given sub-obstacle during the first set of interviews;
- column 5 indicates the average weight respondents attributed to a given obstacle or sub-obstacle during the second set of interviews; this was done on a five-point scale in ascending order of importance;
- column 6 indicates the number of responses on which the data of

column 5 is based, namely, how many second set interviewees gave a weight to the particular obstacle under consideration.

As discussed in Appendix 1, difficulties were encountered in asking executives to attribute weights for the data presented in column 5. It was thus necessary to condense the list of obstacles (i.e., solicit responses on a limited number of items);[2] this is why only certain obstacles have a weight in column 5. Further, certain interviewees resisted the exercise altogether. Column 6 indicates how many responses were actually obtained on a given obstacle.

NOTES

1. In view of these limitations, it was felt it would be meaningless to test this data for statistical significance.

2. Clearly the data on the first set of interviews are also a synthesis of the bulk of the obstacles discussed by executives. (See the discussion on the data processing in Appendix 1.)

CHAPTER 2: LEGAL AND FISCAL ISSUES: DETERMINING THE JURIDICAL STRUCTURE

1	2	3	4	5	6
PAGES	OBSTACLES AND SUB-OBSTACLES	OBSTACLE PER CENT	SUB-OBSTACLE PER CENT	WEIGHT	NUMBER OF RESPON-DENTS
17–21	Impossibility of doing a *de jure* merger	74		1·6	21
18	Set-up fiscal problems	66		1·9	19
29–31	Operating fiscal problems	71		3·0	20
29–30	• double taxation		69		
30	• withholding tax		41		
30	• impossibility of deducting losses of one company from the profits of the other		17		
41–47	By-products of the legal format	58		3·0	13
41–42	• effects of differing company laws on organizational structure		18		
42–46	• effects of lack of information		36		
46–47	• misconceptions		33		

Chapter 3: Other Regulatory Obstacles

1 PAGES	2 OBSTACLES AND SUB-OBSTACLES	3 OBSTACLE PER CENT	4 SUB-OBSTACLE PER CENT	5 WEIGHT	6 NUMBER OF RESPONDENTS
53–63	Antitrust	59		1·9	12
53–59	● technical barrier *per se*		54		
59–63	● barriers deriving from confusion about regulations		38		
64–65	Exchange controls	32			
65–66	Accounting: Problems created by conflicting legal regulations	37			
66–67	Restrictions on the free flow of people	24			
67–68	Disparity in technical standards for goods and services	40			
68–70	No monetary union	42			
68–69	● impedes concentration for banks		26		
69–70	● uncertainty in managing with various units of account		27		
70–74	State ownership in industry	41			

Chapter 4: Bureaucratic Obstacles

1 PAGES	2 OBSTACLES AND SUB-OBSTACLES	3 OBSTACLE PER CENT	4 SUB-OBSTACLE PER CENT	5 WEIGHT	6 NUMBER OF RESPONDENTS
78–93	Negative attitude of national governments	66		3·6	17
79–80	● direct pressure by governmental agents		59		
80–81	● favouritism with regard to national firms		27		
81	● encouragement of domestic concentration		28		
81–82	● render bureaucracy more cumbersome		34		
82–83	● indirect influence		23		
97–98	Perceived slow progress towards European integration	19			
98–99	Bureaucracy	37			
99–101	Informal relationships between public and private administrators	36			
101–104	Environmental uncertainty	48			

Chapter 5: Socioeconomic Obstacles

1 PAGES	2 OBSTACLES AND SUB-OBSTACLES	3 OBSTACLE PER CENT	4 SUB-OBSTACLE PER CENT	5 WEIGHT	6 NUMBER OF RESPONDENTS
107–108	Accounting: Problems created by conflicting business practices	43			
109	Differences in business practices regarding the banking sector	8			
110–112	Finance	46			
110	● capital markets		14		
110–111	● banks and 'other' financial institutions		38		
112–119	Markets	53			
113–115	● consumers' nationalism		36		
116	● dissimilarities in market demand		28		
117–118	● misconceptions about markets		31		
118–119	● lack of market data		13		
119–125	Labour	52			
119–122	● labour opposition to concentration		47	2·9	10
123–125	● managerial problems deriving from labour		18		
125–127	Opposition of stockholders	17			
127–128	Opposition of general public	19			

Chapter 6: The Human Side of the Enterprise

1	2	3	4	5	6
PAGES	OBSTACLES AND SUB-OBSTACLES	OBSTACLE PER CENT	SUB-OBSTACLE PER CENT	WEIGHT	NUMBER OF RESPONDENTS
132–134	Language	60			
132	● comprehension		57		
132–133	● by-products		31		
134–135	Lack of relationships among top executives	29			
135–136	Different ways in which work is organized	40			
136–138	Appraisal gap	37			
138–140	Lack of professional skills	45			
140–144	Resistance to change	67		4·1	20
140–141	● resistance to change with regard to working methods		41		
141–142	● resistance to change in working environment		57		
144–149	Perceived threat of concentration	60		3·8	17
144–145	● reluctance to lose one's independence		48		
145–147	● fear of rationalization or of loss of personal opportunities		47		
147–149	● fear deriving from one's country's economic weakness		28		
149–153	Nationalism	68		3·6	22
149–150	● animosities *vis-à-vis* particular foreigners		42		
150–153	● ethnocentrism		59		
153–155	Misconceptions	58		3·6	15

Chapter 7: Corporate Strategy

1	2	3	4	5	6
PAGES	OBSTACLES AND SUB-OBSTACLES	OBSTACLE PER CENT	SUB-OBSTACLE PER CENT	WEIGHT	NUMBER OF RESPONDENTS
162–178	Inadequate strategic planning for transnational concentration	41		4·0	15

APPENDIX 3: MEMBER STATES' SYSTEM OF TAXATION APPLICABLE IN THE CASE OF INTERNATIONAL MERGERS[1]

In Germany, Belgium, and Luxembourg when a national company is absorbed by a foreign one, the national company is considered dissolved. This gives rise to the taxation of the benefits of liquidation (i.e., capital gain taxes). In Germany and Luxembourg, if a national company absorbs a foreign one, it has to pay the contribution of assets taxes (in Germany, the so-called *Kapitalverkehrssteuer*). In Belgium the merger between a foreign company and a national one, and the absorption of a foreign company by a national one, entails the registration tax—as long as the new company or the absorbing company has its registered office in the country. The rate of this tax is 2·50 per cent except if the absorbed or the merged company belongs to another EEC country. In this case the rate is reduced to 1·25 per cent.

In Italy, the absorption of a national company by a foreign one entails in principle a capital gain tax. An exception is made for the company's permanent establishments which are kept in Italy.[2] The absorption of a foreign company by a national one entails registration taxes on the conferred assets.

In France the absorption of a French company by a foreign one entails, in principle, capital gain taxes on the benefits of liquidation. However, in pursuance of the principle of the territoriality of taxation, no corporate taxes will be levied on the company's foreign permanent establishments. Moreover, the operation may take advantage of a preferential tax treatment, if it has obtained the clearing of the Finance Ministry which is based on the recommendation of the 'Commissaire Général du Plan et de la Productivité'. Finally, subject to the Finance Ministry's approval, the capital gains realized by stockholders when they exchange their shares of the absorbed company with those of the absorbing company, are not considered as an income of the shareholders and are thus not taxed. The absorption of a foreign company by a French one entails a contribution of assets tax which is reduced if the operation has been cleared by the Finance Ministry.

In Holland a national company which contributes its assets to a foreign one may either be liquidated or remain in existence as a shell or holding corporation. By transferring its assets to the foreign company and receiving shares from the latter in exchange, the company incurs the *Vennootschapsbelasting* on the capital gain of this exchange. This tax is also applied in the case of dissolution of the national company. The absorption of a foreign company by a Dutch one gives rise to the registration tax relative to the incorporation of new companies and the increase of equity capital.

NOTES

1. The main source of this appendix is 'Les Fusions Internationales de Sociétés dans la Communauté Economique Européenne', Union des Industries de la Communauté Européenne (UNICE), Brussels, 1967.

2. For the EEC Commission's definition of a permanent establishment, see 'Annexé' in: 'Proposition de Directive Concernant le Régime Fiscal Commun Applicable aux Fusions, Scissions et Apports d'Actif intervenant entre Sociétés d'Etats Membres différents', COM (69)5 final, Brussels, January 15, 1969.

BIBLIOGRAPHY

Books

Aszkenazy, Heinz. *Les grandes sociétés européennes*. Brussels: Centre de Recherche et d'Information Socio-Politique (CRISP), 1971.

Barzanti, Sergio. *The underdeveloped areas within the Common Market*. Princeton, NJ: Princeton University Press, 1956.

Bauchet, Pierre. *La Planification française*. Paris: Editions du Seuil, 1962.

Blake, Robert R.; Shepard, Herbert H.; and Mouton, Jane S. *Managing intergroup conflict in industry*. Houston, Texas: Gulf Publishing, 1964.

Calmann, John. *Co-operation in arms procurement in Western Europe*. London: Institute for Strategic Studies, 1967.

Cannell, Charles F. 'Interviewing'. In Gardner Lindzey and Elliot Aronson, *The handbook of social psychology*, Vol. 2, Reading, Mass.: Addison-Wesley, 1968, pp. 526–95.

Chenot, Bernard. *Les entreprises nationalisées*. Paris: Presse Universitaire de France, 1963.

Davis, William. *Merger mania*. London: Constable, 1970.

de Hoghton, Charles. *The company: law, structure and reform in eleven countries*. London: Allen and Unwin, PEP, 1970.

√ de Hoghton, Charles. *Cross-Channel Collaboration: A Study of Agreement between British and Continental Firms*. London: PEP, 1967.

Deschampsneufs, Henry. *Selling in Europe*. London: Business Publications, 1963.

Dichter, Ernst. 'The world customer'. In John J. Coyle and Edward J. Mock, *Readings in international business*. Scranton, Pa.: International Textbook Company, 1965, pp. 225–37.

Drayton, Clarence I.; Emerson, Craig; and Griswold, John D. *Mergers and acquisitions: Planning and action.* Cambridge, Mass.: Financial Executives Research Foundation, 1963.

Einaudi, Luigi. *Lo scrittoio del Presidente.* Torino: Giulio Einaudi, 1956.

Einaudi, Luigi. *Prediche inutili.* Torino: Giulio Einaudi, 1969.

Einaudi, Luigi. *Saggi sul risparmio e l'imposta.* Torino: Giulio Einaudi, 1965.

Etzioni, Amitai. 'Social-psychological aspects of international relations'. In Gardner Lindzey and Elliot Aronson, *The handbook of social psychology.* Vol. 5, Reading, Mass.: Addison-Wesley, 1969, pp. 538–601.

Fano, P. P. 'The Italian labor movement and collective bargaining'. In Alfred Kamin, ed., *Western European labour.* Washington: The Bureau of National Affairs, 1970, pp. 99–108.

Feld, Werner J. *Transnational business collaboration among Common Market countries—Its implication for political integration.* New York: Praeger, 1970.

Forbes, R. J. *A chronology of oil* (with special reference to the Royal Dutch/Shell group of companies). The Hague: BIPM, 1965.

Friedrich, Carl J. *Europe: An emergent nation?* New York: Harper & Row, 1969.

Granick, David. *The European executive.* New York: Doubleday, 1962.

Haas, E. B. and Whiting, A. S. *Dynamics of international relations.* New York: McGraw-Hill, 1956.

Hackett, John and Hackett, Anne-Marie. *Economic planning in France.* Cambridge, Mass.: Harvard University Press, 1963.

Haire, Mason; Ghiselli, Edwin E.; and Porter, Lyman W. *Managerial thinking: An international study.* New York: Wiley, 1966.

Hermanns, Ferdinand; Knauss, Fritz; and Vogel, Otto. *Unternehmenskonzentration in der westlichen Welt. Stand, Entwicklungstendenzen und Vergleiche.* Koeln: Verlag Carl Heymann, 1967.

Holden, Paul E.; Pederson, Carlton A.; and Germane, Gayton E. *Top management.* New York: McGraw-Hill, 1968.

Holt, Stephen. *The Common Market: The conflict of theory and practice.* London: Hamilton, 1967.

Iannuzzi, Mario. *Il diritto delle società per azioni nella Comunità Economica Europea.* Roma: Associazione fra le Società Italiane per Azioni, 1972.

Jensen, F. B. and Walter I. *The Common Market: Economic integration in Europe.* Philadelphia: Lippincott, 1965.

Jurgensen, Harald and Berg, Hartmut. *Konzentration und Wettbewerb im Gemeinsamen Markt—Das Beispiel der Automobilindustrie.* Goettingen: Vandenhoeck and Ruprecht, 1968.

Kerlinger, Fred. *Foundations of behavioral research—Educational and psychological inquiry.* New York: Holt, Rinehart and Winston, 1963.

Kitzinger, Uwe W. *The European Common Market and Community*. New York: Barnes & Noble, 1967.
Kormann, Hermut. *Die Steuerpolitik der internationalen Unternehmen*. Duesseldorf: Verlag Buchhandlung d. Instituts der Wirtschaftspruefer GmbH, 1969.
Krekel, N. R. A.; Van der Woerd, T. G.; and Wouterse, J. J. *Mergers—A European approach to technique*. London: Business Books, 1969.
Laulan, Yves. *Marché Commun et conjoncture concertée*. Paris: Société d'Editions d'Enseignement Supérieur, 1963.
Layton, Christopher. *Cross-frontier mergers in Europe*. Bath: Bath University Press, 1971.
Layton, Christopher. *European advanced technology—A programme for integration*. London: Allen & Unwin, 1969.
Linowes, David F. *Managing growth through acquisition*. New York: American Management Association, 1968.
Luchterhandt, Hans Friedrich. *Deutsches Konzernrecht bei grenzueberschreitenden Konzernverbindungen*. Stuttgart: Muenchner Universitaetsschriften, Ferd. Enke-Verlag, 1971.
Lutter, Marcus. *Empfehlen sich fuer die Zusammenfassung europaeischer Unternehmen neben oder statt der europaeischen Handelsgesellschaft und der internationalen Fusion weitere Moeglichkeiten der Gestaltung auf dem Gebiete des Gesellschaftsrechts?* Muenchen: Verlag C. H. Beck, 1970.
Mace, Myles L. and Montgomery, George G. *Management problems in corporate acquisitions*. Cambridge, Mass.: Graduate School of Business Administration, Harvard University, 1962.
Massé, Pierre. 'National planning and business enterprise in France'. In George A. Steiner and Warren M. Cannon, *Multinational corporate planning*. New York: Macmillan, 1966.
McArthur, John H. and Scott, Bruce A. *Industrial planning in France*. Boston, Mass.: Division of Research, Graduate School of Business Administration, Harvard University, 1969.
Meynaud, Jean and Sidjanski, Dusan. *L'Europe des affaires. Rôle et structures des groupes*. Paris: Payot, 1967.
Moon, Ronald W. *Business mergers and take-over bids*. London: Gee, 1968.
Most, Kenneth S. 'How bad are European accountants'. In K. B. Berg; G. G. Mueller; L. M. Walker, *Readings in international accounting*. Boston: Houghton Mifflin, 1969, pp. 208–22.
Northrop, F. C. S. and Livingstone, H. H. *Cross-cultural understanding: Epistemology in anthropology*. New York: Harper & Row, 1964.
Parsons, Robert Q. and Baumgartner, John S. *Anatomy of a merger—How to sell your company*. Englewoods Cliffs, NY: Prentice-Hall, 1970.

Roelans, Jacques Y. *Régimes fiscaux applicables aux fusions de sociétés dans les Etats Membres de la C.E.E. et perspectives communautaires.* Brussels: Bruylant, 1970.

Rowley, Charles K. *The British Monopolies Commission.* London: Allen & Unwin, 1966.

Sampson, Anthony. *The new Europeans.* London: Hodder & Stoughton, 1968.

Sanders, Peter. *The European stock corporation.* Chicago: Commerce Clearing House, 1969.

Schelling, Thomas C. 'Bargaining, communication and limited war'. In Harold J. Leavitt and Louis R. Pondy, *Readings in managerial psychology.* Chicago: University of Chicago Press, 1964, pp. 422–41.

Servan-Schreiber, Jean-Jacques. *The American Challenge.* New York: Atheneum, 1968.

Shanks, M. and Lambert, J. *The Common Market today and tomorrow.* New York: Praeger, 1962.

Short, Robert A. *Business mergers—How and when to transact them.* Englewood Cliffs, NJ: Prentice-Hall, 1967.

Soelter, Arno. 'Grenzueberschreitende Konzentration—Grundsatzfragen—Verkaufsniederlassung, Fertigungsstaette, Beteiligung'. In *Handbuch der Unternehmenszusammenschluesse.* Muenchen: Verlag Moderne Industrie, 1972.

Stacey, Nicholas. *Mergers in modern business.* London: Hutchinson, 1970.

Swann, Dennis. 'Cartels and concentrations—Issues and progress'. In G. R. Denton, *Economic integration in Europe.* London: Weidenfeld & Nicolson, 1969.

Swann, D. and McLachlan, D. L. *Concentration or competition. A European dilemma.* London: Chatham House, PEP, 1967.

Thompson, Dennis. *The proposal for a European company.* London: Chatham House, PEP, 1969.

Trevor-Brown, J. 'Practical, legal and tax problems of international company link-ups'. In Mark Weinberg, *On take-overs and mergers.* London: Sweet & Maxwell, 1971.

Weil, Gordon L. *A handbook on the European Economic Community.* New York: Praeger, 1965.

Whiting, John W. 'Methods and problems in cross-cultural research'. In Gardner Lindzey and Elliot Aronson, *The handbook of social psychology*, Vol. 2. Reading, Mass.: Addison–Wesley, 1968, pp. 526–95.

Wight, A. *Handbook on cross-cultural training.* Estes Park: Colorado Center for Research and Education, 1969.

Wilson, Charles. *The history of Unilever.* London: Cassell, 1954.

Wyatt, Arthur R. and Kieso, Donald. *Business combinations: Planning and action.* Scranton, Pa.: International Textbook Company, 1969.

Yannopoulos, George N. 'Economic integration and labour movements with reference to the E.E.C. countries'. In G. R. Denton, *Economic integration in Europe*. London: Weidenfeld & Nicolson, 1969.
Zahn, Ernest. 'The European market-place: Social change and consumer choice'. In Philip R. Cateora and John M. Hess, *International Marketing*. Homewood, Ill.: Irwin, 1971, pp. 136–41.
Zenoff, David B. and Zwick, Jack. *International financial management*. Englewood Cliffs, NJ: Prentice-Hall, 1969.

Journal articles—titled

Allegri, Vincenzo. 'Una proposta della Commissione C.E.E. al Consiglio dei Ministri della Comunità in tema di società anonima europea'. *Rivista delle società*, Anno XV, Fascicolo 6, 1970, pp. 1248–1260.
Armstrong, Lindsay. 'Cross-frontier mergers: No need to wait for the blue-print from Brussels'. *Vision*, February 1971, pp. 80–84.
Austin, Douglas V. 'We contemplated no changes in personnel'. *Mergers and Acquisitions*, September–October 1971, pp. 20–21.
Ball, Robert. 'The Common Market is still good news'. *Fortune*, December 1971, pp. 80 ff.
Bartolini, Anna. 'Reciproco riconoscimento di società giuridiche'. *L'industria lombarda*, No. 9, 26 February 1972, p. 11.
Blake, Robert B.; Mouton, Jane S.; Greiner, Larry E.; and Barnes, Louis B. 'Breakthrough in organization development'. *Harvard Business Review*, November–December 1964, pp. 133–55.
Blansfield, M. C.; Blake, R.; and Mouton, J. 'The merger laboratory—A new strategy for bringing one corporation into another'. *Training Directors*, May 1964, pp. 2–10.
Blass, Walter P. 'Economic planning European style'. *Harvard Business Review*, September–October 1963.
Brault, D. 'Les vues françaises sur la coopération des entreprises au regard du Traité de Rome'. *Revue du Marché Commun*, No. 126, September 1969, pp. 409–19.
Brosio, Guido. 'National tax hindrances to cross-border concentration in the European Economic Community'. *Harvard International Law Journal*, II, 1970, pp. 311–57.
Brown, Robert L. 'The Common Market: What its new consumer is like'. *Printers' Ink*, 31 May 1963, pp. 23–25.
Burck, Gilbert. 'The merger movement rides high'. *Fortune*, February 1969, pp. 79 ff.
Campbell, Mary. 'The top 300'. *The Banker*, June 1971, pp. 628–97.
Cannellos, Peter C. and Silber, Horst S. 'Concentration in the Common Market'. *Common Market Law Review*, Vol. 7, No. 1, January 1970, pp. 5–35 and Vol. 7, No. 2, April 1970, pp. 138–66.

Carré, Michel A. and Bouvard, Philippe M. 'The courtship and honeymoon of successful mergers'. *European Business*, April 1970, pp. 36–43.
Cheris, S. D. and Fischer, E. R. 'The European company: Its promise and problems'. *Stanford Journal of International Studies*, Vol. 6, Spring 1971, pp. 113–45.
Cochetti, Franco. 'Problemi relativi al coordinamento delle legislazioni nazionali sulle fusioni delle società nei Paesi del Mercato Comune europeo'. *Banca, borsa e titoli di credito*, No. 2, 1970.
Colombi, Carlo. 'L'accordo Pirelli–Dunlop: verso una società multinazionale europea'. *Mondo economico*, No. 10, March 1970.
Colonna di Paliano, Guido. 'Industrial policy, public procurement and multinational industry'. *European Community*, September 1970, pp. 3–5.
Colonna di Paliano, Guido. 'Why Europe needs continental-scale firms'. *European Community*, September 1968, pp. 3–4.
Conard, Alfred F. 'Corporate fusion in the Common Market'. *American Journal of Comparative Law*, Vol. 14, 1966, pp. 573–602.
Damant, D. C. 'Investment evaluation, mergers and take-overs'. *European Business*, May 1967, pp. 14–31.
Davis, Richard E. 'Compatibility in corporate marriages'. *Harvard Business Review*, July–August 1968, pp. 86–93.
de Bettignies, H. C. and Rhinesmith, S. H. 'Developing the international executive'. *European Business*, January 1970, pp. 52–57.
de Jong, H. W. 'Concentration in the Common Market'. *Common Market Law Review*, Vol. 4, 1966, pp. 166–79.
de Jong, H. W. 'Spécialisation, concentrations et Marché Commun'. *Revue de l'Economie du Centre-Est*, X, 40, April–June 1968.
Delmas, Jacques. 'Un cadre juridique nouveau pour la coopération interentreprises: le groupement d'intérêt économique'. *Revue du Marché Commun*, November 1970, No. 138.
Denoix, Bernard. 'Une expérience de coopération internationale: l'IBM en Europe'. *Revue du Marché Commun*, No. 109, January–February 1968, pp. 124–30.
de Pamphilis, Nicola. 'Azione sindacale e concentrazioni industriali'. *Conquiste del lavoro*, 18–24 November 1968.
Diepen, F. J. L. 'The E.E.C. and the European aerospace industry'. *Common Market*, August–September 1970, pp. 204–7.
Drancourt, Michel and Lepage, Henri. 'Obstacles psychologiques (et politiques) aux concentrations et aux fusions intracommunautaires'. *Revue du Marché Commun*, No. 109, January–February 1968, pp. 131–42.
Dreyer, H. Peter. 'E.E.C. key to European mergers'. *Journal of Commerce*, 8 March 1966.
Faucheux, C. 'Théorie et technique des groupes de diagnostic'. *Bulletin de Psychologie*, No. 158, 1959, pp. 397–420.

Ficker, Hans Claudius. 'A project for a European corporation'. *The Journal of Business Law*, April 1970, pp. 156–69.
Fornasier, Raffaello. 'Towards a European company'. *Columbia Journal of World Business*, September–October 1969, pp. 51–57.
Franceschelli, Remo. 'Obstacles tenant au droit interne des sociétés'. *Revue du Marché Commun*, No. 109, January–February 1968, Communication, pp. 337–48; Intervention, pp. 420–25.
Garcin, William. 'Obstacles tenant au droit interne des sociétés', Communication. *Revue du Marché Commun*, No. 109, January–February 1968, pp. 349–73.
Gaudet, Michel. 'Obstacles sociologiques et psychologiques aux coopérations, concentrations et fusions'. *Revue du Marché Commun*, No. 109, January–February 1968, pp. 97–98.
Giscard d'Estaing, Olivier. 'Coopération et fusion des entreprises françaises et allemandes'. 31 *Politique étrangère*, 1966, pp. 136–56.
Godino, Roger M. 'A propos du Séminaire international sur le long-range planning'. *European Business*, No. 4, February 1965, pp. 18 ff.
Godino, Roger M. 'The importance of advanced management education for Europe'. *European Business*, No. 17, April 1968, pp. 54–59.
Goldman, Berthold. 'La concentration des entreprises à l'échelon européen et le droit des sociétés'. *Rivista delle società*, 1968, pp. 1005–7.
Goldman, Berthold. 'Obstacles tenant au droit interne des sociétés'. *Revue du Marché Commun*, No. 109, January–February 1968, pp. 297–316.
Goldmark, Francis M. 'Europe catches the merger fever'. *Columbia Journal of World Business*, March–April 1969, pp. 49–54.
Guarino, Giuseppe. 'Raisons et préalables d'une société de droit communautaire'. *Revue du Marché Commun*, No. 109, January–February 1968, pp. 374–91.
Guyénot, Jean. 'Les groupements d'intérêt économique concurrents des sociétés commerciales'. I and II, *Banque*, February 1970, pp. 155–63; and March 1970, pp. 261–73.
Hall, D. J. and de Bettignies, H. C. 'Training better executives: Problems and progress'. *European Business*, January 1968, pp. 25–31.
Hein, Leonard W. 'The auditor and the British companies acts'. *The Accounting Review*, July 1963, pp. 502 ff.
Heymann, Philippe. 'Une question de vie ou de mort: une politique industrielle européenne'. *Communauté Européenne*, No. 140, March 1970, pp. 25–30.
Hofman, E. A. 'The dual structure of Unilever group of companies and the equalization agreement'. *Journal for Companies, Associations and Foundations*, Special Number on groups of companies, September 1968.

Hogatry, Thomas F. 'The profitability of corporate mergers'. *Journal of Business*, 43, July 1970, pp. 317–27.

Houssiaux, Jacques. 'Limites économiques des concentrations et fusions'. *Revue du Marché Commun*, No. 109, January–February 1968, pp. 51–80.

Jaume, René. 'Entente et coopération entre entreprises (ententes et positions dominantes)'. *Revue du Marché Commun*, No. 124, June 1969, pp. 317–24.

Kauffman, Joseph. 'Obstacles tenant au droit fiscal', Rapport. *Revue du Marché Commun*, No. 109, January–February 1968, pp. 449–66.

Kindleberger, Charles P. 'European integration and the international corporation'. *Columbia Journal of World Business*, Winter 1966.

Kitching, John. 'Why do mergers miscarry?' *Harvard Business Review*, November–December 1967, pp. 84–101.

Klatt, Gerhard. 'Steuerliche Probleme einer sogenannten "europaeischen Gesellschaft"'. *Europaeische Steuerzeitung*, No. 47, August 1971, pp. 67–76.

Klein, Philip A. 'The development of planning in European business firms'. *European Business*, No. 4, February 1965, pp. 30–41.

Knauss, Robert L. 'International security markets'. *The Vanderbilt International*, Vol. 3, No. 1, Winter 1969, pp. 35–43.

Lamy, Emmanuel. 'Processus de concentration industrielle', Speech by the President of Banque de l'Union Parisienne. *Humanisme et Entreprise*, April 1971, pp. 17–30.

Layton, Christopher. 'European advanced technology: A programme for integration'. *European Business*, July 1969, pp. 33–36.

Layton, Christopher. 'Europe: It's industry that counts'. *Vision*, May 1971, p. 7.

Lecerf, Jean. 'Perchè le società europee non si fondono?' *Rassegna della stampa estera*, December 1970.

Lecourt, Robert. 'Concentrations et fusions, facteurs d'intégration'. *Revue du Marché Commun*, No. 109, January–February 1968, pp. 6–24.

Levinson, Harry. 'A psychologist diagnoses merger failures'. *Harvard Business Review*, March–April 1970, pp. 139–47.

Loussouarn, Yvon. 'Les sociétés et la Communauté Economique Européenne'. *Revue du Marché Commun*, No. 140, January 1971, pp. 59–77.

Mailander, Peter K. 'Mergers and acquisitions in the Common Market: Problems under corporate tax and antitrust law'. *New York University Journal of International Law and Politics*, Vol. 1, No. 1, April 1968, pp. 19–36.

Marchal, André. 'Nécessité économique des concentrations et fusions'. *Revue du Marché Commun*, No. 109, January–February 1968, pp. 25–50.

Marchini-Camia, Antonio. 'Facilitating transnational business within the E.E.C.: Progress to date'. *Cornell International Law Journal*, Vol. 3, No. 1, Winter 1970, pp. 9–31.

Markert, Kurt E. 'Antitrust aspects of mergers in the E.E.C.' *Texas International Law Forum*, Vol. 5, No. 1, Spring 1969, pp. 32–70.

Markert, Kurt E. 'Mitteilung'. *Revue du Marché Commun*, No. 109, January–February 1968, pp. 254–57.

Mattson, Robert N. 'Mergers: European style'. *Mergers and Acquisitions*, Spring 1971, pp. 27 ff.

McMillan, Claude. 'The swap as a hedge in foreign exchanges'. *California Management Review*, Summer 1962, pp. 57–65.

Minervini, Gustavo. 'Un recente progetto di società di tipo europeo'. *Rassegna economica*, No. 5, September–October 1967, pp. 1163–72.

Mintz, Norman N. 'Toward a common European currency'. *Columbia Journal of World Business*, January–February 1971.

Motte, Bertrand. 'Obstacles tenant au droit interne des sociétés'. *Revue du Marché Commun*, No. 109, January–February 1968, pp. 392–98.

Moussis, Nicolas S. 'L'entreprise internationale européenne est-elle nécessaire et pourquoi?' *Revue du Marché Commun*, No. 117, November 1968, pp. 950–54.

Notari, Benedetto. 'Le società multinazionali: fenomeno dell'economia moderna'. *Cooperazione di credito*, January–February 1971.

Pagès, Max. 'Le T-group ou groupe de diagnostic'. *Hommes et techniques*, 1959, Vol. 15, No. 169, pp. 116–25.

Parker, Alan. 'The European company'. *European Community*, September 1968, pp. 5–6.

Perlmutter, Howard V. 'Super-giant firms in the future'. *Wharton Quarterly*, Winter 1968.

Piccione, Ugo. 'Cross-border Banking'. *European Community*, May 1971, pp. 14–15.

Pirelli, Leopoldo. 'Motivations, development and prospects of the multinational company'. *Banco di Roma's Review of the Economic Conditions in Italy*, Vol. XXVI, No. 3, May 1972, pp. 173–83.

Remacle, Francis. 'La politique industrielle et les concentrations d'entreprises'. *Reflets et perspectives*, 1971, pp. 247–60.

Rockwell, Willard F. 'How to acquire a company'. *Harvard Business Review*, September–October 1968, pp. 121–32.

Sacle, Armand. 'Coopérations, concentrations, fusions d'entreprises dans la C.E.E.' *Revue du Marché Commun*, No. 109, January–February 1968, pp. 105–23.

Sadoux, Rémi and Arnaud, Rémy. 'Les fusions jugées par ceux qui les font, par ceux qui les subissent'. *Entreprise*, No. 851, December 1971, pp. 52–57.

Sassen, Emmanuel M. J. 'Competition policy: more than "anti trust"'. *European Community*, No. 128, October 1969, pp. 3–5.

Schneider, Uwe-Helmut. 'Ueber die Notwendigkeit, neben der SE und der internationalen Fusion, weitere gesellschaftsrechtliche Formen zur Zusammenfassung europaeischer Unternehmen zu schaffen', Anmerkungen zu den Verhandlungen der gesellschaftsrechtlichen Arbeitsgemeinschaft des 48. Deutschen Juristentag in Mainz. *Die Aktiengesellschaft Zeitschrift fuer das gesamte Aktienwesen*, No. 7, July 1971, pp. 209–14.

Schoellhammer, Hans. 'Corporate planning in France'. *European Business*, July 1969, pp. 22–31.

Sheperd, Richard K. 'Dunlop–Pirelli merger'. *European Community*, No. 135, June 1970, pp. 13–14.

Sherif, Muzafer. 'Experiments in group conflict'. *Scientific American*, CXCV, 1956, pp. 54–58.

Siekman, Philip. 'Now it's the Europeans versus IBM'. *Fortune*, August 15, 1969, pp. 86 ff.

Silcher, Friedrich. 'Obstacles tenant au droit fiscal', Intervention. *Revue du Marché Commun*, No. 109, January–February 1968, pp. 534–536.

Smith, G. Maitland. 'Obtaining a stock exchange quotation'. *Accountancy*, January 1964, pp. 23–28.

Stewart, Michael B. 'Transnational enterprise: The European challenge'. *Columbia Journal of World Business*, July–August 1972, pp. 5–13.

Streeter Hatch, Ruth. 'Mergers and men'. *Mergers and Acquisitions*, Fall 1966, pp. 28–37.

Summers, Clyde W. 'Labor relations in the Common Market'. *Harvard Business Review*, March–April 1965, pp. 140–60.

Tabatoni, Pierre. 'Remarques sur les obstacles psycho-sociologiques à la coopération internationale'. *Revue du Marché Commun*, No. 109, January–February 1968, pp. 99–104.

Taylor, Fred W. 'Anatomy of a merger'. *Mergers and Acquisitions*, November–December 1970, pp. 8–19.

Teitigen, Pierre-Henri. 'Rapport de synthèse'. *Revue du Marché Commun*, No. 109, January–February 1968, pp. 539–52.

Thiesing, Jochen. 'Obstacles tenant à la législation communautaire sur les ententes et "positions dominantes" ', Diskussionsbeitrag. *Revue du Marché Commun*, No. 109, January–February 1968, pp. 292–293.

Thompson, Dennis. 'The creation of a European company'. *International and Comparative Law Quarterly*, Vol. 17, January 1968, pp. 183–91.

Trebuth, Guenter. 'Hindernisse auf Grund des Steuerrechts'. *Revue du Marché Commun*, No. 109, January–February 1968, pp. 508–23.

Turq, André. 'Obstacles tenant au droit fiscal'. *Revue du Marché Commun*, No. 109, January–February 1968, pp. 524–33.

Urciuoli, Arthur J. 'Toward a European equity market'. *Columbia Journal of World Business*, September–October 1970, pp. 17–22.
Von Clemm, Michael. 'The rise of consortium banking'. *Harvard Business Review*, May–June 1971, pp. 125–42.
Von der Groeben, Hans. 'Vers des sociétés anonymes européennes—Nécessité et possibilité de créer une société de type européen'. *Revue, trimestrielle de droit européen*, 1967, pp. 224–37.
Wakefield, B. R. 'Mergers and Acquisitions'. *Harvard Business Review*, September–October 1965, pp. 6 ff.
Warden, James B. 'International banking in the seventies'. *Columbia Journal of World Business*, July–August 1972, pp. 67–72.
Weber, A. P. 'Les mouvements de concentration en Europe et la pénétration industrielle et commerciale'. *Direction*, No. 148, March 1968, pp. 262 ff.
Wierzynski, Gregory H. 'G.E.'s $200 million ticket to France'. *Fortune*, June 1, 1967, pp. 92–96 and 159–62.
Worms, H. G. 'How does German industry plan?' *European Business*, February 1967, pp. 20–30.

Miscellaneous—titled

Abs, Hermann J. 'The European security and new issues market with a view to international financing', Report presented to the Institut International d'Etudes Bancaires at its 28th Session on 6 November 1964 (Knokke, Belgium).
Agnelli, Giovanni. 'The changing world scene and the international automotive industry', Speech by the Chairman of Fiat SpA, Detroit, 12 January 1972.
Agnelli, Giovanni. 'Creating Europe's industrial giants', Speech by the Chairman of Fiat SpA, New York, 2 December 1970.
Agnelli, Giovanni. 'The economics of the motor industries', Speech by the Chairman of Fiat SpA, London, 26 October 1971.
Ardoino, J. 'Le groupe de diagnostic, instrument de formation'. Institut d'Administration d'Entreprises de l'Université de Bordeaux, 1962.
Barsanti, William P. 'Accounting pitfalls in foreign acquisitions', Speech by an officer of Arthur Andersen & Co., New York, 23 May 1968.
Bieberstein, Jorg. 'The German Cartel Law and its administration: role of the Federal Cartel Office in regard to the E.E.C. antitrust provisions'. Economic Concentration, Hearings before the Subcommittee on Antitrust and Monopoly of the Committee on the Judiciary, United States Senate, 90th Congress, pursuant to Senate Resolution 233, Part 7A, at pp. 4038–58.
Campbell, D. T. 'Ethnocentric and other altruistic motives'. Nebraska Symposium on Motivation, 1965.
Chevrier, Jacques. 'Les entreprises publiques dans une société libre:

expérience d'Electricité de France'. VII Congrès de l'Economie collective, 1965.

Collin, Fernand. 'The formation of a European capital market', Lecture delivered by the Chairman of Kredietbank. Brussels, 1962.

de Jong, H. W. 'Economic concentration'. Judiciary Committee, U.S. Congress, Part 7, April 1968.

Erdmann, Ernst-Gerhard. 'The myth of codetermination'. Bundesvereinigung der deutschen Arbeitgeberverbaende. Koeln, 1970.

Flory, Jean. 'Coopération et concentrations dans le cadre de la Communauté Européenne', Exposé par le Directeur de la Direction Générale des Affaires Industrielles de la Commission des Communautés Européennes. Paris, June 1971.

Goldberg, Paul Morton. 'The evolution of transnational companies in Europe', Ph.D. Dissertation, Massachusetts Institute of Technology, Sloan School of Management, Cambridge, Mass., 1971.

Gramberg, Barbara. 'Die Konzentration im Bereich der chemischen Industrie (Historische Entwicklung)'. Verband der chemischen Industrie (Unpublished study). Frankfurt, 1962.

Grapin, Jacqueline. 'Il n'y a pas que des mariages heureux . . .', *Le Monde*, 5 September 1972, p. 17.

Greenwood, Allen. 'The 19th R. K. Pierson Memorial Lecture'. Weybridge, 24 November 1971.

Gropkopp, Wilhelm and Schmacke, Ernst. 'Die grossen 500—Deutschlands fuehrende Unternehmen und ihr Management'. Droste, Koeln, 1970.

Hermann, A. H. 'Continental Can Company v. Commission of the European Communities'. Legal Reports (International), 86 Queen Victoria Street, London, 1973.

Hochmut, Milton S. 'The effect of structure on strategy: the government sponsored multinational joint ventures', DBA Dissertation, Graduate School of Business Administration, Harvard University. Cambridge, Mass., 1972.

Kain, Walter. 'Activities of American chemical companies in Europe'. Baden-Baden: Verlag Walter Kain, 1970.

Kroener, William; Mazzolini, Renato; and Mignon, Patrice. 'Transnational concentration in the EEC'. (Unpublished paper). Stanford, March 1971.

Lovell, Enid B. 'Nationalism or interdependence: The alternatives'. International Survey of Business Opinion and Experience. The National Industrial Conference Board, New York, 1969.

Lutter, Marcus. 'Recht und Steuer der internationalen Unternehmensverbindungen'. Bertelsmann Universitaetverlag.

Malmlow, Eric G. 'Industrial mergers in Western Europe'. Long-range Planning Service, Stanford Research Institute, Menlo Park, Calif., 1970.

Marsh, R. 'The Dunlop–Pirelli Union', Speech given at the Institute of Chartered Accountants, Summer Conference. Oxford, July 1971.

Mazzolini, Renato. 'Generating an unconventional hypothesis: Stockholders' personal objectives as motivating forces for international concentration—The Italian case'. (Unpublished paper). Stanford, May 1971.

McConnell, G. D. 'Behavioral factors in world consumer markets'. Long-range Planning Service, Stanford Research Institute, Menlo Park, Calif., July 1970.

McFadzean, F. S. 'The operation of a multi-national enterprise'. The company and its responsibilities, Third paper in the 1971 programme. Industrial Educational and Research Foundation. London, 1971.

Melodia, Giuseppina. 'Evoluzione della politica comunitaria di concorrenza—Orientamenti della giurisprudenza della Comunità Economica Europea in tema di applicazione delle norme di concorrenza del Trattato di Roma'. Confederazione Generale dell'Industria Italiana. Roma, November 1971, pp. 1–18.

Melodia, Giuseppina. 'Orientamenti della giurisprudenza della Comunità Economica Europea in tema di applicazione delle norme di concorrenza del Trattato di Roma'. Confederazione Generale dell'Industria Italiana. Roma, August 1968.

Melodia, Giuseppina. 'Orientamenti della giurisprudenza della Comunità Economica Europea in tema di applicazione delle norme di concorrenza del Trattato di Roma'. Confederazione Generale dell'Industria Italiana. Roma, October 1969.

Raphael, Winifred and Zimmerman, M. W. 'After the take-over—A study of reactions of employees in a group of companies'. National Institute of Psychology, London, 1963.

Rhinesmith, S. H. and Nylen, D. 'A behavioral approach to international management training'. Graduate School of Public and International Affairs, University of Pittsburgh, 1969.

Rodière, René. 'La fusion des sociétés commerciales dans les pays du Marché Commun', Document de travail 7, pp. 78–87. Communauté Economique Européenne.

Seybold, Geneva. 'Communicating with employees about mergers'. National Industrial Conference Board, New York, 1968.

Vits, E. H. 'Die Neuordnung der Beziehungen zwischen AKU und Glanzstoff', Ansprache des Vorsitzenden des Vorstandes der Glanzstoff AG. Wuppertal, 16 July 1969.

Von Fieandt, Otto. 'Trends in European commercial banking'. Euro-economics, Paris, 1972.

Miscellaneous—untitled

Agfa–Gevaert N.V. 'The Agfa–Gevaert merger'. Mortsel-Antwerpen, November 1971.

Amsterdam-Rotterdam Bank, Deutsche Bank, Midland Bank and Société Générale de Banque. 'Capital markets in Europe', Report published by an economic research group of the above banks, March 1966.

Arrêt du 21 février 1973 de la Cour de Justice des Communautés Européennes du Luxembourg dans l'affaire 6/72: Continental Can Company Inc., et Europemballage Corporation contre Commission des Communautés Européennes.

Bilateral Agreement for the mutual recognition of companies and the transfer of their registered office between West Germany and France of 27 October 1956, and Annexation to the protocol.

Bundesamt fuer gewerbliche Wirtschaft. 'Bericht ueber das Ergebnis einer Untersuchung der Konzentration in der Wirtschaft (Konzentration-enquete)'. Bonn, 1964.

Business International. 'Solving international accounting problems'. New York, 1969.

Business International. 'The European Communities today and tomorrow—New rules for the seventies'. Business International Research Reports. Geneva, 1969.

Centre d'Etudes politiques, économiques et sociales. 'Le problème de la concentration dans le Marché Commun'. Brussels, 1966.

Chambre de Commerce Internationale. 'Les concentrations en Europe'. Paris, 1965.

Chambre de Commerce de Paris—Centre de recherche sur le droit des affaires (CREDA). 'Pour une société européenne à responsabilité limitée'. Paris, 1970.

Comité Européen pour le progrès économique et social (CEPES). *Grenzueberschreitende Unternehmenskooperation in der EWG*. Stuttgart: Forkel Verlag, 1968.

Commission des Communautés Européennes. *Concentration d'entreprises dans le Marché Commun—Memorandum de la Commission de la C.E.E.* Service Concurrence. Brussels, 1966.

Commission des Communautés Européennes. 'La coordination du droit des sociétés et la société européenne'. Service Central de la Documentation. Brussels, 15 June 1971.

Commission des Communautés Européennes. *The Development of a European capital market*. Brussels, 1966.

Commission des Communautés Européennes. 'La politique de concurrence de la Communauté—Extraits du premier rapport sur la politique de concurrence publié par la Commission des Communautés Européennes', No. 114. Brussels, 16 May 1972.

Commission des Communautés Européennes. *La politique industrielle de la Communauté—Memorandum de la Commission au Conseil*. Brussels, 1970.

Commission des Communautés Européennes. 'Das Problem der Unternehmenskonzentration im Gemeinsamen Markt'. Brussels, 1965.

Commission des Communautés Européennes. 'Problèmes fiscaux'. Service Central de la Documentation. Brussels, 1 December 1970.

Commission des Communautés Européennes. *Proposed Statute for the European Company*, Supplement to Bulletin 8—1970, of the European Community, Brussels.

Commission des Communautés Européennes. 'Proposition de directive concernant le régime fiscal commun applicable aux sociétés mères et filiales d'Etats Membres différents'. COM (69) 6 final. Brussels, 15 January 1969.

Commission des Communautés Européennes. 'Proposition de directive concernant le régime fiscal commun applicable aux fusions, scissions et apports d'actifs intervenant entre sociétés d'Etats Membres différents'. COM (69) 5 final. Brussels, 15 January 1969.

Commission des Communautés Européennes. 'Proposition de troisième directive sur les fusions de sociétés anonymes', Supplément au Bulletin 5, 1970 des Communautés Européennes, Brussels.

Commission des Communautés Européennes. 'Les règles de concurrence dans la Communauté Européenne'. Information. Brussels, 21 October 1971.

C.ie Lambert pour l'Industrie et la Finance. 'La dimension des entreprises européennes', Annexé au Rapport de l'exercice 1966. Brussels, 1967.

Conseil National du Patronat Français (CNPF). 'La politique industrielle européenne', Document de travail préparatoire, January 1971.

'Convenzione sul reciproco riconoscimento delle società e persone giuridiche—Bruxelles, 29 febbraio 1968'. *Jus Gentium—Diritto delle Relazioni Internazionali*, Vol. 8, No. 4, Rome, 22 May 1971, pp. 380–84.

DBG. 'Codetermination rights of the workers in Germany'. June 1967.

The Dunlop Company Limited. 'Dunlop–Pirelli: A European experiment', Paper No. 442, London, 1971.

Dunlop House. 'Proposals to effect the Union of the operating activities of the Dunlop Company Limited, and Pirelli SpA and Société Internationale Pirelli SA'. London, 1970.

Dunlop House. 'The Dunlop Company Limited Union with Pirelli SpA and Société Internationale Pirelli SA—Proposed revisions to the trust deeds constituting the first and second debenture stocks'. London, 1970.

EFTA Bulletin, Vol. XI, No. 7, September–October 1970. 'Company Law: EFTA studies for the case of a supranational company'.

Les ententes à l'échelle européenne, Séminaire organisé par l'Institut d'Administration des Entreprises de l'Université de Paris et l'Association pour le Développement des Etudes de Gestion des Entreprises. Paris: Dunod, 1967.

European Community. 'Criteria outlined for cooperative agreements in line with communities' competition rules'. August 1968, pp. 15–17.
European Community. 'European company law'. August 1970, pp. 4–6.
European Community. 'Common industrial policy'. April 1970, pp. 4–5.
European Community. 'Direct tax harmonization plan outlined'. July–August 1967, p. 22.
Fédération des Industries Belges. 'Adaptation des structures des entreprises et coopération', Memorandum de la Fédération des Industries Belges au Gouvernement. Brussels, November 1971.
Fédération Européenne des Associations EUR d'Analystes Financiers. 'L'analyse financière et la concentration des entreprises en Europe'. 6ème Congrès. Montreux, October 1970.
Hoesch–Hoogovens. 'Bericht ueber den Zusammenschluss'. Dortmund, April 1972.
Journal Officiel, 'Décision de la Commission du 9 décembre 1971 relative a une procédure d'application de l'article 86 du Traité CEE', Commission des Communautés Européennes, Brussels, 8 January, 1972.
Journal Officiel, No. C75, 29 July 1968. Communication officielle—Commission des Communautés Européennes, Brussels.
Journal Officiel, No. 533. Regulation 19—Commission des Communautés Européennes, Brussels, 1965.
Journal Officiel, No. 204. Regulation 17—Commission des Communautés Européennes, Brussels, 1962.
Kredietbank. 'La société européenne', Bulletin Hebdomadaire, 25e année, No. 5, 30 January 1970, pp. 50–54.
Opera Mundi Europe. 'L'interpénétration dans le Marché Commun'. (Unpublished study) Paris, 1970.
Successo. 'Il consulente aziendale in Italia', No. 12, December 1968, pp. 133 ff.
Treaty establishing the European Economic Community (referred to as *Rome Treaty*). Secretariat of the Interim Committee for the Common Market and Euratom. Brussels, 1958.
Treaty establishing the European Coal and Steel Community (referred to as *Treaty of Paris*). High Authority of the European Coal and Steel Community, 1951.
Union des Industries de la Communauté Européenne (UNICE). 'Politique de la Commission Européenne en matière de règles de concurrence'. Brussels, 9 September 1970.
Union des Industries de la Communauté Européenne (UNICE). 'L'Europe face à la concurrence de l'entreprise mondiale'. Lausanne, 1965.
Union des Industries de la Communauté Européenne (UNICE). 'Les fusions internationales de sociétés dans la Communauté Economique Européenne'. Brussels, 28 October 1967.

Union des Industries de la Communauté Européenne (UNICE). 'La politique industrielle de la Communauté'. Brussels, 10 September 1970.
'Vertrag zwischen AKU N.V., Arnhem/Niederland und 1) Glanzstoff AG, Wuppertal, und 2) Enka N.V., Arnhem'. 16 July 1969.
Vita. 'L'impresa transnazionale nel MEC'. No. 614, January 1971.
Wirtschaftliche Rundschau. 'Konzentrationstendenzen in der europaeischen Wirtschaft'. No. 6, 20 March 1969.

INDEX

PRINTED IN GREAT BRITAIN BY ROBERT MACLEHOSE AND CO. LTD,
PRINTERS TO THE UNIVERSITY OF GLASGOW